When Conscience Calls

When Conscience Calls

Moral Courage in Times of Confusion and Despair

KRISTEN RENWICK MONROE

The University of Chicago Press
Chicago and London

The University of Chicago Press, Chicago 60637
The University of Chicago Press, Ltd., London
© 2023 by Kristen Renwick Monroe
All rights reserved. No part of this book may be used or reproduced in any manner whatsoever without written permission, except in the case of brief quotations in critical articles and reviews. For more information, contact the University of Chicago Press, 1427 E. 60th St., Chicago, IL 60637.
Published 2023
Printed in the United States of America

32 31 30 29 28 27 26 25 24 23   1 2 3 4 5

ISBN-13: 978-0-226-82907-4 (cloth)
ISBN-13: 978-0-226-82909-8 (paper)
ISBN-13: 978-0-226-82908-1 (e-book)
DOI: https://doi.org/10.7208/chicago/9780226829081.001.0001

Library of Congress Cataloging-in-Publication Data

Names: Monroe, Kristen Renwick, 1946– author.
Title: When conscience calls : moral courage in times of confusion and despair / Kristen Renwick Monroe.
Other titles: Moral courage in times of confusion and despair
Description: Chicago ; London : The University of Chicago Press, 2023. | Includes bibliographical references and index.
Identifiers: LCCN 2023009342 | ISBN 9780226829074 (cloth) | ISBN 9780226829098 (paperback) | ISBN 9780226829081 (ebook)
Subjects: LCSH: Courage. | Ethics.
Classification: LCC BJ1533.C8 M665 2023 | DDC 179/.6—dc23/eng/20230512
LC record available at https://lccn.loc.gov/2023009342

In loving memory of
My father, James Oliver Monroe, Jr. and
My maternal grandfather, Robert Hart Renwick
Who first showed me integrity and moral courage.

He who learns must suffer. And, even in our sleep,
pain that cannot forget falls drop by drop upon the heart,
and in our own despair, against our will,
comes wisdom to us by the awful grace of God.
　　　AESCHYLUS, *Agamemnon*, episode 1, line 176

　　Take your broken heart. Make it into art.
MERYL STREEP, Golden Globe Awards, January 2017

Contents

Preface: One Very Small Candle xi

Introduction: What Is Moral Courage? 1

PART I Moral Courage as a Concept

1 Moral Courage: What We Know and What We Need to Know 9
2 Stories of Moral Courage: Data and Research Methodology 28

PART II Understanding Moral Courage

3 "We're Going to Do What's Right. We May Pay a Price for It, but That's Fine": Steve Zimmer on Protecting Undocumented Students 41
4 "No One, Not Even the President, Is Above the Law": Erwin Chemerinsky on Suing President Trump 49
5 "If We Organize, We Can Change the World": Heather Booth on Social Activism 54
6 "I Am Going to Do This. I Am Going to Do This to the End!": Kay Monroe on Caring for the Elderly 75
7 "The Courage You Have ... It's Not Something You Consciously Think About": Amal on Anti-Muslim Bullying 96
8 "It Would Be a Violation of the Public Trust to Not Do All I Could to Stop the Wrongdoing": Loretta Lynch on Speaking Truth to Power during the Enron Crisis 108
9 "Nothing Else ... Would Enable Me to Look in the Mirror the Next Day": Vikram Tej on Fighting Caste in India 128

PART III A Richly Faceted Moral Courage

10 When Nobody's Watching   135

Conclusion: Learning from the Lives of Others   174

Acknowledgments 205
Notes 207
Bibliography 227
Index 235

PREFACE

One Very Small Candle

This book would not have been written had Donald Trump not become president in 2017. Like many other liberal American academics, I was both shocked and horrified at his election. For several days after November 8, 2016, I had students in my office and in my home, asking me to explain what had happened and what they should do about it. I had no answer. I was as disheartened as they were.

Sometime in January 2017, however, I remembered something Albert Hirschman once told me.[1] "After the fall of France," he said—although I am paraphrasing from memory—"many intellectuals felt it was the end of the world. The barbarians had taken over. There were many suicides." Hirschman paused. "I couldn't live that way. If I had believed things were that bad, I would have had to kill myself, too. So, I always tried to find—because I HAD to find—something to smile about, to laugh about, something good in a world seemingly going mad. This is why Varian Fry called me Beamish because I was always smiling, laughing, beaming even."[2]

I understood what Hirschman meant. Innately someone who sees too much ugliness in life, I find it an act of faith, akin to a religion, to be able to find some good on which to focus. Better to light a single candle than to curse the darkness. If this is not true, then one might as well give up and pack it all in.

So I went to my students and offered them a proposition. "You know, in this class, you absolutely can hold any opinion you like. You know I will be totally open and honest with you about my opinions but in exchange for this, you must agree that we all understand you will never be penalized for disagreeing with me. Nor should you be intimidated when my views differ from yours. You must be willing to disagree with me and not fear any reprisal if we are to be open and honest with each other. If you're okay with this, I would like us to discuss openly our feelings about Trump, and about what those of us who are upset about his election and concerned by his presidency can do that is positive."

Thus began the discussion that produced this book. The course, called "The Moral of the Story," was one on ethics in which I asked how people learn about ethics through stories—bedtime stories, Bible stories, fables, parables, television shows, movies, novels, autobiographies—and then use stories to work through their own issues about how to navigate life, finding their own moral compass. For example, we read Harper Lee's *To Kill a Mockingbird*, along with *Go Set a Watchman*, her earlier draft of *Mockingbird*, in which the father is a more flawed character, probably even a racist or a racism sympathizer—certainly not the inspirational paragon that Atticus Finch was in Lee's masterpiece.[3] Discussing what the shift in Lee's fictionalized memoir tells us about her own views of her father led the class to ponder how they relate to their parents. Do we change our views of our parents over time? How and when does this recalibration occur? Can we still love imperfect parents, forgive them for being so fallible, and even continue to respect them? How does our ability to recraft our view of, and our relationship with, our parents affect our own lives? These were the kinds of issues we discussed in class, into which stories—both real-life and fictional—can lend insight.

For the final project, the initial syllabus asked each student to conduct an in-depth interview with someone whose life story revealed something of interest to the student about moral choice. After the class discussions of our own views of politics and ethics in the age of Trump, however, I agreed to add a second option to the original assignment. Option 1 remained the same: students could follow the original assignment and conduct an interview with someone they respected and ask about that person's moral choices. For Option 2, however, students worked together with me to interview people we believed demonstrated moral courage. The value of doing an interview was captured beautifully by one of the speakers, whose story was analyzed but is not presented in full here. Richard Ceballos, a Los Angeles assistant district attorney who sued his own office over corruption and free speech, noted:

> Now in a classroom setting, the answers are relatively easy because it's just a classroom setting. There are no real consequences for wrong answers. But in the real world, it's far different. When you have a family to provide for; a car payment to make; a mortgage payment to make; kids to put through school; and promotions you are looking forward to getting, these are factors

you suddenly have to consider when faced with an ethical decision. It makes the decision that much more difficult. I would be lying to you if I didn't tell you that I thought about all these things when I was faced with my ethical decision. I did consider keeping quiet and not saying anything and just giving in to what my bosses and the Sheriff's department wanted. But after thinking about it some more, I knew it wasn't the right thing to do. I had to stand firm and insist on doing things the right way even though I knew it would have consequences for me. And even after everything the office put me through, I can still hold my head high and know I did the right thing.[4]

The interviews proved both instructive and fascinating, and they were fun for the students. I am deeply grateful for the time and generosity of those interviewed for this project.

As we gathered the interviews, the class had many discussions about the meaning of moral courage. We refined our ideas as the course progressed to focus on a shared, if perhaps general, understanding of moral courage as the strength of character that impels one to take action for moral reasons, even when one knows doing so incurs a risk of suffering adverse consequences. Moral courage thus includes both the strength to stand up against political wrongs and the small, quiet acts of bravery that help us affirm who we are as a people and what is important to us. Eventually, we realized moral courage emanates from values we hold so dear that they effectively form our central core; these core values constitute our sense of who we are. To fail to act in defense of these values is to betray one's sense of self. The trick then becomes to determine what these values are. This topic is discussed more fully in chapters 1 and 10, but initially we agreed to include only stories of moral courage driven by values we as a class found commendable. Later, as I reviewed the literature on moral courage, I realized two things:

1. Discussions of moral courage almost always reflect the values shared by the analyst.
2. Contemporary analyses of moral courage tend to reflect liberal, democratic, humanistic values.

This observation raised further interesting questions. If, as I shall demonstrate, moral courage reflects the actors' foundational values—those so deeply held that they constitute the actors' identity—can we recognize acts of moral courage that do *not* reflect our own values? Can we find moral courage in a society that shares only some of our own values? And what about moral courage driven by values we find morally repugnant? Can we call these values morally courageous? What about distinguishing between acts of moral courage and acts of betrayal or fanaticism? These questions are important, but, owing to space constraints, a full discussion of them is held for a later volume designed to lend insight into whether moral courage can exist outside the liberal, democratic framework.[5]

Our first task here—in the first volume of what will eventually become a trilogy on moral courage—is the establishment of a baseline for moral courage as scholars traditionally analyze it. Most contemporary scholars work out of the liberal, democratic, humanistic traditions. Hence most of the literature in the field, and all the stories I include here, reflect our own standards of what is right and good in a moral sense. These standards reflect our own values, which can be best characterized as liberal, democratic, humanistic. I thus came into the project recognizing that I would have to address the concept of an "objective" standard on this issue. I was conscious that moral courage almost inherently involves subtle issues of loyalty and betrayal, and I was fearful of the logical and analytical weakness in having to decide what objectively distinguished one person's courage from another's fanaticism or betrayal. Fortunately, and to our surprise, the empirical analysis lent insight into this issue of an objective standard for moral courage; this important finding is discussed in the book's conclusion.

Discussions of these issues continued, for me anyway, long after my class ended. I conducted more interviews throughout the summers of 2017 through 2022 in an internship program I run each summer for high school and college students through the University of California, Irvine [UCI] Ethics Center.[6] Designed to show students how to do research, the internship involves students in actual research through a mentoring program in which they can design their own projects or work with me on one of my projects.[7] I included the summer interns in the project on moral courage for the same reasons I began the project with my UCI students. One of the most important of these reasons was a desire to help not only the students but also myself feel more empowered and less helpless as the political world seemed to cycle out of control—a feeling exacerbated in 2020, when the COVID-19 pandemic struck the United States, adding to the confusion already in place from the political uncertainty engendered by the election of Trump. This entailed discussions of agency, a concept more familiar to philosophers than to political scientists.

Agency refers to the sense that one matters in the world, that one can have an impact on things, that each of us has a part to play in the world, and that we can take actions that count. While realizing I could not address all the issues raised by a chaotic political environment and the uncertainty of COVID-19, I hoped that by asking the students to consider what moral courage meant, I could encourage them to think about how courage played out in their own lives. I wanted them to step outside their comfort zones and think about times when they had demonstrated moral courage—if only in a small matter—and how that had made them feel; but I also wanted them to think about those times when they felt they had sought refuge in their group, or had given way to anger and fear of new people or new behaviors. I promised I would do the same, and I did.

Although I was as much a novice as the students in understanding moral courage, I did have a bit of an agenda. First, I wanted the students to realize that courage is not the absence of fear. Rather, courage is acting even when we are afraid. Second, I wanted students to be reminded that they too can make a difference, and that developing a moral compass starts early. We do not have to be powerful people to demonstrate moral courage.[8] The ability to demonstrate small, quiet acts of moral courage occurs every day, if we only notice them. I wanted students to think about the times in their own lives when they needed moral courage. Although I was uncomfortable doing it, I made myself share with them a time in third grade when I was a member of a small clique of girls. Three of the girls were "cool"; I was definitely not, or so I feared. A fifth girl wanted to be part of the group and one of the cool girls made fun of her, excluding her by ridiculing the way she dressed. I felt bad about this but I kept quiet. I was so frightened that my own place in the cool-kid group would be jeopardized that I did and said nothing. Even today, I am embarrassed by this, ashamed of my own cowardice. Yet I wondered if it was the acknowledgment and owning of this failure that helped me later take bolder stands. So I wanted the students to recognize that failure can help us grow.

Finally, I also wanted the students to think about their own values as we moved through the project. We soon realized, as we analyzed the interviews, that moral courage derives from our sense of who we are; a story of moral courage thus is ultimately a story about ourselves. "What is it that is important for you?," I asked each student; "What or who would you risk embarrassment, unpopularity, or censure for?" "Do you think you have the capacity to make a difference in the world?," I asked them to ask themselves. "If not, why not? What makes you less worthy of doing great things than someone else?"

I hope the students and interns felt empowered by the project. I believe they did. Their interviews with people they knew—their fellow students, neighbors, or people in their own church or family—taught them that just one seemingly inconsequential act of moral courage can increase the sense of what a single individual can accomplish. I call this *moral muscle*.

The interviews, conducted by individual students and by me, sometimes in conjunction with students, also struck a deeper chord, however—one that harks back to the initial impetus for the project.⁹ We learned—or were reminded—that America as a country is not defined by the president, by the person at the top. America is not the project of any one individual, but of each of us, working together to affect the world for the better, as we see it.¹⁰

President Obama was fond of quoting Martin Luther King, Jr.'s comment that "the arc of the moral universe is long, but it bends toward justice." Obama also quickly added his own insight, however, that the arc does not bend on its own. The arc needs people to move it in the direction of justice, kindness, and generosity, and toward all the other values we hold as a country.

A book on moral courage thus, above all else, reminds us that we, as individuals and as a people, always have a choice.¹¹ If there were no tough times, if progress were assured, we would never need moral courage. But there are, it isn't, and so we do. Considering what constitutes moral courage and what drives it—the two main scholarly goals of this project—forced the students to think about who they are, what they care about most in life, what values drive them, and who they want to become as they compose a life. Asking people the students admired and, in many cases, already knew and cherished helped them understand how other people made their moral choices, where those choices took them, and what the sum of our choices leads us to become as people.

How did I do this, and what does this project contribute to the literature on moral courage? This is the subject in part 1. Chapter 1 reviews the literature on moral courage. Chapter 2 outlines my own theoretical approach: that of the political psychologist relying on narrative interpretation as a methodology, collecting oral histories of moral exemplars and then asking them how they came to perform their acts of moral courage. In doing this, I deliberately conceptualized moral courage broadly. I included public acts of moral courage, of course. I also examined acts of moral courage that are quiet, flying under the radar, designed to pick up the gist of moral courage that includes holding one's tongue, refusing to fight back, or that occur behind the scenes, in the home and hence not in the public domain. Part 1 also explains the narrative research methodology and describes my full data set.

Part 2 presents the stories of some of the people my students, interns, and I interviewed. I wanted the reader to be able to enter into the minds of just a few people who demonstrated moral courage. The stories in chapters 3–9 are fascinating, but reading them also has a critical analytical goal: it allows the reader to view the raw data, as it were, encouraging readers to determine for themselves whether or not my analysis is accurate.

Part 3 presents my analysis of these interviews, suggesting both what conducting these interviews taught my students and me about moral courage as a concept and what drives moral courage in practice. The conclusion offers some broad thoughts about particular questions to be addressed in future work as I seek greater insight into moral courage. This conclusion also makes a plea for teaching ethics by drawing on emotional as well as analytical intelligence and describes what both the students—and the professor—learned about ethics and their own values through participating in this project.

INTRODUCTION

What Is Moral Courage?

Two closely related concerns drove the writing of this book. The first is a straightforward scholarly one: what is moral courage, and why is it important? To answer this question, this book explores moral courage in difficult political times through interviews with individuals who performed acts most of us would agree look like moral courage. The book then offers a conceptual definition of moral courage and argues that moral courage cannot be understood without reference to the core values that constitute one's identity or character. Indeed, the way we traditionally think about moral courage ties so closely to our own values that most of us lack an objective method for distinguishing acts of moral courage from acts of fanaticism or betrayal. My first task thus is to address three interconnected and fundamental questions: what does moral courage look like in much of today's contemporary world? What drives it? And why should we care about moral courage?[1]

The second concern is both darker and more existential; it is reflected in the book's subtitle: *Moral Courage in Times of Confusion and Despair*. Sometime in 2016 my need to understand, to truly comprehend and appreciate, moral courage took on a highly personal note. What would I do in response to what felt like a national and ethical crisis precipitated by the presidential election of 2016, when someone I considered unfit, both by experience and character, was elected to the highest office in my country? I was horrified, in shock at the ugliness of political life as practiced by many Trump supporters—and some of his opponents—and deeply troubled about the nation's future, sensing that democracy was under threat throughout the world. I remained alarmed as I searched in vain for an appropriate response to the despair and heartache this engendered in me.

As a scholar, I knew that the literature on moral courage needed the stronger empirical analysis and underpinnings the exploration in this book produced. As a teacher, I realized that most of my students were feeling as lost and disoriented as I was. As a human being, I understood that if I could find the strength to reveal my own anguish and vulnerability, provided by Trumpian politics, my sharing at a more personal level might help others in what would surely be an analogous search for strength and an appropriate ethical response in times of confusion and despair. As a result, this book weaves personal thoughts into the more objective, scholarly analysis, in the hope that both can inform the reader.

A mixture of the personal and the objective seems an appropriate approach to the topic of moral courage. Difficult times are not rare in political life. Wars, genocide, totalitarian abuse, political repression, and cruelty—all these force us to ask, what do sensitive, humane people do when the world around them goes a bit mad, when tolerance, decency, and compassion go missing, truth becomes a rarity, and the norms of civilized democratic discourse seem more a distant ideal than a working reality? How do we explain why certain individuals find the moral courage to speak out, while so many others retreat into the islands of their own world or become cynical and bitter? What kind of person resists falling into the refuge of a clan or tribe? Who refuses to succumb to anger, to fear of people who don't look like us or worship as we do? Who stands up to hate, in others *and* in ourselves? Who finds the strength to fight back against dogma, including our own? Who finds the restraint and sensitivity to listen, to find common ground, to avoid the cheap retort, petty annoyance, and hostility?

Our analysis begins first by stipulating that courage is not the absence of fear; courage is mastering fear and acting in spite of it. Courage involves digging deep into ourselves and finding the strength to do the hard things even when we are uncertain, scared, anxious, or tired, and when we feel unequal to the task but manage somehow to do it, nonetheless.

Second, the traditional view in contemporary Western philosophy misleads us: moral courage need not necessarily involve moral reasoning. Instead, an Aristotelian analysis—finding examples of what most of us accept as moral courage and then asking what these examples have in common—suggests that moral courage derives from our sense of who we are. So a story of moral courage is ultimately a story about ourselves—about our identity, values, and agency, and our capacity to believe we can make a difference. I have lived long enough to realize that this process is not simply about politics. We all experience moments of personal loss so great that they engender bewilderment, chaos, uncertainty, and disorientation, instances when we are overwhelmed and feel adrift. One response to any existential crisis in life lies in recognizing that by looking deep into ourselves, we may find our potential and use all we have to survive these times with our humanity intact. We can use our personal experience with pain and despair to help us find greater sympathy for others, to slowly grasp something important about what it means to be a human being.

Third, in a time of cynicism, we need to understand why some people believe they possess the ability to change things. Beyond this, however, we ought to be asking different questions from those conventionally found in the literature on moral courage. Why do some people act even when it is unpopular? Even when it is costly to them? Even when there is no reward, or their good deed goes unnoticed? Conscience and standards of morality and ethics can be stronger than our fear of scorn, our anxiety about failure, our dread of public censure or reprisals. When does this happen, and why?

Because of the complex nature of moral courage, this book has grown to become the first volume in a trilogy on moral courage. The analysis here mostly avoids stories of courage by political actors, saving them for a later volume in which moral courage will be examined in a more explicit and institutional political context. If moral courage inherently involves a disagreement over values—and forces us to confront issues of betrayal versus loyalty—what does it look like in extremely contentious political times, such as those that plagued America during the Trump years, and that remain with us still? Can moral courage exist in polities and societies whose moral values we reject or even find morally repugnant? These are the questions addressed in the second and third volumes. Volume 2 considers moral relativism and asks whether moral courage can exist in societies whose values we do not share or even find morally reprehensible. Volume 3 focuses explicitly on the double-edged aspect of moral courage: isn't every act of moral courage also an act of betrayal? How, then, do we distinguish what to me constitutes an act of moral courage from what to you is an act of betrayal or fanaticism?[2] Interestingly, all three volumes suggest how moral issues and moral courage relate to a polarization of political life and reveal that how we conceptualize issues—our moral cognition—strongly influences our political life.[3]

In this book, however, our focus is on providing a baseline understanding of moral courage. We begin by examining the everyday acts of ordinary people. One story concerns a schoolteacher who quit her job and devoted thirteen years to caring for her mother. Kay's story illustrates how normal people work to help others, often through small, unnoticed acts of bravery and devotion, performed quietly and on a daily basis that can—as one sees one's own life dribble away—feel like an eternity.[4] At one point, Kay knew her own health was in jeopardy—she has a serious heart condition—but she said she simply didn't care if her time devoted to her mother killed her; she was *not* walking away from her mother. While Kay's story certainly entails many other critical forces—love and duty chief among them—it also entails moral courage, here expressed in a quiet form but one with great power to affect another's life in critical ways. Stories like Kay's remind us that courage need not always roar; it can be a quiet voice at the end of a long day, reminding us we can try again tomorrow.

Themes in Kay's account of her life surfaced in other stories. Born worlds away from Kay's midwestern America, Vikram Tej risked his job to fight caste discrimination in India, emphasizing the importance of empathy in moral courage and explaining his actions thus:

> It was not easy for me to do that [sue the government for discrimination]. I had two children I was addressable to, and their futures depended on their father working. In India, once you get fired from the government, no one else will hire you. But I decided this was the type of case that was so wrong that if I didn't say anything, I couldn't go to work. So I spoke out and tried my best, and thankfully the system worked.
>
> Q: *So you were never scared you would get fired? Fearful of what would happen to your children?*
>
> Tej: Parenting isn't always about giving your children money. Parenting is about leading your life in a way that you would want your kids to lead [theirs]. (129)

Heather Booth, a political and social activist who began her work as a student with the 1964 civil rights Freedom Summer and the founding of the Jane movement and continued through the Affordable Care Act and the 2017 MoveOn Resistance Summer, also highlighted the private, undramatic aspect of moral courage:[5]

> You are pursuing acts of courage, instances where people act on their moral values. Often those are projected in intense moments of great conflict that are dramatic. Like Jane [abortion assistance], or like [Freedom Summer in 1964 in] Mississippi. But I think that there's another way to look at moral courage. It has to do with, "Do you do the work every day? Do you do the work every day, when it's often boring, or you're too tired, or it's too hot, or you're too cold, or you didn't get enough sleep last night? Do you do the work every day that builds organizations and supports others and yourself to act? That moves forward even when you're not sure what to do, when you're insecure, when you feel, 'Will this be good enough?'" The moral courage required to take those steps every day is at *least* as important as the moral courage in times we often

romanticize, the overly dramatic and important actions where people stand up against unaccountable and unjust power. (64)

Other themes ran throughout our interviews. One was that moral courage becomes a habit: just one otherwise inconsequential act of moral courage can increase the sense of what a single individual can accomplish. People often develop what I call their moral muscle in small, seemingly insignificant ways. Our interview with Amal (chap. 7), who first demonstrated moral courage as a Muslim teenager attending a Christian grade school, highlights this process.

Above all, studying moral courage reminds us that we, both as individuals and as a people, constantly have a choice.[6] Our best hope in troubled times is to dig deep within ourselves, within our own character, to ask what our personal values are and what we care about enough to make us put aside self-interest when duty calls or conscience demands.

This book details the journey of seven people who did this. My analysis in this book is based on a sample of over fifty individuals,[7] but for reasons of space I present the full stories of only seven individuals whose narratives beautifully capture the broad themes found in the larger sample.[8] Some of these speakers were semi-public figures, like Steve Zimmer, who protected undocumented students as head of the Los Angeles Unified School District, or Loretta Lynch, who as California's Commissioner of Public Utilities withstood pressure from both the Clinton administration and California's Governor Gray Davis to "go along" during the Enron crisis. Others are people who hold no political office and define themselves only as private individuals, such as Amal, the young woman who in high school fought bullying and prejudice against Muslims. All of these individuals would classify themselves as normal, ordinary people.

As I completed my analysis, I was struck by the critical relationship between moral courage and basic values—core values held so deeply that they effectively shape and mold the essence of who the individual is, thus creating an identity or character that requires compliance with these core values. In doing so, however, I realized most work in this field fails to note the complicated but tight association between moral courage as traditionally analyzed and liberal, democratic, humanistic values. To speak more directly to the existing literature, this volume focuses on moral courage in the societies traditionally examined by scholars: those with liberal, democratic, and humanistic values, the kinds of societies in which most scholars today work.[9]

My analysis here concludes with a discussion of the close bond between moral courage and its consideration by scholars working in liberal, humanistic democracies. We discuss the complex relationship moral courage has with such societies and use this evaluation to present a kind of baseline for moral courage. Doing so provides a framework from which to analyze moral courage existing in societies that do not share such values. This theoretical scaffolding helps move us closer to touching the ambiguous heart of moral courage: its uneasy tension between moral courage and betrayal, disloyalty, or even fanaticism.

After a brief introduction to explain how I put together the research, I construct a narrative interpretive analysis of interviews with seven individuals, suggesting what listening to these stories teaches us about what constitutes moral courage and why moral courage matters to us all. Part 1 reviews the literature and presents my research design and data description. Part 2 presents my data: the stories of seven individuals that illustrate moral courage concretely, up close and personal. Part 3 analyzes my entire data set to flesh out our knowledge of moral courage as traditionally conceptualized. The conclusion summarizes my findings and discusses the impact this study had on both students and the professor.

PART I

Moral Courage as a Concept

Courage is not the absence of fear, but rather the assessment that something else is more important than fear.
FRANKLIN DELANO ROOSEVELT

1

Moral Courage:
What We Know and What We Need to Know

Introduction

The tumultuous last days of the Trump presidency and the inaugural period of the Biden administration made much of the term *moral courage* as the fate of American democracy often seemed to rest precariously in the balance, depending on the actions of a small number of individuals. The post-election period of 2020 was filled with news media discussions bemoaning the lack of moral courage among Republicans who failed to challenge a president on his way out, and praising the moral courage of the Republican sitting secretaries of states for honestly doing their job in counting votes, despite pressure from the sitting president of the United States (*New York Times*, November 29, 2020). Indeed, the entire Trump presidency was one in which US senators such as Mitt Romney and congressional representatives such as Liz Cheney were praised—or vilified, depending on one's perspective—for putting principle above party affiliation. Voters in many states exhibited moral courage by risking the health threat presented by COVID-19 in order to vote or to participate in peaceful protests against racial injustice in Black Lives Matter marches. Election officials were praised for their moral courage in ignoring death threats and continuing to count ballots fairly. Finally, we had health-care professionals and lifetime public servants—like Dr. Anthony Fauci and Dr. Rick Bright—similarly lauded or punished for arguing that science should not be subject to politics. The death threats these people received remind us of the importance of moral courage in many walks of life.

But what exactly is moral courage? Why is it so important? And what role does it play within a liberal, democratic society? Answering these questions is the topic of this book. The first step in that process is to review the literature on moral courage to understand what we do know and which areas need to be examined more fully.¹ In doing so, we move beyond the literature in the obvious fields—philosophy and political theory—to include work in areas as diverse as nursing, social psychology, and social science, where moral courage remains a subject too seldom addressed directly by political scientists. As will be evident, the existing literature on moral courage is noteworthy in two regards: (1) the wide range of definitions of moral courage and (2) the extent to which contemporary analysts address the definitional questions of moral courage by assuming that the existence of liberal, democratic, humanistic values both form and drive acts of moral courage.

MORAL COURAGE AND LIBERAL DEMOCRACY

One of the main questions in this field concerns the relation of moral courage to liberal democracy. This argument emanates from ancient discussions of moral courage, held to be a virtue fundamentally in tension with the core values of liberal democracy.² The essential thrust of this argument holds that courage is too deeply intertwined with its origins on the battlefield to lend itself to democratic values. A liberal populace that venerates physical or martial courage will likely be hoodwinked by their leaders into supporting imperialist adventures abroad while finding the space for criticism at home narrowly circumscribed. In other words, within a democratic society, a love of courage can too easily lead to a politics of militarized patriotism. Furthermore, courage has been made a principal component of a variety of decidedly illiberal political and social systems and creeds. For example, courage played an outsized role in the cultures of ancient Sparta and Nazi Germany. In the latter case, in particular, courage was intimately linked with a ruthless disregard for human suffering.

It is not just that courage, in being a fixture of these societies, keeps bad moral company. Courage itself involves a great deal of moral ambiguity. We can identify reprehensible acts that require tremendous physical and moral courage and point to individuals willing to put others to death for their beliefs who nonetheless demonstrated tremendous courage in defense of their own values. (Consider Thomas More, canonized by the Catholic Church, which conveniently overlooked More's keenness for torturing and executing Protestants.) The animating spark of courage is a virtuous and principled defense of one's values. Because it depends on whose values are being stood up for and which way of life is being protected, courage can aptly be deemed largely audience-relative.

Ultimately, I find that an exploration of moral courage both links the concept to a discussion of the critical values within society and makes clear that moral courage can exist in a wide variety of moral systems. Indeed, I find that while most scholars argue that liberalism and courage are a poor fit, moral courage distinctively suits citizens of a liberal, democratic order—since moral courage is, at its core, connected with the personal values of integrity, authenticity, and truthfulness—and that liberal, democratic institutions and values reinforce moral courage, and vice versa.[3] The audience-related aspect of moral courage and the lack of empirical work focusing on how moral courage might differ according to the moral society in which it exists is why I make both an extensive empirical examination of moral courage in general (part 2 of this book) but also in moral systems whose values differ significantly from our own (treated in volume 2 of a forthcoming trilogy on moral courage).

ORGANIZATIONAL FORMAT

Our review of the existing literature on moral courage proceeds as follows. Part 1 begins by outlining my working model of courage. Perhaps the best work, and certainly the most extensive, emanates from philosophy and political theory and in social and moral psychology. The literature on courage in social psychology unfortunately remains deliberately vague about just what courage is, or how it could be operationalized for the purposes of measurement. Unsurprisingly, moral philosophy is equally flush with mutually incompatible accounts of the virtue of courage. By cross-pollinating the two kinds of literature, I have arrived at a provisional definition of courage, drawn in large part from a study of an individual's moral intuitions on the topic.[4] This definition emphasizes five central components.

1. A courageous action must, fundamentally, involve some degree of intentionality or internal deliberation on the part of the agent.
2. The agent must experience some degree of fear in performing their action.
3. The action needs to be done for the sake of some noble or well-intentioned goal.
4. The action must involve some awareness of the amount of risk.
5. The review highlights the irreducibility of value to the concept of courage. In particular, it conceptualizes the concept of courage as care, which locates the personal values and commitments of agents in the foreground of acts of courage.[5] The end of part 1 examines some of the ways in which this provisional conceptualization could benefit from revision.

After examining these thorny definitional questions, part 2 turns to the conceptual structure of the virtue of courage. Psychologists and philosophers have articulated at least three distinctive kinds of courage—physical, vital, and moral courage.⁶ Though my focus in this book is predominantly on moral courage, one must set this focus in a broader context of both physical and vital courage, explaining their scope and the virtues of character with which they are associated. Ultimately, both seem unsuitable, at least when compared to moral courage, for serving as an explicitly political concept of courage in a liberal polity. We thus must turn to the concept of moral courage itself. We identify its connection with the attributes of integrity, truthfulness, and authenticity. Moral courage—as opposed to physical courage—is a decidedly internal form of courage, focused concretely on agents' relationship to themselves and their values. In finding moral courage largely internal, I make no claim that it is apolitical or purely concerned with notions of self-realization or self-mastery. I touch briefly, in fact, upon moral courage's connection with shame and publicity within a liberal society. But the key finding is that the actualization of moral courage is prompted by situations in which individuals look inward to the values individuals care for most—values prompted by the demands of integrity, truthfulness, and authenticity to undertake a selfless or courageous action.

Following this discussion, part 3 turns to moral courage's connection with democratic and liberal values. In the first instance, I consider Athenian democracy, which contained some of the most fruitful reflections on the capacity of moral courage. Pericles, Demosthenes, and even the Platonic Socrates upheld the virtues of integrity and truthfulness as part of a uniquely democratic form of moral courage. The decidedly more modern liberal values (post-1500) are highlighted by two liberal theorists, Bernard Williams and Judith Shklar, who developed accounts of the core values of liberalism that were directly connected with the virtues of moral courage. The core argument in this section is that the virtues of moral courage and liberal democratic values are mutually reinforcing, with each set of values nurturing and strengthening the other. The structure of liberalism and democracy serves to inculcate the virtues of integrity, truthfulness, and authenticity, while these values, if widespread enough among the citizens, make liberalism and democracy both possible and far more stable.

The chapter concludes by tying together the three streams of thought outlined above and then presenting a brief examination of the definition of courage itself. The chapter concludes with some additional reflections on the nature of courage in illiberal democratic politics.

Toward a Model of Moral Courage: The Vagueness of the Concept

In the aftermath of the insurrection on January 6, 2021, America has been inundated with harrowing accounts of how close the rioters came to being able to act on their murderous desires. The baying mob assembled gallows outside the US Capitol and evidently had every intention of carrying out summary executions, even of the sitting vice president. In this, they followed a long tradition of American antidemocratic vigilantism. Fortunately, individual acts of courage thwarted the goals of the haphazard attack by members of the January 6 mob. Officer Eugene Goodman—a Black man—stared down the Confederate flag–waving mob, going so far as to shove one of the rioters, thus successfully inducing the mob to retaliate.[7] In doing so, Goodman achieved his goal: steering the rioters away from the Senate chamber. It is not hyperbolic to view Goodman's personal risk to his own well-being as an attempt to save the institutions of American democracy.

Some may be skeptical that such examples of courage are necessary within a democratic society. This is because courage has acquired a negative reputation owing to its typical conflation with martial prowess; it has therefore acquired a decidedly masculine and elitist reputation.[8] It is of course easy to dismiss the example of Officer Goodman as a model of simple physical courage, something we cannot reasonably expect everyone to be able to demonstrate. Indeed, as a matter of political philosophy, until recently, the relative lack of scholarly interest in moral courage may stem from liberal suspicion of theories of virtue and perfectibility. Theories of courage share a generally inegalitarian nature with any theory that places outsized emphasis on virtues suspected to be rare by their very nature.[9] As an empirical matter, the psychological study of courage has been hindered by the preoccupation of social psychology with the failings, prejudices, and shortcomings of human beings as opposed to their signature strengths.[10]

Yet if we step back, we realize courage occupies a place of unquestioned importance in popular parlance. Even within the fraught partisan climate of contemporary American politics, it is one of the few political virtues saluted on both sides of the aisle.[11] Moreover, it is clearly a contested and multifaceted concept, and one that is correspondingly difficult to define. Indeed, Shane Lopez and Charles Snyder offer eighteen separate conceptualizations of courage proposed by philosophers, psychologists, and other theorists of the human condition.[12] In a study of undergraduate students, Christopher Rate, Jennifer Clarke, Douglas Lindsay, and Robert Sternberg found the vast majority believed four components were essential to any definition of courage:[13]

- intentionality or deliberation,
- personal fear,
- a noble goal, or well-intentioned reason for action, and
- clear personal risk.

More scholarly studies, of both a psychological and philosophic bent, validate the wisdom of the undergraduates Rate and his colleagues studied, although neither their original study nor any subsequent work has reached a clear consensus about what an operational definition of courage would entail. Some, for example, additionally emphasize perseverance or endurance in the face of exacting circumstances or confidence in one's eventual success.[14] The range of definitions does not end there, though. For Hobbes, courage was a social vice, a lack of justified fear that made its bearer a danger to the social order.[15] For Aristotle, courage lay at the appropriate mean between reckless abandon and cowardice and could be possessed by only a select few.[16] This definitional question is inescapable, so I tentatively endorse the working definition that Rate and his colleagues provide.

Though it is difficult to arrive at a definitive meaning of courage, the literature suggests that the intuitions of individuals on the subject provide a working foundation on which to build. It is clear that courage, at its base, is concerned with values and, more specifically, with care for those values. A common theme connects courage philosophically with care. As Alasdair MacIntyre argues: "If someone says that he cares for some individual, community, or cause, but is unwilling to risk harm or danger on his, her, or its own behalf, he puts in question the genuineness of his care and concern."[17] Another common theme suggests that courage presupposes one has fundamental commitments, things for which one would be willing to die.[18] Courage, then, is ultimately a form of radical care or regard for fundamental commitments. Without making the stakes life or death, it is clear that even courage in the face of social scorn or through a struggle with illness involves care for the values or constitutive commitments that make one's life meaningful.

Conceptual Structure: Three Types of Courage

Putting aside these definitional points for a moment, what does the literature suggest about an abstract conceptualization that tells us what circumstances make an act courageous? While most scholars agree that courageous individuals are necessary in a political order—that we need brave soldiers and politicians who scrupulously adhere to principle—there are real questions of who should count as truly and rightfully courageous, and under what conditions they qualify. Cicero claimed that "the courageous deeds of civilians are not inferior to those of soldiers."[19] Nevertheless, any conception of courage that does not contend with its military dimension is "hollow to its core," and any understanding of courage must remember that its roots originate on the battlefield.[20] Along these lines, and thinking about the battlefield, it is important to remind ourselves that the ancient Greek *andreia* referred to the explicitly masculine bravery of soldiers during wartime.[21] This has led some to conclude that courage is incompatible with modern liberal norms of gender equality and the liberal polity's generally pacific nature.[22] However, while the study of courage may have begun with the grizzled warrior, modern understandings of the concept reveal several distinct conceptions of courage that apply just as seamlessly to the principled politician and the cancer patient alike. In what follows, it is useful to engage the tripartite model of courageous behavior employed by most researchers within the field of social psychology. This schema of courage differentiates between physical, vital (or medical), and moral courage.[23] We document the defining virtues of each before examining the importance of moral courage within the modern liberal state.

Physical courage. Within this system of classification, physical courage is often presented as concerned with successfully overcoming subjective fear in situations that involve substantial risk to one's bodily integrity.[24] Research within this tradition has primarily looked to such figures as decorated soldiers and members of bomb squads, essentializing a certain conception of maleness within courage as it evolves as a concept. This understanding of courage as essentially physical owes much to Aristotle's influential treatment of courage as one of the quintessential components of his theory of the virtues. For Aristotle, only on the battlefield does one have the opportunity to practice the physical excellence and nobility in combat he believed were inextricably linked with the exercise of courage,[25] because it was only on the battlefield could one earn the honor and glory attached to displays of military heroism. This conceptualization excludes noncombatants and women from the exercise of courage; it consigns those facing illness or trying circumstances outside of combat to an inferior category of bravery.[26] This intimate and perhaps even universal connection between physical courage, martial skill, and honor has subsisted across time, as analysts identify instances of physical courage transcending the boundaries between ally and enemy on the battlefield.[27] Recounting the honors soldiers afforded to their sworn enemies during both World War II and the American Civil War, Richard Avramenko writes: "War is not always conducted on the field of hate; on the contrary, the bonds it creates can dispel unexamined antipathy and even hatred. Courage closes the gap between individuals, be they friend or foe."[28] In total, the defining excellences of physical courage have to do with skill on the battlefield, with disregard for the risks an action poses to one's physical integrity, and with a distinct concept of honor.

In contrast, liberal theorists and philosophers have long held that physical courage is a dangerous virtue for a democratic society. The traditional virtues associated with courage form "a life that sustains and enlarges their particular excellences, creating situations in which their virtues can be given the fullest play."[29] In other words, a society that venerates feats of military bravery and the virtue of honor is likely to engage in expansionist behavior and resemble polities such as the antebellum South in its adherence to a reactionary politics of social status.[30] This understanding of traditional courage has led numerous liberal thinkers to reject *physical* courage while affirming that *moral* courage has a role to play within liberal society.[31] A preoccupation with physical courage has caused many theorists to mistakenly conclude that courage is a virtue that can be dispensed with in a liberal, democratic society.[32] But this highlights the distinction between courage and moral courage. I shall argue below that moral courage is indispensable to a democratic society. For now, however, consider the second critical aspect of courage: vital courage.

Vital/health courage. If physical courage is the oldest conception of courage, vital courage is the newest. Aristotle notes that those who suffer from illnesses exhibit bravery of a sort, though he was quick to reject this, considering it necessarily inferior to martial bravery. By contrast, physicians and patients both rely on a distinctive version of courage.[33] The courage of patients centers on facing one's own mortality, developing the courage to "surrender the good of life for the good of death," and generally enduring the tribulations of living with illness.[34] Physicians, on the other hand, need courage to admit their own "finitude and uncertainty" and provide the appropriate "care and concern" to help patients realize their "capacities to negotiate reality" in making decisions about the course of their care.[35] The work of nurses and other caregivers is irreducibly linked to courage, with nurses willing to undertake risky behavior to provide care to patients even when faced with threats from communicable diseases and pandemics.[36] One could argue that patients who live with and accept the threat of chronic health conditions exhibited a particular kind of courage.[37] Indeed, empirical work finds the presence of strong values or role models in the lives of individuals was a substantial predictor of vital courage.[38] Aside from those with long-term health issues, all manner of individuals exhibit psychological courage when they attempt to reorient their lifestyle to avoid stress and other damaging psychological pressures.[39] The importance of vital courage in the face of pandemics, such as COVID-19, is even clearer.

The defining features of vital courage, then, have to do with endurance in the face of adversity, a realistic acceptance of what one can do—to help others as well as oneself—in situations of human precarity. It must be stressed that while vital courage is a critical form of courage—indeed, it may be the one most of us witness or exhibit over the course of our lifetimes—it is in many cases a decidedly private or personal form of courage. Vital courage certainly has facets essential for a political community, especially its connection to values and its promotion of an outlook of honesty. However, as I demonstrate below, these features are not unique to courage. In fact, they are among the central virtues of the concept of moral courage, as seen in chapters 6 and 7.

Moral courage. Finally, let's turn to the most central component of this inquiry: moral courage. The literature finds moral courage most centrally concerned with the virtues of integrity, authenticity, and what I term *truthfulness*.[40] Unlike physical courage, which is concerned with one's external circumstances, moral courage is almost exclusively concerned with honesty to oneself and one's values. Truly, one could posit that individuals ought to be fundamentally committed to developing and protecting their autonomy.[41] Individuals need to protect their true or authentic selves from external influences—especially malign social forces.[42] This approach leads to a close corollary in that individuals exhibit moral courage by refusing to subvert their values in the face of negative consequences and social pressure. So, courage is quintessentially concerned with the reaffirmation of the self in a world hostile to existence.[43] This makes moral courage about (a) affirming one's existence and core values and (b) about an unwillingness to surrender to the reality that an independent and principled life within the world almost invariably entails anxiety and suffering. This latter facet of moral courage was central to Plato's account of this virtue, with philosophers being capable of the highest form of courage since they alone were willing to pursue an uncomfortable truth to its logical conclusion.[44] The notion exists in the works of Mencius, a Confucian philosopher who identified courage as a quintessentially moral virtue and drew a connection between the principled refusal to be a party to injustice and the well-being of the soul.[45] For Mencius, only the individual who could defy the unjust orders of a king, with full foreknowledge of the likely consequences, could truly claim to be virtuous.

Hallmarks of moral courage—integrity, truthfulness, and authenticity—are evident in the stately "profiles of courage" that captivate the American imagination, as well as in the whistleblowers who expose criminality within the halls of power. Moral courage is the defining trait of Henry David Thoreau's celebrated refusal to be a party to what he considered an unjust and expansionist war.[46] It can be found among individuals who stand up to unfair employment practices or other forms of workplace mistreatment.[47] It is also evident among individuals who refuse to tolerate acts of discrimination and bigotry or student protestors opposed to American involvement in wars such as Vietnam. Moral courage is made possible by an agent's values and their connection to a defined sense of self. Agents who are morally courageous express proper care for their core values and commitments and refuse to forsake them, even when they expect to suffer as a consequence.[48] The truthfulness moral courage demands prevents agents from performing any action that would not demonstrate this sense of care. This strong commitment to core values necessarily involves a theory of authenticity and integrity. A morally courageous individual must have, at least implicitly, certain core goals and projects they value above all else; they must have a core moral identity to which they can be true. In standing up for what they believe, or refusing to be complicit in something they reject, the morally courageous are guided by the demands of authenticity—what Harry Frankfurt calls "the reasons of love."[49]

Indeed, the quintessential examples of moral courage undoubtedly concern "practical necessities" or "ethical incapacities"—actions one simply must take or things one could never do and retain any self-respect.[50] This is why moral courage links closely with the emotion of shame, the feeling that one has failed according to standards one wishes to uphold.[51] The interactions between moral courage and shame are twofold. First, the morally courageous individual wishes to avoid the shame of undermining their deepest convictions and so must act with truthfulness and integrity. In this form, shame is pointed inward and sees agents pressured by their own ideals and internalized social expectations.[52] The second form shame takes is outward-facing. In an open, liberal society in which transgressions can, in principle, be made public, morally courageous agents confront those whom they oppose with their own venality. They shame the others, then, through the example set by their actions, with their comparative lack of integrity, and often for their lack of care toward shared social values. The particular cast of characters in these situations can vary, with some principled politicians refusing to toe the party line and protestors risking bodily harm and arrest to publicize blatant injustice. Nonetheless, liberal moral courage will—at its core—always retain this close connection with truthfulness and shame. This is why moral courage is so critical to a liberal, democratic society. These societies are defined by the plurality of different conceptions of the good that inhere within them.[53] However, without those who feel bound to stand up for the principles of fairness and the rule of law—such as Black Lives Matter protestors, whistleblowers, or heroes such as the dedicated Capitol policeman Eugene Goodman—it is unlikely the citizenry as a whole will retain a commitment to liberal values. The temptations of self-deceit and/or political and personal advantage are too great to resist for many of us, at least some of the time. Consequently, we may need to be shamed into living up to the values we share as citizens of a liberal democracy. This is not a new idea; in the archetypal democratic society, the Athenian polis, the power of moral courage was explicitly linked with its capacity to shame those who failed to live up to the democratic ideals of their city.[54]

The Relation of Democratic Liberal Values to Moral Courage

The literature reveals deep interconnections between democratic values and the virtue of moral courage. This is evident even in the history of the values of classical Athens. One might expect Greek conceptions of courage to be of limited use in helping us understand the importance of courage in the politics of contemporary America. Instead, the origins of moral courage—within the Athenian polis—actually provide a clear set of examples of how moral courage and democratic values are uniquely suited for each other.

MORAL COURAGE AND DEMOCRACY: THE CASE OF ANCIENT ATHENS

It is commonly believed the ancient Greeks viewed courage as an exclusively martial virtue. I find this to be a misconception. Aristotle held that the courageous person "stands firm against what is and appears frightening to a human being; he does this because it is fine to stand firm and shameful to fail."[55] Aristotle draws strikingly hard boundaries between what is appropriately frightening and what is not, and his examples are chosen in a way that consciously diverges from Plato's discussion of explicit moral courage in *Laches*. Aristotle emphasized the centrality of bravery in the face of death, typically during wartime. This stilted conceptualization renders the Greek notion of courage too conceptually narrow to be properly incorporated into the fabric of modern civic and social life. However, even granting the problematic nature of Aristotle's concept of courage, this account of militaristic courage fails to account for the nuances of Aristotle's view, let alone that of the rest of Greek antiquity.[56] Although the combat-centered term *andreia* was one part of the Greek understanding of courage, the concept of moral courage as one that can serve decidedly democratic ends clearly existed in the Greek world.

Undeniably, classical Athens provides a wealth of insights into the nature and scope of truly democratic courage. Athenians from Homer to Pericles and Demosthenes articulated a model of democratic courage that connected the freethinking and independent nature of the Athenians with courage, in explicit contrast with the Spartan militaristic courage.[57] Athenian courage was predicated on both self-ownership and the constellation of democratic values that made individual acts of bravery worthwhile and laudable.[58] Pericles' celebrated funeral oration makes courage the virtue enabling individuals "to put into practice their underlying ideals and their explicit rational judgments in the appropriate way."[59] Democratic courage, then, is distinctively practiced in defense of values and made possible by one's self-aware commitment to those norms. Both Demosthenes and Pericles shared a belief that democratic institutions—such as freedom of speech, and the egalitarian culture, debate, and discussion that defined life in Athens—were necessary to create courageous citizens.[60] Further, democracy was possible, the Athenians believed, only because of the revolutionary moral and physical courage of specific individuals.[61] Pericles notes—and Socrates later claims it in Plato's *Apology*—that the democratic norms of Athenian life were mutually reinforcing with the integrity and truthfulness moral courage requires. The Socrates of the *Laches* defends his method of dialectic as a means of forcing Athenians to confront their own mistaken beliefs and demands a spirit of truthfulness from them.[62] This public engagement and intellectual shaming chastised those who did not display the proper sense of integrity regarding the city's defining values of free inquiry and truthfulness. It was a process possible only in a society that not only permitted but in fact celebrated the free exchange of ideas and philosophic dialectic. Rather than being antithetical to a democratic way of life, then, moral courage seems uniquely actualized by democratic citizens.

Plato's *Laches*, a text to which numerous studies of courage return, expands upon some of these same themes. Here Socrates presses his interlocutors, the generals Laches and Nicias, on the question of the precise nature of courage. These two leading figures in Athenian politics and military affairs stay noticeably entrenched in their preferred understanding of courage, resorting alternately to insults and attempts to flatter Socrates, or simply parroting confusing platitudes in the hope of sounding impressive; the dialogue ends abortively, with no clear resolution. However, the structure of the dialogue, and its jarring and abrupt conclusion, have led scholars to conclude that Plato wished to highlight the intertwined relationship between wisdom and courage.[63] Socrates's companions are not courageous precisely because they refuse to challenge their own beliefs and pursue the truth.[64] According to Dobbs, Plato intends for the reader to conclude that the pursuit of the good and the true in politics requires a certain courage, and that this courage is "not merely the virtue of the sacrificial lamb, but the fundamental excellence which the good citizen and the good philosopher necessarily share."[65] In *The Republic*, Plato expands his definition of courage to distance it even further from more traditional understandings of virtue. In particular, Plato articulates a conception of courage open to both men and women.[66] This model of courage concerns balance and the rightful organization of the soul. It is the quintessential virtue, allowing one to face down one's passions and, in the phrase made famous by the filmmaker Spike Lee, "do the right thing."[67] This philosophic form of courage, manifested as an unflinching commitment to the truth, provides one basis for the value of moral courage. Those who put principle over political expediency in a democratic society, and who ignore the social consequences of adopting this posture of integrity, often are the same individuals who evince the moral courage Plato describes in *Laches*.

BEYOND THE POLIS: MORAL COURAGE AND LIBERALISM

While the mutually reinforcing features of democracy and moral courage can be glimpsed most clearly in ancient Athens, the literature also reveals a wealth of contemporary proponents of moral courage within a liberal society. Why does the morally courageous individual fit the liberal polity like a hand fits a glove?[68] Liberalism, in all its various forms, is basically committed to the inviolability (or the purity) of the individual, the rule of law, and a political system of truthful publicity.[69] This is why adherence to the rule of law, respect for individual rights, and belief in the importance of public transparency are among some of the most central, contemporary, liberal values. Even liberals who remain skeptical of the more optimistic pretensions of liberalism recognize liberalism as the form of government most effective at preventing institutionalized cruelty and humiliation.[70] Certainly moral courage plays a critical role in helping liberalism achieve these ends, with the values of liberalism helping foster citizens who exhibit this kind of courage. The structure of liberalism provides the space for truthfulness as a social virtue by (a) preserving an institutional framework of criticism and (b) encouraging individuals to be suspicious of claims to authority.[71] Additionally, (c) liberalism's particular emphasis on individual identity provides the protections to the individual that preserve the space for authenticity.[72] In more traditional societies, the individual's ability to form an authentic individual identity was limited by the forces of tradition, group, or caste.[73] Liberalism allowed a level of identification with one's identity, and its potentially dynamic and shifting particulars, beyond what was possible in more traditional social arrangements. In these ways, liberalism and what I have called the virtues of moral courage are closely aligned.

If the citizens of a liberal society are to "protest and block any sign of governmental illegality," then they must have "a fair share of moral courage, self-reliance, and stubbornness to assert themselves effectively."[74] Citizens in a democratic society must refuse to be parties to "passive injustice" and stand up in the face of even the most ordinary and everyday forms of harmful misconduct.[75] By refusing to be complicit parties to passive injustice, democratic citizens strengthen their faculties for moral courage and answer the democratic demand to "treat each expression of injustice not just fairly according to the actual rules but also with a view to better and potentially more equal ones."[76] Life in a liberal society—and repeated experiences with its core values of individual rights, transparency, and rule of law—thus provides citizens with an education in moral courage. The structure of the institutions, and the corresponding suspicion of political mendacity and wanton government power they promote, help inculcate a disposition of courage among liberal citizens when these vices manifest themselves. Unless morally courageous citizens are willing to step up to defend these values, the whole institutional structure of liberalism could collapse, and the antihumanist forces of reaction and superstition, with their disregard for human well-being, could prevail. The distinctive virtues of moral courage have been sustained by liberalism.

This is clearly evidenced in contemporary American democracy. Liberalism needed morally American public discourse to not vilify one's opponents, a tendency fully evident not just in Trump's tweets and rallies but also in the intractable culture wars within American academia and across social media. I find this in the debates over "cancel culture," by which I mean a contemporary form of ostracism that thrusts someone out of social or professional circles via social media or online sources. Those so ostracized are said to be "canceled." Both sides of the ongoing war over cancel culture claim the mantle of courage.[77] One side argues that courage is basically concerned with the expression of unconventional and even controversial views. Their opponents claim that this rejection via public shaming and ostracization amounts to the stifling of an altogether different form of democratic courage: the drive to hold the powerful to account for their misbehavior and misuse of their platform. (Although in slightly different form, this use of moral courage is found in early Greek consideration of its role, as discussed earlier in this chapter.) The anti–cancel culture coalition believes their opponents are unruly online trolls, practicing a form of political correctness with Stalinist undertones. Those opposed to this point of view describe their opponents as understrappers of bigots and abusers, cronies who would willingly protect those who espouse racist, homophobic, and transphobic ideas. While I can neither settle this dispute conclusively nor feel optimistic about its prospects for being resolved in the near future, it is true that the commitment of both sides to the virtues of moral courage suggests it could ably serve democratic ends. However, without a commitment to liberal tolerance—and the concern for the virtues of truthfulness and discussion in good faith—the staunch courage of both sides may ultimately become self-destructive. If neither side can accept the other as basically concerned with seeking the truth, as opposed to being motivated by ideology and hidden animus, then the politically bracing aspects of moral courage, saluted by theorists such as Judith Shklar and Bernard Williams, will not be realized. The alternative to a truthful liberalism is likely to be a reactionary politics of superstition.[78] Minus the courage necessary to resist self-deception and outright falsehoods, a liberal citizenry is likely to behave as many Americans have during the pandemic and into 2023, refusing to accept the seriousness of the pandemic and the reality of President Joe Biden's victory. Whatever else needs to be done to shore up America's institutions in the face of its accelerating democratic backslide, the strengthening of American citizens' capacity for moral courage will play a key role.

Conclusion

Moral courage remains an important topic within popular culture, the media, and our imagination, even if scholars must range far afield academically to seriously study moral courage as a concept. Before beginning our own empirical examination of moral courage, I will remind the reader of the importance of virtue ethics for moral courage and then note five critical aspects of moral courage itself.

VIRTUE ETHICS

The most useful philosophical perspective for understanding moral courage is embedded in a virtue approach to ethics, an approach too often relegated to a secondary place in contemporary scholarly circles. Emanating from Aristotle and reconfigured in the early 1950s, virtue ethics focuses on character and virtue rather than doing one's duty through the conscious deliberation of acts or rules that guide one to good consequences.[79] Virtue ethics focuses on the individual rather than on decision-making or establishing rules for behavior. It looks at how the moral character of the person carrying out an action develops, rather than at ethical rules or duties, or even the consequences of particular actions. Virtue ethics encourages individuals to think about what constitutes a good life. Rather than prescribing rules to live by—such as the Ten Commandments—virtue ethics asks people to think about the kind of person they are, and the kind of person they want to be and should become. It is this process of reflection, virtue ethics holds, that will naturally produce the habits that then develop the positive character traits that result in good decisions. What is key is the constituting of stable, internal tendencies and habits that produce the good outcomes, not duty or following particular rules of behavior. A virtue ethics approach thus contrasts with deontological and consequentialist ethics, which emphasize identifying universal principles that may be applied to any moral situation. A further philosophical gap exists between virtue ethics and approaches such as Kantian or utilitarian ethics that stress conscious, deliberative ethics, and rules for behavior.[80] The centrality of identity allows moral courage to fit well into a philosophical framework of virtue ethics.

Beyond this, I find several major aspects concerning moral courage that I should note as we begin our analysis.

AGENCY AND KNOWLEDGE OF HUMAN BEHAVIOR

At one point, courage was concerned almost exclusively with martial skills and battlefield heroics. However, a careful review of the literature reveals that courage is not inextricably linked with war and warfare. In fact, even in Greek antiquity, Plato, Aristotle, and Pericles all helped reframe courage in terms that led the way to a broader conceptualization of moral courage. Pericles' rhetoric reframed the virtue of courage in terms that connected it with the performance of democratic citizenship.[81] Similarly, the ambiguous ending of Plato's *Laches*, where everyone leaves stumped, underscores how courage should be viewed as concerned with asking hard questions of one's own beliefs and meeting tests of intellectual bravery, as much as military ones.[82] Aristotle's account of courage does not map onto an ethnology of reckless abandon in combat.[83] To be sure, Aristotle's individuals must, through a semirational process, act for right, noble reasons in the interests of their souls. So it is necessary to explicitly uncouple courage from nationalist fervor and armed conflict.[84] Taken all together, and alongside other readings within this subset of my research materials, I conclude by noting several key themes in the literature on moral courage.

Theme 1: Courage is intimately linked with a theory
of agency and a knowledge of human behavior.

Concern for others. Moral courage is intimately associated with care.[85] Courage presupposes one has fundamental commitments, things for which one would be willing to die or at least make serious sacrifices to protect. It is therefore a form of radical care or regard for one's fundamental commitments, a conceptualization that in contemporary times owes much to feminist care ethics,[86] which argues that courage is *not* inherently sexist in nature if conceptualized correctly.[87] Nor do analysts find it inconsistent with a commitment to liberal democracy.[88] Several of my readings substantiated the general association of courage with care (Avramenko) and identified instances of moral courage in the workplace (Sekerka and Bagozzi), the sporting green (Corlett), and even in the wards of a hospital (Lindh, Barbosa da Silva, Berg, and Severinsson).[89]

Theme 2: Courage requires attachments to ideals, causes, or other individuals.

Link to liberal values. Courage is often portrayed as inconsistent with life in a liberal democracy. Expecting citizens to be courageous might be thought to violate liberal hostility toward the virtues more generally. This would run against Madison's admonition that human history reflects the folly in searching for virtuous leaders, as well as the necessity of preparing "auxiliary precautions" for when the wicked were inevitably in power.[90] For Hannah Arendt, all political action (which entailed the bringing of something new into the world) required courage.[91] Political action was about great deeds done in the public sphere, all of them necessarily ephemeral. Arendt was by no means an archliberal, and I began this inquiry uncertain as to whether a distinctive model of liberal courage existed. However, reviewing the literature problematized the superficial contrasts between liberal democracy and courage. In fact, liberalism has a particular conception of and need for courage, even if it enjoys what has been called an ambivalent relationship toward it.[92] Alexis de Tocqueville, in fact, argued that the peculiarly American form of self-interest and love of individual achievement had created a new democratic concept of courage, one particular to a democratic temper.[93]

Theme 3. Liberal courage entails self-sacrifice in the interests of the well-being of a liberal, democratic state.

Liberal courage can be a "catalyst for responsible political behavior: It can compel "bold and pragmatic officeholders [to make] tough and unpopular decisions or give other officeholders unwelcome but necessary advice." "[94] Indeed, within a liberal polity, many individuals can be capable of courageous acts and the burden of courage falls on all citizens.

SOCIAL-PSYCHOLOGICAL LITERATURE

When we turn to social psychology, the single most important body of contemporary empirical work to offer both a complex, well-thought-out conceptualization of moral courage *and* a thorough examination of the contributing factors leading to moral courage is Ervin Staub's work on heroes, altruism, and genocide.[95] Staub defines moral courage as "acting on one's values in the face of potential or actual opposition and negative consequences."[96] He notes four issues relevant to my empirical work. First, Staub observes that "people can and do hold values they regard as moral that give rise to immoral goals and harmful and destructive acts. For example, obedience to authority is often held as a moral value, even when the authorities are destructive."[97] Second, Staub's work on altruism and heroism distinguishes between heroism as a single act (e.g., jumping on train tracks to save someone from an oncoming train) and as persistent action (e.g., hiding Jews during the Holocaust). Third, Staub distinguishes between acts requiring immediate action and heroism that makes deliberation possible. Finally, Staub observes that moral values can give rise to immoral goals and destructive acts, such as when obedience to authority constitutes a moral value but the authorities themselves are evil and destructive. For all these problems, Staub advocates restricting "the meaning of moral courage to people acting on genuinely moral values which serve moral ends."[98] Unfortunately, Staub fails to specify the definition of moral values or moral ends. My empirical work is geared toward this end.

CENTRAL COMPONENTS OF MORAL COURAGE

Although there thus are different ways to think about moral courage, a review of the literature suggests most include five central components.

1. Moral courage entails acts based on the actor's core values.
2. The actor is aware there are personal risks involved for the actor in taking the morally courageous act and may feel personal fear at having to act.
3. The actor nonetheless knowingly disregards these risks, thus intentionally or deliberately demonstrating a willingness to endure hardships, including some of which the actor recognizes he may not know in advance.[99]
4. Most conceptualizations distinguish between costs and risks and make the actor's values key to the action insofar as the act reflects the actor's most strongly held and central values.
5. Moral courage is usually in pursuit of a noble goal or a well-intentioned reason for action which involves care for the values or constitutive commitments that make one's life meaningful.

Most of the prior literature on moral courage is set in the context of the liberal, democratic polity, although many analysts find moral courage incompatible with liberal, democratic systems. I found that liberalism, in all its various forms, is basically committed to the inviolability of the individual, the rule of law, and a political system of truthful publicity.[100] This is why adherence to the rule of law, respect for individual rights, and belief in the importance of public transparency are among some of the most central contemporary liberal values. Yet, as Staub makes clear, moral courage can exist in societies whose values differ significantly from those of democratic, liberal humanism. Indeed, moral values can give rise to immoral goals and destructive acts, such as when obedience to authority constitutes a moral value but the authorities themselves are evil and destructive. Thus, moral courage is a complex phenomenon, and many questions need to be answered if we are to gain greater understanding of the concept. To do so, we must broaden our understanding of moral courage through an empirical analysis of individual acts of moral courage. Let us turn now to a discussion of how I constructed such an empirical examination.

2

Stories of Moral Courage: Data and Research Methodology

Data

To construct the analysis, I conducted interviews with people who had performed acts that seemed morally courageous according to the general conceptualizations found in the literature summarized in chapter 1. The interviews included nearly one hundred individuals. For reasons of space, I can print only a few full interviews here; the ones I chose were selected both because the interviewees' demographics reflect the members of the broader sample and because their conversations articulate so well the main substantive themes I found explained moral courage. These individuals include:

1. Steve Zimmer, head of the Los Angeles Unified School District (LAUSD) when we interviewed him. Zimmer has worked his whole life to help immigrants and as head of the LAUSD took action to protect undocumented students.
2. Erwin Chemerinsky, founding dean of the University of California, Irvine's School of Law, who sued President Trump over violation of the emoluments clause. Chemerinsky is now dean of the law school at the University of California, Berkeley.
3. Heather Booth, a well-known American civil rights activist, feminist, and political strategist, often described as "the most important person you've never heard of" because she so often works behind the scenes. While in college, Heather participated in the 1964 Freedom Summer and established the Jane Collective to provide safe abortions in the pre-*Roe* era. After the birth of her children, Booth established the Action Committee for Decent Childcare (ACDC) and founded the Midwest Academy, a training organization inspired by the work of Saul Alinsky, to teach grassroots community organizing. She continues to work for civil and human rights, immigration and voter reform, and the rights of women and minorities,

in areas ranging from health care to economic reform. Her work is documented in *Heather Booth: Changing the World*.
4. Kay Monroe, a schoolteacher who retired early to care for her mother through fourteen years of Lewy body disease (LBD), leaving her financially and physically vulnerable owing to a heart condition.
5. Amal (pseudonym), who showed moral courage as a teenager in the face of bullying and anti-Muslim sentiment.
6. Loretta Lynch, former head of the California Public Utilities Commission, on withstanding pressure from both Governor Gray Davis and the Clinton administration to forgo public hearings after the energy crisis that later evolved into the Enron/energy crisis.
7. Vikram Tej (pseudonym) on fighting caste discrimination in India, not against himself but against members of other castes.

My goal in printing the full interviews is fourfold. (1) Each interview presents a detailed picture of a real human being who exhibits moral courage. These people are neither saints nor archetypes nor abstractions; they are normal people we might meet in our own lives, people with whom we have much in common and to whom we can relate. If they can perform acts of moral courage, perhaps so can we. (2) Beyond just capturing the reader's imagination, the stories perform another crucial function: they slow down the reader long enough to open the door to the possibilities of alternate scenarios. The idea of a different way of seeing the world might sneak in and thus make readers receptive to later scrutiny. While large chunks of the interviews are repeated in part 3 as material for analysis, I intend this repetition to provide the emphasis necessary to prepare the reader for the consideration of important new arguments. (3) The stories provide the critical context within which to view the process that drives moral courage while revealing vital details about how the moral self developed in these seven people and what shaped it. Consequently, these narratives provide the historical background for the later analysis. By reading the details surrounding moral courage, I hope readers can feel they are coming back to familiar ground when I analyze moral courage in chapter 10. (4) Finally, and perhaps most important, having access to the complete interview allows readers to form their own opinions of moral courage. By presenting the data in full, I hope to reassure readers that I am not cherry-picking quotes or shading the data to serve a hidden agenda of my own. The essence of scientific work is to analyze and share evidence that can be evaluated carefully and independently. Omitting the full stories thus would deny readers the chance to examine the data themselves and perhaps find fault with my analysis. In an age where truth is questioned and "alternate facts" are offered willy-nilly, it is absolutely indispensable to intelligent discussion that people have easy access to the evidence necessary to disagree with any scholar.

Although I try to keep analysis tightly focused on these seven individuals, I do occasionally quote others from the broader sample when a particular passage is especially insightful.[1] The other people quoted here include:

1. Choo Tee Lim (pseudonym), who tells of being sold into slavery as a child in China and fighting tradition by refusing to sell one of her own children after her husband died leaving her with nine children to raise.
2. Nini, a Dutch woman who as a teenager rescued Jews during the Holocaust. Nini later became a psychoanalyst in Chicago. She was interviewed for an earlier project but asked that her full interview be shared only after her death.
3. Sophal Ear, a Cambodian activist, on speaking out against the Cambodian government.
4. Janusz Reykowski on offending friends in the Polish trade union Solidarność (Solidarity) and the last communist government of Poland by helping organize the Round Table Talks, which smoothed the way for a peaceful transition to Polish democracy in the 1980s.
5. Richard Ceballos, a lawyer and whistleblower who sued colleagues in the Los Angeles district attorney's office over corruption.
6. Senator Joe, a California state senator who broke with the leaders of his political party over matters of principle.

COLLECTION OF STORIES

The narrative interviews analyzed here were collected during three main periods: (1) the initial course for which this project was devised in the winter of 2017; (2) two summer internships in 2017 and 2018; and (3) my own individual interviews, most of them collected between January 2017 and fall 2019. The two exceptions were interviews with Nini and Kay. Nini's interview was done for another project on altruism,[2] and my interview with Kay began before this project, simply as an oral history with a friend (in this case, also my cousin). Kay's initial interview was supplemented by a follow-up interview done by a student. Nini asked to have her interview held back until after her death. She has since died.

Some stories were analyzed but not quoted from directly in order to protect the speaker's identity. (This group includes people who had been sex-trafficked or were undocumented students.) Most of the interviews were conducted by me or by friends and/or former students. We obtained interviews by word of mouth, in what might be best described as a modified snowball sample. Also called non-probability sampling or chain-referral sampling, snowball sampling is a non-probability sampling technique utilized when the samples have rare traits that make them difficult to find. Existing subjects provide names of other people who share their characteristics. For this research, we modified the snowball sampling to include personal referrals from friends and from our general reading/knowledge of people who had performed acts that seemed, at least on the surface, to fit the general criteria of moral courage found in the existing literature on that topic. (For example, I learned about Zimmer from catching a short news story about his refusal to let immigration officers come onto LAUSD property. I knew of Chemerinsky's suit against Trump; two students in my class were taking a course with Chemerinsky and asked to interview him.)

All interviews were recorded, transcribed, and the transcriptions then shown to the speaker for corrections and approval. Surprisingly, few changes were requested. A few interviewees wanted to be anonymous; others preferred pseudonyms. It was important to include some stories in full, however, so the reader can examine what are essentially data in the form of stories. Sharing a few specific original interviews also provides concrete illustrations of how we interpret the narratives to reach conclusions about the common themes driving moral courage and the themes that suggest how the speakers—the people who demonstrate moral courage—think about what moral courage means as a concept.

How did I decide which stories to publish and which to use only as part of my analysis, sometimes quoting from them but mostly drawing the quotations from stories included in full in the book? First, I never included stories that might harm the speaker if published. This means several DREAMer stories were omitted, as was a fascinating story of someone who had been sex-trafficked and now works to help prevent sex trafficking in California. Secondly, sometimes the speaker wanted to share the story for background purposes but did not want to be quoted directly or preferred to be included only anonymously. Choo Tim Lee and Vikram Tec are two such speakers. In a few cases, I had gotten approval to include the stories but could not later contact the speaker or the interviewer to obtain final approval for the completed manuscript because the speakers' real names had been deleted. To address this issue, when I draw on such stories I have given the speakers pseudonyms and disguised their stories slightly. Thirdly, I tried to balance the speakers in terms of demographics, such as gender, nationality, and so on. I also tried to balance the type of moral courage, using stories of both private moral courage (such as Kay's caring for her mother) and political moral courage (such as Sophal Ear's protest against the Cambodian government). I also include some stories that fall in between (such as the accounts of Erwin Chemerinsky and Heather Booth). Not all the stories have the same critical dimensions, then. Finally, some interviews were simply too compelling, the speakers too articulate and insightful, for me to omit those interviews entirely. (Reykowski, for example, a social psychologist, is accustomed to thinking and writing about topics similar to moral courage. His interview was priceless in helping me understand the intricate complexities of moral courage as a concept, and I am grateful to him for his expertise in addition to his willingness to share his own individual story of moral courage.)

Each interview was recorded, transcribed, edited, and then sent to the speaker for approval, including comments, deletions, additions, and anything else they wished to have excluded or included, from substantive clarification to spelling corrections. I never pushed anyone to have their story made public and indeed pulled several stories when the speaker wished to have them remain private, or in one case, simply failed to respond to many attempts to locate him for approval and confirmation of the interview. (As noted above, two of the stories included here were approved and allowed for inclusion, but I still changed identifying characteristics and names.)

Narratives

Narrative analysis is by now widely accepted as a research tool in social science.[3] I have discussed its value, uses, and challenges elsewhere.[4] But it is important to remember that stories reflect and refract people's lives in a way that no other text can, making the abstract concrete. This is not to minimize the value of other methods of political analysis. Political science—indeed, all of social science—has long relied on numbers, statistics, and other forms of formal methods and modeling to capture political reality and political life. All of these are legitimate approaches. But just as a diamond has multiple facets, political and social reality has multiple dimensions. Statistical and quantitative methods, for example, will not capture all of those facets any more than narrative analysis can capture every aspect of political life. There is a place for methodological pluralism in political science.[5] But overreliance on numbers or even historical textual analysis can ignore the people, the real live human beings, who stand behind these numbers. Narrative analysis can get at this. Narrative can bring into the foreground the actual persons who create, transform, and act in historical contexts. Narrative paints pictures; it brings emotions and passions into the center of our focus. I try to use narrative to get to the heart of what psychodynamic psychology brings to the understanding of moral courage and its relation to ordinary human beings.

My underlying assumption thus is that analyzing the stories a speaker creates to explain an event will reveal the subconscious and unconscious factors in the speaker's mind and behavior. Perhaps not perfectly, but enough to help us begin to better understand how that individual's psychology affects the speaker's personality, perception of the world around them, and their actions, including acts of moral courage.

We hold a cultural stock of stories that reduce things into bite-size pieces without reducing their complexity. Narratives are present at all times, in all places, in all societies. It is not an exaggeration to note that the history of narrative corresponds with the history of mankind. It is hard to think of a people without thinking of them in the context of a narrative.[6] The question is, how do narratives help us recognize ourselves in other people's stories? Sharing stories creates the enigma of social change, builds community, and increases the moral imagination. When we read the narratives of moral courage in this book, we will find reflected and concretized, and thus made more intelligible, many of the questions about moral courage posed in the first chapter. So, in thinking about the stories of moral courage, we should hold in mind several key questions guiding our analysis:

- What are the specifics of the story that is happening?
- To whom is it happening?
- Why is it occurring?
- Do we see ourselves in the story?
- How do the stories relate to each other? Do we find counternarratives, and, if so, what are they?
- How do the stories themselves change through negotiation and retrospective recasting?[7]

Beyond these guiding questions, I also asked and attempt to answer, as best as possible:

- How do we interpret other people's implicit meaning?
- What is not mentioned? How do we tackle this silence and discover its significance?
- Does this silence reflect a narrative unconscious?
- Is there a consequential linking by, for example, the use of phrases such as "that" and "then"?
- How do we avoid overinterpreting these connections, finding linkages that might not exist for the speaker?

As readers consider these stories, they should focus on who the "we" is, and whether, when, and how the meaning of this "we" shifts, if indeed it does. What is taken for granted in the narrative, and what does this reveal about the speaker, and his or her situation? About the culture? When speakers talk with us, who do they believe is their audience?

Stories of moral courage—indeed, all stories—are about the storytellers' lives. But this also includes the community, however that community gets defined. There are national stories, and in some cases universal stories. We find this in the individual stories here. For example, when chapter 4 describes Erwin Chemerinsky suing Trump for violating the emoluments clause of the Constitution, what kind of statement is he making about our country? Our president? Our past? When Kay tells us (chap. 6) how people treated her mother while she was in a nursing home, what is the context? The time and culture surrounding the story can be critical, as Kay's story illustrates, especially because current norms for caring for elderly family members have shifted dramatically from a hundred years ago, when most widowed parents who became infirm lived until their death with their children. Today, more elderly go into assisted living. Stories also reveal a great deal about the complex relationship between micro- and macro-narratives. We find an illustration of this phenomenon when Chemerinsky argues that it is Trump who has broken trust with the people and with our shared American history. A structural transformation of the private sphere into the public domain can also occur, as we find when Vikram Tej tells us (chap. 9) how his conscience led him to sue the Indian government for caste discrimination because such discrimination—by an officer working for the government—violates the spirit of the Indian freedoms as embodied in the Indian constitution, a document Tej holds sacred. When Heather Booth argues (chap. 5) that we are all entitled to clean air, safety, and education, is her statement a universal one? Is she positing that all human beings should be entitled to such rights simply as part of being born? Or is she saying that this right is limited to Americans?

As we read these stories of moral courage, we should consider how the construction of political narratives speaks to ethics and politics and remember that almost all narratives addressing how we deal with others should be defined as political. This broadening of the political extends the political analysis to include personal relations between any two individuals. Usually associated with feminist theory,[8] the idea that personal experiences result from social structures or inequality originates in C. Wright Mills's 1959 work *The Sociological Imagination*. Mills argued that the personal is inextricably linked to greater social and historical contexts. Betty Friedan, for example, in her 1963 work *The Feminine Mystique* picked up on this idea and associated

1950s women's unhappiness—the "problem that has no name"—with the narrow, rigid position of women in postwar American society. Second-wave feminists such as Carol Hanisch, fed up with the chauvinism of the leftist movement in the 1960s and '70s, used Mills's and Friedan's approach to reject arguments that posited an opposition between personal and political issues. (Discussing "personal" problems was dismissed by many men at the time as "grumbling" or "therapy.") Feminists countered that "the personal *is* the political," especially, they argued, since these so-called personal problems were caused by women's inequality, and individual women were not to blame. Further, because these so-called personal problems emanate from deep-seated societal inequalities, they can be resolved only by social change, not by personal solutions. Feminist organizations, such as the Redstockings, and Black organizations, such as the Combahee River Collective, which focused on the link between racism and sexism, embraced this idea of a class hierarchy based on gender. The idea of the personal as political influenced both later feminist theorizing and feminist activists. (Hanisch advocated an interplay between action and theory, or praxis.) Hence, we find that contemporary feminist theory adopts a broader conceptualization of the political.[9]

Our conceptualization of politics to include personal acts between two people seems both sensible and advantageous. By thinking of politics in this broader sense, we can then ask a whole series of new questions designed to provide insight into moral courage.[10] For example: how does the strategic use of narrative construction serve to move people from a traumatic past into a future that is richer and more peaceful or more destructive and violent?[11] How does the construction of one particular narrative versus that of another lead the speaker—or the listeners—to a happy outcome in which their sacrifices (in this case in the form of moral courage) seem to have served a purpose—for example, to have ennobled a person? Or has the narrative left the speaker trapped by the past, sad and alone after an event that went wrong? One could argue that truth and reconciliation commissions perform that function, or are intended to do so. But this can happen even at the micro-level. Kay's story provides a remarkable illustration of how her care for her mother shaped the rest of Kay's life. But Booth and Tej also speak of the political as including quiet family moments and the caring for others that is also a hallmark of moral courage.[12]

Sometimes we tell our stories in order to bridge a gap between ourselves and others. In this sense, stories can become communicating and bonding experiences.[13] Storytelling also can be a bridge between the personal and the public. (Zimmer's experience as head of the LAUSD, where he worked to protect undocumented students, makes clear how his acts as a public official were informed and shaped by his more personal experience, growing up close to grandparents who were themselves immigrants.) Finally, storytelling can recreate history as alternate possibilities; stories can trigger the moral imagination, suggesting new options. This idea held true for Reykowski, whose sponsoring of the Round Table Talks in Poland helped establish a new democracy without bloodshed but meant Reykowski had to risk losing his credibility with Solidarity when he served on the Politburo in order to oversee this peaceful transition to the new democracy. Indeed, when I sent Reykowski the transcribed interview to approve, edit, and correct, he wrote to me asking how soon I needed the corrections. At the time he was eighty-eight years old, yet he was still working assiduously to establish a liberal think tank in Poland that could provide the intellectual influence to further Polish democracy, again under attack in 2018 as it was when he first helped put democracy back on track in the 1980s.[14] I find these seemingly little things immensely touching and helpful in bringing into concrete form the more general theoretical concepts academics like to toss around for our students and our own edification.

The importance of listening to stories of moral courage thus cannot be overestimated, especially when we consider the role stories play in pointing out alternative routes to action. A story of moral courage can inspire by example but also by helping the reader imagine alternative scenarios to the one the listener might otherwise fall into or accept as the norm. Narrative imagination accordingly can create a sense of the possible. It extends the idea of the potential and helps us in imagining the other and thus see different possibilities. It lets us reach beyond our own limits to grasp different scenarios, different possibilities, and different actions.[15] After listening to Booth's determined outlook—"cynicism of the intellect, optimism of the will," she said, quoting Antonio Gramsci—I wished I could spend a month with her. I hope some of the spirit and bravery of these speakers will rub off on and inspire readers as well as they did the students who participated in this project.

There are many other intricacies of narrative; the literature now has grown so vast that one cannot raise all these issues here.[16] We need to ask: how is the story told? When is the story told? Under what circumstances? To whom? Reykowski never wanted to tell his story, saying he had done nothing of importance. At age eighty-eight, he told his story to his grandniece Zosia because he loved her, just as Vikram Tej told his granddaughter his personal story but would not, perhaps, have given it to anyone else. The context of Reykowski's story is relevant. I had read his initial interview with his grandniece Zosia. I then happened to visit him in Warsaw in the spring of 2018. I asked to supplement this interview with Zosia with additional questions.

Why, this modest man asked me, would anyone care about his story? I responded honestly, saying that just hearing one story of moral courage from a normal person could inspire others to think they too might find the strength to do one brave thing. Hearing this, Reykowski recognized that others might want to know about his story, to know about his life. Our twenty-some-year friendship also helped establish the element of trust necessary for an unpretentious man to share his story, and I did several additional interviews during my weekend visit. But the external world also mattered, and the fact that Reykowski was willing to communicate his story at a time when the Polish democracy he had helped nurture and midwife was under attack was not, I believe, irrelevant. Thus, personal stories told to a dear friend or family member involve not only trust, but also a desire to set the record straight for someone you love and who you believe should know the truth, especially in times when similar acts of moral courage may again become morally salient.

In this sense, stories are gifts from the speaker to the listener. These stories should be cherished and interpreted with great care. I trust I have done this here. I hope the insight these stories provide into moral courage in the age of Trump will help us all understand moral courage as a more general phenomenon, useful whenever we encounter times of confusion and despair, nationally or personally.

PART II

Understanding Moral Courage

I just try to do what I think is morally and ethically correct. I don't consider it courageous at all, actually.
STEVE ZIMMER

3

"We're Going to Do What's Right. We May Pay a Price for It, but That's Fine": Steve Zimmer on Protecting Undocumented Students

> I treat these issues as if they were affecting my own family, for it *is* our family. It may not be my mom or dad but it's *someone's* mom or dad. When you dehumanize these issues, that's when you get policies like the executive orders of this president, President Trump.
> STEVE ZIMMER, March 22, 2017

Q: Let me begin by telling you the background for this project. Some of my students were extremely upset about the 2016 presidential election and I was trying to console them a little bit. I said, "Take your heartache and turn it into art"—something like that, the idea being that none of us can avoid bad times but we can use our own unhappiness and despair to gain greater understanding and compassion for other peoples.' So we decided to do a project together that would involve collecting stories of people who've demonstrated what we think of as moral courage, people who took a stand on an issue that wasn't necessarily popular and that might cost them their own lives but which they [took] out of principle. You were one of the people we thought about, and that's why we want to interview you. We'd like to record your story, if you're okay with that. We'll send you a copy so you can review it and determine whether there's anything you want to add, subtract, correct—anything you're not happy with. Only if you're happy with the interview would we then analyze it. Please don't answer any question you're at all uncomfortable with, and feel free to stop me at any time. You're a human being, not a research subject, and your privacy is a prime concern, okay?

Basically, we'd like to begin by asking people to tell us a little bit about themselves, because not everybody knows who you are. Then we'd like to ask you about anything you've done in your life, any time when you've confronted actions that required moral courage. As a child, for example, some people confront bullying or discrimination. We're interested in hearing about times when you did what you wanted to do and other times, maybe,

---

Steve Zimmer is the former head of Los Angeles Unified School District.

when you didn't do something and felt bad about it afterward. That's basically the project.

Okay, well I'm honored to be considered for this. Let's go ahead.

To begin, I grew up in Bridgeport, Connecticut. My mother was an educator. My father was a blueprinter. I grew up with the family business from a very young age. I remember working in that business in whatever capacity we could help. That's what you did in the family business. I became a teacher because I wasn't a very good student; at some point, I realized most of the teachers, while they were certainly great people and wonderful educators, they became teachers because they were good at school, not because they were struggling at school. I thought it would be important for someone like me to consider a career in teaching. That's why I became a teacher. I taught English as a second language. Then I taught any subject they would let me teach, to students who were either failing in school or were recent immigrant students. That's my educational background.

I never planned to run for elected office. I was asked to do so. I said no a couple of times. Then in a momentary lapse of reason, I gave in [*laughter*]. I found myself on the Los Angeles School Board and have tried to do right by the students and families I worked with over the years. I never imagined I would be in the position to do the things I've done. I've tried to do my honest best in this job for the last eight years.

Q: So you ended up in politics the way a lot of good people do. They don't intend to do it, but they realize they want to do something. Now you are head of the school board in Los Angeles, isn't that right?

That's correct, I am.

Q: Tell me a little bit about the action that you took. I don't know how it happened or if you were the driving force, but I know there was an action taken quickly after the 2016 election to protect LA students who might be undocumented. Can you talk about that?

Sure. I've been very blessed throughout my career to have been able to work directly with the immigrant rights community. My grandmothers were the first in their families to be born here in the United States. They both, along with my grandfathers, grew up in a monolingual Yiddish-speaking family. Then, because of labor unions and the opportunities of the public school systems, my parents' generation, the first generation really, were able to break out of the cycle of poverty. I don't think of myself as a 2.5 generation or third generation. Most of us who are white don't think of ourselves that way, but I am. My grandparents were monolingual Yiddish speakers; they were English learners.

They came from Austria-Hungary on my father's side and eastern Poland on my mother's side. They got out before World War I, between 1912 and 1915. It was that wave of immigrants. My grandmothers were the first to be born here in the United States. My grandfathers arrived here as infants.

Q: Okay, got it. The point is that you're aware of what education can do for newcomers.

That's right. When I arrived in Los Angeles and began working in the recent immigrant community, I have to tell you, it was like coming home, really. I felt more connected to the history of my family than I ever had previously. So I began a long-standing working relationship with the immigrant rights community. In the early 1990s I started teaching. There was a wave of extreme xenophobia and extreme actions against our immigrant communities, so I became involved politically, in many ways, based on that. I started working with the immigrant rights community in 1993–94 and have worked with the immigrant rights community ever since. At various points in my career, I have been able, both as a teacher and as a board member, to be very involved, very engaged with the community. Before the 2016 election there was a wave of enforcement—raids, actually—under the Obama administration. I wrote a policy that banned cooperation between the school district and the immigration authorities. Late 2016 is when I wrote this last policy, but this was not new. I had been working on this issue for quite some time. I've been involved in the DREAMer movement for undocumented college students since the late 1990s. It was February 2016 when we passed what's basically a sanctuary schools bill; immediately after the election, we reiterated that policy. We just made very proactive direct statements to our kids and their families that all schools in Los Angeles would be safe. We would make absolutely sure we would not cooperate with ICE [United States Immigration and Customs Enforcement] and would use our schools as resources.

Q: Was everyone on the board in agreement with this? I would imagine this was not a totally uncontroversial policy.

We have a pretty progressive board as it relates to immigrant rights. But yes, I definitely had to bring some people along. There's always a lot of outrage whenever you do something like that. That's part of it.

Q: How do you deal with the outrage? What happens when someone says: "Look, I pay tax dollars. These are my schools. People who don't pay any taxes, why should their kids get to benefit from my work?" I'm assuming that's one of the arguments you've heard.

Sure. People came at me all the time. I do a lot of things that are unpopular. I'm used to people yelling at me. I just try to do what I think is morally and ethically correct. I don't consider it courageous at all actually. I feel very, very strongly that we're a nation of immigrants. The courageous people are the immigrants themselves, especially our unaccompanied youth. My God, it's incredible what our kids go through. What we're doing around this issue is the least we can do. I don't think we're doing anything heroic. We're just doing what's right. The children and their families are trying to follow the same dreams my grandparents were trying to follow . . . the dreams they had for my mom, my dad, my aunts, and my uncles. I don't think the families I work with in Los Angeles deserve anything less than my family does.

Q: So this is a pretty straightforward moral issue for you? It's not something predicated on the idea that the country will be better off if we have immigrants? It's more that this is just the right way to treat people?

Yes. Look, I make decisions as a policy maker as if it were my own children in a classroom. If they were my son or my daughter who was affected by an instructional policy, an equity policy, or whatever it is. If my son or my daughter were at our most highly impacted school in this district and I were deciding about this school or our curriculum or whatever it is, I make the decision as if it were my own kid. When it relates to our employees, I also make decisions as if it were my mom or my dad working in the cafeteria or driving a school bus. So it is for issues around immigration: I treat these issues as if they were affecting my own family, for it *is* our family. It's not some community like, "those kids over there." This is our family. What would we want for our own family? What were the dreams my grandparents and my great-grandparents had? Well, it turns out it's the exact same dream a hundred years later. So I'm just doing what I would hope anyone would do if it were their own family, which is treating it as if the issue were affecting your own family. It may not be my mom or dad, but it's *someone's* mom or dad. When you dehumanize these issues, that's when you get policies like the executive orders of this president, President Trump.

Q: *Let's talk a bit about that. Are you concerned that there may be, at some point, literally, federal agents at the door of the school? I mean, Los Angeles is not your small town in the middle of nowhere. This is one of the most important and largest school districts in the country.*

Yeah. I don't know what to expect from this administration. I wake up in the morning; I read more and more things every day. I have no idea what to expect. All I know is that as long as the leadership of this city takes this very personally and behaves as if it is our own families on the line, we'll be okay. We will stand up for and defend the rights of our kids and their families. We'll defend their dreams, and we'll defend their hopes and aspirations. Hopefully, we will, in two years, have a Congress that can legally stand in the way of this new policy of Trump.

Q: *I can remember television pictures of integration in the South where there were Southern leaders literally standing at the door barring children from coming in and federal troops coming in and trying to enforce the law. Are you at all concerned there may be something like this in reverse, where there may be federal agents literally coming in, saying, "We're going into the school," and you are standing there, barring the door saying, "No, you can't go into our schools." How far are you prepared to go?*

I think dramatic scenes like that very quietly play themselves out and have been playing themselves out for the last couple of decades, as it relates to immigration. To be very clear, the heroes and heroines in this story are not myself or Jerry Brown or Eric Garcetti, or anybody else. The heroes and heroines are peoples whose names we'll never know, who have taken an extraordinary personal risk to bring their families here to escape oppression, to stand up to racism and xenophobia. There is not going to be any hero at the schoolhouse door. We're going to do what's right. We may pay a price for it, but that's fine. It's not going to nearly be what others paid; it's not going to be the price my elders paid. I feel very lucky to have a chance to take a stand. Most people don't have that opportunity in their lifetime. But as it relates to standing up to the federal government or standing up to oppression, this is our Selma, in some ways. But there is no John Lewis. There's no Martin Luther King. These are just regular people going about their lives with very brave, ordinary acts of courage every day. The job of the high-profile people is to just stand at their side and make sure they can continue to be the courageous people they are in their own lives and their own ways, to show that the American dream still means something. Those of us who have been the beneficiary of it from a previous generation have an obligation to stand up for it for a new generation. Those people who don't do this either don't understand history, don't understand their own family, or they have abdicated their obligation to pay back this country for the opportunities their own families had.

Q: So you're really driven by your own sense of morality and a sense of feeling that you're genuinely connected with these people, that they are you. They are like family.

Yes. Look, I understand white privilege. I understand the opportunities I've had because of that. I also dealt with anti-Semitism in my own life, and it's fine. I actually think that was lucky, in some odd way. I'm very grateful that I was exposed to hate. I feel like being exposed to hate as a child allowed me to both understand what that means on a personal level and to give me the opportunity to understand what my privilege means. I know what it means to not have to face systemic or institutional racism. When I have the opportunity to make decisions where I can use the undeserved privilege I have to take down instruments of institutional or systemic racism or to stand with a community that is facing oppression, a vulnerable group that is facing hate, well, that's a high honor. It's a privilege and a blessing to do it. I don't really think about these things that much. I have to do the job that I have to do. I was elected to be here. I never aspired to be here, but I'm here. I mean . . . you always have to be reflective and to make sure you have a gut check. You have to make sure you're doing things your elders would be proud of. That's all I do. It's not any different than anybody in our own system. My job is just to make sure we can keep having dreams come true through public education.

Q: Let me just ask you one last question and I'll let you go. How do you explain to yourself all the people who voted for Trump for these kinds of reasons? People who said they wanted to protect the country from foreigners, that they didn't like immigrants. How do you explain all the anti-immigrant feeling that is in the country?

How do I explain it?

Q: *Yes. How do you explain it to yourself, and to the kids you teach? How do you change it?*

Hate is present. It's very hard to explain hate to people. I'm not sure it's important we understand hate, other than to know it exists. To try and dissect what causes it, that's great work for sociologists, but it's not how I spend my time. I just think it is important to understand that working folks in this country struggle a lot. That's the reason Donald Trump and Bernie Sanders culminated at the same time. They both, in their own way, appealed to a core discontent in the fabric of our democracy, which is economic inequity, a system that benefits and is stacked precariously in favor of others. These core inequities and these core separations that infect our systems make it so there is a deep strain of discontent that throughout history we find repeatedly turns us upon the "other." The job we have is not necessarily to understand the hate or try to explain it, but rather to be working constantly to eradicate inequity and reduce the savage gaps between those who have and those who do not have in our economic system. It's a strange thing in retrospect, but I firmly believe that if Bernie Sanders had won the Democratic nomination, he would be president of the United States right now. A lot of the rejection of the establishment that was part of the Trump vote was not actually this radically xenophobic, radically deregulatory kind of madness that's going on right now; it was a statement against the status quo. Some people within our electorate believe there is a ruling elite. Donald Trump is not part of that ruling elite; he's part of a different type of elite. But he was able to capture that antiestablishment feeling. I don't think every single person who voted for Donald Trump hates immigrants. I think it means that . . . look, when you're sick, you go to the doctor. If the sickness is serious, you want the doctor to give you medicine. Most of us are not deeply concerned with a multifaceted understanding of what caused us to be sick. We just want to be better. So when you feel the economy doesn't work for you and you're told by a charismatic leader that all we have to do is build a wall and keep other people out and you're going to be okay, well, I don't blame people who want to feel better. It's our responsibility to have the courage to come up with real solutions for economic inequity and create an economy that truly works for the working class.

Hate exists, and it's important to understand it exists. But what is going on right now, I don't think it's an increase in hate. It's an unleashing, licensing and legitimizing the ability to express hate. And that's reckless and should be called out at every turn. But what exists is a situation in which voters, when confronted with a choice between what they thought would be more of the same and a medicine they thought could work, they chose the medicine.

Q: *Well, you may say you don't understand hate, but that was a very good explanation. It's extremely coherent. It also explains to me one of the reasons why you're in education, because if our job is to be working constantly to eradicate inequity in society, then education is one of the best ways to do that, isn't it?*

Well, that's what I've been blessed to be a part of my whole adult life. I'm very thankful I'm able to be in a position of leadership at this moment. I just hope I make my elders proud every day. That's what I try to do.

4

"No One, Not Even the President, Is Above the Law": Erwin Chemerinsky on Suing President Trump

> Real acts of moral courage are done by people who put their jobs or their liberty on the line.
>
> ERWIN CHEMERINSKY, Winter 2017

Q: Could you begin by telling me a little about yourself?

I grew up in Chicago in a working-class family. Neither my parents nor my brother or sister ever went to college. My dad worked a home improvement store. My mom always worked at home. I was always more interested in academics than... well, I was always more interested in sports, but I was terrible at sports. I was always purely academically inclined. I went to Northwestern for college and Harvard for law school. If you had talked to me during college, I would have told you I wanted to be a high school teacher. I took all the classes to become a certified high school teacher. I did student teaching. I became a certified high school teacher but decided to go to law school because I wanted to be a civil rights lawyer. I worked in Washington as a trial attorney at the Department of Justice at a small public office, then became a law professor at DePaul in Chicago, from 1980 to 1983. I taught at the University of Southern California from '83 to 2004, at Duke from 2004 to 2008, and came here [Irvine] in 2008, so I am in my ninth year here. I am married and have four children and two grandchildren.

Q: Can we discuss some of your early instances in your career when you spoke out and stood up for the little guy? In 2000 you conducted a report for the Los Angeles Police Department relating to the Rampart scandal, which involved police officers planting evidence on innocent people and then sub-

---

Erwin Chemerinsky was the founding dean of the School of Law at the University of California, Irvine.

sequently lying in court to gain convictions.[1] *Can you tell us about that case and why you felt it was important for you to be part of it?*

The Rampart scandal was exposed in the spring of 2000 when a police officer named Rafael Perez got caught substituting flour for cocaine in the police evidence room. It turns out he had done that before. He said that in exchange for a plea deal, he would tell the truth about what they were doing. He and his partner, Nino Durden, and others in the Rampart division had been framing innocent people, lying in court to gain convictions. I got a call from the Police Protective League to do a report on the Los Angeles Police Department. I [had] spent two years before as the chair of an elected commission of Los Angeles to rewrite the city charter. I had run for election, gotten elected, and then [been] chosen to be the chair, so they asked me to do the report. I was initially reluctant because the Police Protective League, a police union, has historically not been a force for positive change in the police department. I was skeptical of what they wanted me to do, but over a couple of days, over the weekend, they assured me I could say anything I wanted. I could write anything I wanted, work with anybody I wanted, and whatever I reported to them would be public the moment I reported it to them. I decided to do this and recruited a group of civil rights lawyers to work with me.

The Los Angeles Police Department has a terrible history with regard to civil rights. I thought this was the moment that could bring about reform, and I wanted to be part of that. I spent six months working on the report. I interviewed about a hundred police officers and I released my report, ironically, on September 11, 2000, a year before 9/11.

Q: In 2002 you argued the first habeas corpus case in the country on behalf of Guantanamo detainees in federal district court. The court denied relief on the ground that it could not hear such a challenge. Can you tell us about this case and why you felt compelled to speak up for the detainees?

Over Martin Luther King Day weekend in January 2002 came the first reports of individuals being brought in blindfolded, gagged, drugged, in shackles, and housed in cages in Guantanamo. I spoke that weekend to a civil rights lawyer in Los Angeles. We thought what was being done violated the Constitution and national law. There was no one, at that point, to speak up for them. We filed a lawsuit on Martin Luther King Day in January 2002 on behalf of the Guantanamo detainees. I argued the case in February 2002 in federal district court and in the 9th Circuit [Court] in July 2002. This was the first case on behalf of the Guantanamo detainees. To me, it was all about the country needing to follow the Constitution and the rule of law.

Q: *In 2013 you argued a free speech case in front of the Supreme Court for Dennis Apel's right to protest the US military. Can you talk about that case and your views on free speech?*

We have an appellate litigation clinic here at the UCI law school where students get to brief and argue cases in the Court of Appeals. I always supervise two students per case, so I would supervise one case a year. In 2010–2011, maybe it could have been 2011–2012, the case I supervised involved Dennis Apel, a devout Catholic, who has been involved in a military protest. He lives not far from the Vandenberg Air Force Base.[2] At one point he engaged in an act of vandalism. He was convicted and spent some time in jail. They issued him a bar order saying he could never come on the base. He never went in the restricted areas of the base. But the Pacific Coast Highway, which you're familiar with, runs through the base. There's a public protest area right on the Pacific Coast Highway. He just wanted to be in the public protest area on Pacific Coast Highway. The military said he could not even be there. My students won Apel's case in the federal Court of Appeals. Then the United States government sought Supreme Court review. Those students had since graduated and the Supreme Court doesn't let law students argue anyway, so I represented Apel in the Supreme Court. I lost by the close margin of 9 to 0. It was about free speech. I admired him a great deal. All it was about was his ability to be on that side of Pacific Coast Highway, in a public area, officially designated as a protest area.[3]

Q: *I want to switch over to your work here at UCI law. You've created [the] Civil Justice Research Institute to explore and research ways in which the civil justice system can be more available to more people. Can you talk about what this independent university-based think tank will do and why it is important that courts remain accessible to people?*

Rights are meaningless unless they are enforced. In order for rights to be enforced, people need to have their day in court. Through many different doctrines, the Supreme Court has restricted access to the courts—limiting the ability to bring class-action suits or forcing people to go to arbitration rather than be in court or making it harder to show the facts to get to court. I thought it important there be independent, university-based research on this. Most of the research right now comes from the Chamber of Commerce, and it's very biased research. It's very pro-business and in favor of what businesses want, which is often restricting access to courts. I thought it would be a good thing to have independent research, and that's what the Civil Justice Research Institute is about. We've raised over a million dollars and hired a terrific executive director, Anne Bloom. We have an advisory board from people all over the country and it's off to a great start.

Q: Finally, we would like to ask you about your most recent act of moral courage. You are currently taking part in a lawsuit against President Donald Trump for violation of the emoluments clause. Can you speak to what you hope to accomplish with this suit and what advice you have for the country over the next four years?

Sure. I just want to insert one thing, and you can put it wherever it fits. You are very kind in calling these acts of moral courage. I'm a tenured law professor. I've been a tenured law professor since the spring of 1987. That means it would be very difficult to fire me. You can fire me as a dean; that's a whole different question. There's no tenure there. But I have a guaranteed job and a guaranteed salary. It's not moral courage to stand up for these things. Real acts of moral courage are acts done by people who put their jobs or their liberty on the line. Being a tenured law professor provides wonderful security in life to be able to do these kinds of things. So, yes, people write to the chancellor, I'm sure, saying I should be fired for writing the *Orange County Register* columns I write, or for bringing the emoluments suit, but they're not going to fire me. So I'm not sure I agree that any of these things are acts of moral courage, in the scheme of moral courage. They *are* standing up for things I believe in, though.

The emoluments clause suit—there are two provisions of the Constitution I'm going to talk about, so two provisions that use the word "emoluments." One says that no one who holds a position in the federal government can receive a present or emolument from a foreign government. This was meant to limit the ability of foreign governments to exercise influence over the new nation of the United States. "Emoluments" simply means "benefits." Every day Donald Trump is violating the emoluments clause because he's receiving benefits from foreign governments. To take one example, Trump International Hotel in Washington, D.C. is owned 76 percent by Donald Trump, in his own name. The other 24 percent is owned by his children. We now know foreign governments have rented rooms and facilities in Trump International Hotel, rather than alternative hotels, because it's the Trump hotel. He benefits, every time that happens, from a foreign government. Think about this connection with all of the different properties across the world.

There's another provision of the Constitution that says the president can receive no emoluments from the federal government other than salary. The president can't receive any other benefits from the federal government. The concern was that the president shouldn't be able to use his position to benefit himself financially other than [with a] salary. There are Trump buildings where entire floors are rented to the federal government, and he's benefiting from it. So, I agreed to be co-counsel in this lawsuit, filed on January 23. It's called Citizens for Responsibility and Ethics in Washington—that's the name of the organization against Trump.

You ask me why I am involved. I think one of the most basic aspects of the rule of law is that no one, not even the president, is above the law. Everyone in government has to comply with the Constitution. So President Trump is violating the Constitution. That's just not acceptable.

Q: Do you have any advice for citizens over the next four years? What they should be doing?

Get involved. Obviously, that depends on each person's individual interest. But we all can be more effective working in groups, or organizations, than working individually. So if somebody is particularly concerned about immigration, work with the Center for Human Rights or the Mexican Legal Defense Fund. If they're particularly concerned about reproductive freedom, work with Planned Parenthood. If they're particularly concerned about civil liberties, the ACLU. There are plenty of organizations people can get involved with. If they can afford it, help financially. Or they can get involved by volunteering their time. But the most important thing is to be involved.

5

"If We Organize, We Can Change the World": Heather Booth on Social Activism

> There's another way to look at moral courage. . . . Do you do the work every day, when it's often boring, or you're too tired, or it's too hot, or you're too cold, or you didn't get enough sleep last night? Do you do the work every day that builds organizations, supports others and yourself to take action? That moves forward even when you're not sure what to do, when you're insecure, when you feel, "Will this be good enough?" The moral courage required to take those steps every day is at least as important as the moral courage in times we often romanticize, the dramatic and important actions where people stand up against unaccountable and unjust power.
> —HEATHER BOOTH, Summer 2018 and Summer 2022

I was born into an incredibly loving family that values social justice. I have had incredible luck and fortune to be raised believing we should not only try to live our values, but we should try to make this a world consistent with the values of treating everyone with decency, dignity, and respect. Perhaps I should give some background related to this kind of work I do.

I became regularly active with the civil rights movement starting in 1960, when I joined the people, mostly students, who were protesting discrimination at Woolworths. Woolworths had a lunch counter, and African Americans weren't allowed to sit at their lunch counters in the South. There were protests then. This is how I got involved. I then joined the Student Nonviolent Coordinating Committee [SNCC] and went south to Mississippi in 1964. I learned we make change for the better when we organize—but only when we organize. We still have a long way to go, but this is a key lesson. If we organize, we can change the world.

I became very active in the women's movement and in the antiwar movement, and contributed to the civil rights movement. It was a unified movement for justice and democracy. In Chicago [where I was in school] I was part of a combined Civil Rights Labor Organizing Drive. At one point (when I was not trying to organize) I was fired for standing with others for fair treatment of clerical workers on the job. I won a back-pay suit, and with

---

Heather Booth is a social and political activist.

that funding I started a training center called Midwest Academy, which still exists and does terrific training for organizers. It trains organizers at all sorts of levels and kinds of groups, from NAACP and Planned Parenthood to little groups you may not have heard of. It addresses all kinds of issues. From there I helped to create new models of organizations. We helped to build statewide organizations at a time when there were only community groups and national groups. We formed multi-issue organizations at a time when there were mostly single-constituency groups. You were either an environmentalist or a senior, for example, a labor person or someone working for women's rights. But if you were both, where did you go? To address this issue, we helped create multi-issue organizations. Then, I formed an alliance between labor and community groups because there has been a big division between those that occurred in the 1940s and those in the 1950s. I created the alliance on the energy issue, Citizen Labor Energy Coalition.

In 1980, when President Reagan was elected, I came to realize how important elections are. I had been skeptical of elections before then. I lived in the original Mayor [Richard J.] Daley Chicago, and he gave a shoot-to-kill order during a demonstration after Dr. King was killed. I thought: "This isn't the kind of politics I wanted to do." Plus, in Mississippi, many of the Democrats were hostile to the Black lives, and the Republicans were even worse. Well, I didn't want to be part of *those* politics! But I realized I couldn't continue to think this way when a friend of mine, Alice Palmer, said, "If you don't do politics, politics does you." Since then, I've learned a lot about elections. I set up an electoral training organization (the State and Local Leadership Project) to train grassroots groups on how to incorporate electoral work with grassroots organizing. Before this time almost no grassroots groups (like Sierra Club or NARAL [National Abortion Rights Action League]) did electoral work. I had been running the field operation for Carol Moseley Braun's 1992 Senate race. I then was asked to set up a field operation for the Democratic National Committee. I did that, and I then did the outreach for the Clinton health-care plan, though I was also a single-payer health-care advocate. Then I became the training director of the Democratic Party. In 2000 I was asked to run the advocacy arm of the NAACP, the NAACP National Voter Fund. Julian Bond was the chair of the board of the NAACP, and I knew him from SNCC. He asked me to run the organization. We ran an amazingly effective program in 2000 that helped to increase African American turnout by nearly two million votes. But that was the year the Supreme Court decided the election, and I believe Bush stole the election in large part because of the vast increase of the African American vote in 2000. Then I ended up running large-scale issue campaigns. I was asked to set up the campaign for comprehensive immigration reform. I ran the campaign on the first Obama budget, the AFL-CIO's campaign for the Affordable Health Act, the campaign for health care. Then I ran the campaign for financial reform that won the Dodd-Frank Bill and the Consumer Financial Protection Bureau. I ran the campaign for marriage equality around the Supreme Court decision and many other issue campaigns. I was the strategic advisor for the immigration reform campaign [Immigration Justice Campaign]. That brings us back to today: I still advise and consult in large-scale issue campaigns. The last thing I'll say about my background is that the filmmaker Lilly Rivlin made a film about my life in organizing called *Heather Booth: Changing the World*. I'm taking it around the country to promote this message: if you organize, you can change the world. To change the world, you really need to be related to people joining in together, in organizations following their values and moral directions. Then we are changing the world.

Q: *So how do you feel then about what's going on in Washington today?*

This is a time of great peril and also an inspiring time. Under the current [2018] policies of President Trump, families will be separated. Voting and civil rights will be jeopardized. People will suffer. People may die because of these policies: the destruction of safeguards, guidelines for food, water, and health, on the environment, voting rights, and women's rights. It's an undermining of so many of the protections and caring, welcoming communities we've created over the last fifty years. And it's not just at the federal level in Washington. In fact, over the last ten years there has been destruction of the same kinds of laws at the state and local levels. There has been a rise of forces in many states that are driven more by fear of each other rather than by caring and community. These policies are driven sometimes by hate, race, and antidemocratic tendencies, limiting voting rights rather than expanding small-d democracy. So I think it's also a time of incredible peril.

At the same time, I am actually quite inspired by the resistance going on. The [2017] post-inaugural women's marches were among the largest demonstrations in this country's history, not only in D.C. but around the country, around the world. We see a mobilization on almost every issue: the environment, voting issues, civil rights, Black Lives Matter, the Fight for $15, for labor rights, for human rights. There is a rising young leadership, often young leaders of color, who are coming into their own. I find that inspiring; we need to keep that momentum. The main issue is that the pain, fear and anger about the peril, I think, can be turned into positive action if we stand together and organize.

Q: What do you say to young people when they say, "Come on. Get real! The forces of reaction control both the Houses of Congress. The Supreme Court is highly politicized. The right controls most of the state legislatures, and they are doing gerrymandering so that will continue. Trump is in the White House. All the social activism is just a flop. The bottom line is just that the people who don't care about the environment are remarkably busy systematically dismantling the EPA [Environmental Protection Agency]. They're dismantling the Civil Rights Division of the Justice Department. They have the Justice Department going in to sue on behalf of white students who believe they are being discriminated against in the universities. Immigration policy—that's a farce. The right is getting rid of a lot of people. The whole idea that there was progress being made, it's just made a U-turn and it's just been going back to an older period. A lot of the gains we've made are actually being threatened while some of us were marching in the streets. That's what some of the young people say to me. They effectively tell me, "You are out of it! Do you know what's going on in Washington? Trump's got the government and the politicians who are supposed to be doing things to combat him, [but] they aren't doing anything. You're just kidding yourself going out marching and making yourself feel good."

Well, it is certainly true it is a frightening time in many ways. It's certainly true. There are twenty-five states in which Republicans now control both houses of the legislature and the governor[ship] and in many cases [have] the Secretary of State, which means they decide how you count the votes. In contrast, there are only eight in which the Democrats have control. Now, being Democratic does not equate to good and Republican does not equate to bad, but at least those designations constitute a kind of statement of what priorities are. Do you believe we are a welcoming country, where all of us are in it together? Or do you believe the people are on their own and the government is not there to give a helping hand? But the very fact that ten years ago those figures were almost reversed is an indication that what we do or do not do matters. There *is* human-impacted climate change. To be a climate denier and say, "Well look, the climate is just out there changing and there's nothing we can do about it"—that's not so! We can change the climate if we take action, and the same is true in the affairs of the people. And knowing that ten years ago it was different means we also know that we can make it different now, but only if we act. I go further than that. We saw that the repeal of health care was stopped, and it was not expected to be stopped! There has been a lot of focus on how that happened because of only three votes in the Senate. And yes, those three were especially important votes in the Senate. But those votes happened because people around the country were mobilizing, were demonstrating, and those three people—who *might* have voted with their party instead of with their principles—decided not to vote with their party, for a variety of reasons. Sharing the message with people—what this health-care vote actually meant, what the vote means, the number of people who will lose their health care, the ways in which it could undermine Medicare and Medicaid, the ways in which it will harm the people with a preexisting condition—all this helps to win public support. With public support, we can build political power to not only stop bad things from happening but to win the better vision we care about. Even in the times of greatest crisis, when you think everything seems hopeless and you just can't make a difference, it's often [then] when there is the greatest progress.

In 1964 I went to Mississippi. In 1964, in Mississippi, Black lives did not matter to the white power structure. There were lynchings and people were living really in conditions just a step above slavery, in sharecropper positions. But because people organized, within a year there was the Voting Rights Act, and Mississippi now has more African American elected officials than any other state in the country. There is much, much further to go, much more to be done, but we make progress if we organize.

I do want to give two examples from Mississippi because they underscore my point with pretty dramatic stories. One is that in 1964, in order to draw attention to what was going on in Mississippi, a network of community and civil rights organizations recruited students from the north. I told you I was recruited through SNCC—[the] Student Nonviolent Coordinating Committee—with several hundred other students to come to Mississippi. There was great organizing going on with local people in the state, but more power was needed. The white power structure didn't care about Black lives at that point. Perhaps northern students with additional power, funding, resources—we could shine a light on what was happening in Mississippi. Sadly, the summer project gained notoriety when three young volunteers—Andrew Goodman, James Chaney, [and] Michael Schwerner—were picked up by the sheriff and delivered into the hands of the Ku Klux Klan.[1] For several weeks there was a search for the three young men. The white power structure was saying, "Oh, they're probably laughing at us, hiding off someplace, laughing at us." In fact, the three young men had been murdered. Many people know that part of the story, but what many people do not know is that while they were looking for the bodies of these three young men, they found the bodies of other Black men whose hands had been bound or feet chopped off and had been thrown in the Tallahassee or Pearl River. Those disappearances had not been reported because poor Black people lived in such terror. Even when they found the bodies, the murders were not investigated at the time because people lived in such terror. And yet, within a year there was a Voting Rights Act.

I'll give one other story from Mississippi to give a sense of how seemingly hopeless things were. Also how things have changed, because we often keep thinking about how far we have to go—and it's important to keep thinking of how far we have to go—but we shouldn't lose sight of where we've come from. One of the families I lived with during that summer was the Hawkins family, Andrew and Mary Lou Hawkins, in Shaw, Mississippi. After the summer project, the Hawkins family, along with some other families in Shaw, sued the town of Shaw in a case called *Hawkins v. Shaw*. The case went all the way to the Supreme Court. The issue they focused on was that in the Black part of town, there were no paved roads. There were no sewers. There weren't streetlights or full indoor plumbing in the Black part of town. The town was totally segregated. Black people lived in one part, and there were few public services there. But in the white part of town, there were swimming pools and paved roads and all sorts of wonderful accommodations. The Hawkins family and others sued to say you can't make improvements in the white part of town until you have comparable improvements in the Black part of town. The case is often seen as comparable in importance to *Brown v. Board of Education*. Because the Hawkins family filed that suit and were part of a freedom-fighting, morally driven family, their home was firebombed twice. The second time, one of their sons and two of their grandchildren died. A short time later Mrs. Hawkins was confronted by one of the policemen in town and killed. She was shot to death by a policeman! The people who firebombed the home were never found. I don't know how serious that investigation was, but there was no trial. The policeman who killed Mrs. Hawkins was tried but exonerated. So here you have one family where in effect, four people in the family were killed—were murdered—because they stood up for their moral beliefs. Almost no one even *knows* about that story. So there you have an instance of moral courage that no one ever hears about. If it happened to the Hawkins family, it's likely tragedies like this happened more often, a lot more often, but we didn't know about it. We didn't hear about it.

We are no longer in that kind of situation. Yes, there are murders of unarmed Black people and especially unarmed Black men, and there is an outcry around the country. But there are changes beginning to happen. Right now in California, there are moves around restorative justice, caring for people. Making demands on the criminal justice system. We have much, much further to go. But we make progress. We have made progress and we will make progress when we organize.

Q: *Why do you think you have such incredible faith in people's ability to change things? Why do you think you're such an optimist about all of this?*

Well, first, I've seen it happen. I gave that one story out of Mississippi, but there are *so many* stories. I worked on immigration reform. When I started working on immigration reform, perhaps 30 percent of the country thought there should be a pathway to citizenship. The last poll I saw said about 70 percent of the country thinks there should be a pathway to citizenship. Even in the time of such hatred being stimulated, attitudes change, people change. We must make sure our *power* changes to match those changes of attitudes. Because right now the vast majority of the country believes in expanding democracy, tackling problems of the environment, [and] being a welcoming community. So the majority of the country believes that. But not all the people in all the places whose votes count believe that. This then directs us in what we need to do. What we need to do is to take the moral convictions we have and the interests we have, in addition to our moral values, and act on them. We believe we should have health care for everyone, that no one should be denied care when they are sick because of a previously existing condition or because they are not wealthy. That you should be able to walk on the streets and not be frightened you'll be picked up because of how you look. That you should have an education you can afford that helps gives you resources to make a decent life. So, in addition to the values based on shared interest, we also need to move from mobilization to organizing, connecting with people in communities, listening as well as talking. Engaging people. Helping people see ways that they can take action. Then we need to move that into a political arena so our moral and social power, and organizational power, are converted into electoral power. I use a phrase of a political leader from Italy, whose name is Antonio Gramsci. Gramsci was put in jail by the fascists in World War II and while in jail he wrote some diaries. One of the things he said was that he believed in "pessimism of the intellect and optimism of the will." Pessimism of the intellect says, "Look, this is not good. It is a perilous time. This can go wrong. You're going to face these problems." But optimism of the will says, "We are going to drive ahead and fight for what's right and do what's right." That is more the attitude I try to hold. And as I said, I've seen it work. But it works only if we work at it.

Q: *That's a great phrase. I like that. Let me ask about your own situation, about when you've had to do things requiring some guts on your part to do. I can't imagine it was easy to go down south as a young white girl. Really, you were then just a college student. Yet you go into Mississippi in that time period. You had to know there were a lot of murders and things that happened. You've done a lot of things during college when you helped set up the Jane [abortion] group. I don't know if you want to talk about that. I don't want to get you into any trouble.*

No, no. That's fine. I'm glad to talk about any of it.

Q: *What are some times when you felt you had to demonstrate some moral courage, and what caused you to do that?*

In 1965 I already had the experience of having been in the civil rights movement. Certainly that was transformative in my life and told me that if you have confidence in regular folks, they know what they need, and they can take action to change their lives. I also saw and learned the lesson that sometimes there are unjust laws that need to be confronted and need to be opposed, even if the risk is arrest. I was arrested in Mississippi for doing voter registration!

Q: *Did your parents have any qualms about letting you go down there?*

On the one hand, I think they were very proud I went. They realized I was living the values they had instilled in me. But they were desperately frightened. So frightened that the night before we were to leave for Mississippi, I had a rift with my folks over the strain it was causing. My mother, whom I love dearly, was crying so hard over the phone she basically couldn't breathe. She was so frightened. Even thinking about it almost makes me cry right now because I did love—I do love—my parents so dearly. To know how frightened they were is still painful for me. And yet, I did go down there. I was living the values they had instilled in me. I know they were glad about it. They did actively support the summer volunteers. My father, who was a physician, helped create the Medical Committee for Human Rights, MCHR, which was the medical arm of the civil rights movement. My mother went to lobby and support the summer project to get FBI assistance.

Q: *Let me go back a minute to the phone call. You're on the phone. You're talking to your parents. Your mother can hardly talk, you said, because she's so upset, she's crying so hard. What was it that gave you the drive to go ahead and say to these two people you love dearly, "I'm sorry, I'm going do it anyway"?*

This was both—well, first, they raised me to try and do the right thing. Often, it's not that people want to do the wrong thing; it's that they feel confusion about "what can I do?" I often tell people that when I'm confused—and I'm often confused—I try to center myself with two thoughts. One, what is the right thing to do? Sometimes it's hard to know because it's just things competing for what's right. The second thing is to center yourself in love. And while I have deep love for my parents, I also knew the stories of what was happening to people in Mississippi. They were living with a level of terror, threat, and inequality worse than second-class status. They had absolutely no chance of breaking out. But if the northern students were there to support them, that could provide visibility, provide greater attention so people could hear their stories. So, with great sadness and [despite] the pain it caused my folks, I decided I would go.

Q: *Did you ever talk about that with them later?*

We did. Initially, there was a rift—it was probably the greatest rift we had in our relationship—and I have letters I wrote during the summer, to my brothers, others, and friends, asking them to be loving to my parents. But it was hard to overcome. Then later we had conversations about it, with my parents saying how proud they were of what I did, how they loved and cared for me and were also frightened for me. I would say to them how much I loved and cared for them. But it was sad to the extent I was taking action that was painful to them.

Q: *Well obviously, you got beyond it. I supposed simply because you survived, that does a lot to help assuage your parents' fears. But you did talk about it with them later, I gather.*

Yes, we did, and we were very, very close, really, throughout our lifetimes.

Q: I know. I knew your dad; I didn't know your mother. But I knew how your dad talked about all three of you kids and he was enormously proud of all of you. All right, so let's go back to the Jane experience.

Jane, yes, and then there's this other point I want to make. Let's go through Jane and then you'll see what I mean. I'll come back. So, having learned these lessons from Mississippi civil rights summer: trusting in people, having love at the center, standing up to unjust laws . . . I'm back on my campus, and in 1965 a friend tells me his sister is pregnant, nearly suicidal, and wants an abortion. She is not ready to have a child. He asks if I can find a doctor for her, to perform an abortion. I don't recall thinking about abortion before that. It was a more innocent time. I've never had to face the issue myself. But, almost on the level of doing a good deed—"do unto others"—I went back to the Medical Committee for Human Rights, MCHR, and found a remarkable doctor, Dr. [T. R. M.] Howard. There's a book about him called *Black Maverick*. He was a fiery civil rights leader in Mississippi who left the state when his name appeared on a Klan death list, and he came to Chicago. He set up a clinic for women called the Friendship Clinic. I was then at the University of Chicago, and I contacted him about my friend's sister, and he performed the abortion. I really didn't think about it again. But then word spread a little bit, and someone else called. I made the connection again, and then the word spread again. I realized there really would be a need and maybe I should set up a system. So I set up a system. Because I was living in a dormitory at the time, I told people to ask for Jane. This was at a time when three people discussing having an abortion was a conspiracy to commit a felony. I didn't quite know that at the time, but I certainly knew it was not legal. I set up a system and the number of people started to increase. First it was students at my university. Then it was students in the Midwest. Then it was housewives and children in the city, and then throughout the Midwest. Then the demand for the service was so great, that I realized I needed to pass it on to other people. I recruited others in what became Jane, an underground abortion service. Between 1965, when I made the first call, and 1973 when *Roe* became the law of the land, the women of Jane learned how to *perform* the abortion. The women of Jane performed eleven thousand abortions themselves between 1965 and 1973.

Q: They learned to perform abortions themselves? How did you do this? How did you train them?

I didn't train them in the procedure; I trained them initially in *counseling*. "Here's who we call. This is the fee. This is how we negotiate on it. This is what I'm told how women feel. Here are the precautions to take. Here's how to advise them. Here's how to support them. This is what they do beforehand. This is what they do afterward. Here's how you follow up." After a while, Dr. Howard died, and there was this other provider I found, Mike. I trained people in counseling about abortion. Then I left Jane for a variety of reasons. I was terribly busy with many other things: I was getting a graduate degree. I was working full-time. I still had movement work. I had little kids at home, and so other women took it on. There's a play, a book and a movie about Jane. I'm told now that there are two film producers who have optioned the story for Hollywood. So that was the development of Jane.

Q: So, you said you wanted to say something surprising . . .

Yes, I did. You are pursuing acts of courage, instances where people act on their moral values. Often those are projected in intense moments of great conflict that are dramatic. Like Jane, or like Mississippi. But I think there's another way to look at moral courage. It has to do with, "Do you do the work every day? Do you do the work every day, when it's often boring, or you're too tired, or it's too hot, or you're too cold, or you didn't get enough sleep last night? Do you do the work every day that builds organizations and supports others and yourself to act? That moves forward even when you're not sure what to do, when you're insecure, when you feel, 'Will this be good enough?'" The moral courage required to take those steps every day is at *least* as important as the moral courage in times we often romanticize, the overly dramatic and important actions where people stand up against unaccountable and unjust power. One way I capture this idea is in reference to the civil rights movement. People often asked each other, "Are you willing to die for freedom?" I thought about it a lot and though I very much wanted to live, I thought I would be willing to die if that was what happened while I was struggling for freedom and justice. But now the question is a little different. People may still die in the struggle for justice and the struggle to live moral values. But the better question is, "Are you willing to *live* for justice? Will you live for freedom, live your values?" Not just as an individual, as important as that is. We all want to be good individuals. But will you do the hard work, the inspiring work, the important work every day? Will you be able to continue the work of mobilizing, building the organization, moving it into elections, building others' confidence, and making the change that leads us to a more just and decent world?

Q: I'm very glad you just said that. I'm finding a disconnect between the scholarly emphasis on dramatic, conscious agonistic choice and the empirical reality as I talk with people. Take the example of John McCain, flying in from brain surgery to vote in a history-making Senate vote. This kind of moral choice where people make a conscious choice in a difficult and dramatic situation is not the way it happens most of the time. What I found, in fact, was that most of the time these things evolve out of your sense of who you are, that your identity simply leaves no options for you but to do something. That the hard work is deciding who you are as a person, what kind of life you want to lead and building that life in a small, inch-by-inch, daily way. Some of these big decisions are not decisions at all, then, so much as a reflection of who you are, of the person you created yourself to be. I use the analogy of a figure skater who has trained for years to do certain things. Once she's out there on the ice, competing, her body knows whether she can make the third turn or whether she needs to stop at two turns. I'm finding a lot of our moral muscle works like that, too. People think about things every day, sometimes exceedingly small, seemingly inconsequential matters, as you said. "Are you too tired to go out to a rally? Are you too hot to go out and do something in a crowd? Is it boring to fill out forms and collect data and things of that kind?" But I'm finding those are the little issues that build a kind of moral muscle, if you will, that becomes critical. Little things give you the ability to not just act later, but to see that something needs to be done. So what you said was especially important, and I'm very much in agreement with the idea that it is this concept that captures the way people actually operate. If you look at real human beings and real situations, not just the general theoretical, philosophical texts, you find something quite different. So thank you for saying that. It makes a lot of sense to me and it resonates with what I found with other people I've been interviewing. That moral courage, it's really who you are. It's a kind of identity issue. What kind of person are you? Are you happy? Is this who you want to be as a human being? That explains the kind of situation you're talking about with your parents, which you said was so difficult. It's a situation where they gave you these values and then you had to operate on them, even if it meant you're going to make them unhappy. So let me just ask—

Kristen, I love you talking about the moral muscle. I really love that.

Q: *Well, it's very much a kind of virtue-ethics approach. It's not as common and as popular in philosophical and academic circles today as the kind of Kantian approach, where everything is very rational, and we assume people have a kind of conscious deliberation before we act. But I think as I've looked at people—and this is one of the things that the UCI Ethics Center does—we try to look at empirical reality rather than what we assume occurs, or what we work out theoretically and logically in our own minds. That's fine to do, but we also need to look at how real people operate in the real world. As I did that, it was like everything I had been taught was wrong, or at least a little off. It isn't how real people operate. Their choices—even life-and-death moral choices—were driven by who they were. Certain options were simply not on their moral menu in the same way that if you go to a Japanese restaurant, it's difficult to get spaghetti Bolognese. It's just not on the menu. So after doing all these interviews, I see things differently. Certain things you just can't do because it's not on your moral menu, if you will. It's not who you are.*

So, let me ask you if there's one example of a time when you had to do something that was difficult. The Jane example—was that difficult for you to do? Were you concerned? I mean, going down to Mississippi sounds as if in some ways it wasn't that difficult for you. It was difficult to give your parents pain, but that was a situation where you felt eventually they would understand and realize you were acting out of the values they had given you. In the example of Jane, was there any aspect of it that gave you pause, or was it something that you did kind of automatically, without really thinking about it?

You know, in Mississippi, you had to be accepted to be on the summer project. I remember filling out forms. You had to raise $500 in case you were arrested. That money was used as bail bond money in case you got arrested. Now $500 for a college student in 1964 was a great deal of money, and I really struggled to raise it. Then, ironically, when I was arrested, there was no bail bond for me! I didn't care by that point because I already had made that commitment.

Q: *When were you arrested? Where? What happened there?*

There are three cities. Three towns, all small. Rowville, when I was with Ms. Hamer, Fannie Lou Hamer, who is a moral icon. Her innate sense of right and wrong was amazing. She was the co-chair of the Mississippi Freedom Democratic Party, which was set up when the Democratic Party was rejecting participation by African Americans. At the Democratic

[National] Convention, the summer culminated with a demonstration at the convention saying they should not be the all-white delegation, but they should be integrated—racially integrated. The Mississippi Freedom Democratic Delegation was key, and Fannie Lou Hamer was co-chair of that delegation, along with the Reverend Ed King. She did not accept the compromise position that would have given the Freedom Delegation two seats. She said, "We won't take two seats because we're *all* tired." Again, I almost cry when I think about it; it's such a statement of moral clarity.

With Jane, I didn't see it as a moral issue, except as one in which you're doing a good deed for someone else. It's only if the golden rule is a moral guide. You should treat others as you would want to be treated. Do not treat others as you would not want to be treated. Although I never faced the issue of abortion, I felt that if I were desperate and wanted an abortion, someone should be there to help support me. But I didn't even think of it in personal terms. I just thought, "Someone else is in need; I'll do what I can."

Q: But you knew that you could be prosecuted for a felony.

Well, I knew it wasn't legal. I don't know that I focused on it very much. I tried to be cautious. I didn't discuss it with a lot of people. I wanted to help a friend in need.

Q: Were you frightened at all? Were you scared you could get into trouble?

I was cautious. I don't know if I was frightened. At one point, actually–when I was pregnant with my first child and still doing Jane—someone thought it would be clever to have the shower for me by giving me the code that we agreed to use if something went wrong. If something went wrong, whether it was a police arrest or whether it was a medical problem, or whatever happened, there was a signal if something went wrong. Someone called and gave me that signal. I was absolutely terrified at that moment. As I'm walking over to the house where we all agreed to meet, I'm literally eating all the records. I'm ripping up little pieces of paper, eating the records, throwing one little set here and another set there, so there are no records, so no one would be harmed. So there was all this adrenaline. It was a false alarm. I then arrived and they said "Surprise!"

Jane provided medically safe procedures. In fact, a section of the University of Illinois did a study of the medical impact of Jane, compared to later abortions done in medical facilities; Jane had a better medical outcome on almost every standard. In part, since it wasn't legal, the women were being particularly careful. Further, it was a women's culture that said we are here to support women. It wasn't a profit-making culture.

Q: So, there were times when you were frightened. But you just really didn't listen to the fear, it sounds like.

I say this about fear and what I call insecurity. There's a kind of fear: "What will happen to me?" There's another kind of fear that's an insecurity that says: "Am I good enough? Do I know enough? Will it come out right? What do I really do? What if there's a problem?" I think the insecurity, believing we're not good enough, often holds us back from acting. It's one of the reasons I'm for training and support of people. But I'm also for people knowing and spreading a strong message: we *are* good enough. We *are* the leaders we have been waiting for. We need to support each other. If we act, if we organize, we *will* change the world. I'm for action that is in a context of a thoughtful plan for making a difference. There are all sorts of organizations that are doing that right now. When you're around others and you see them changing the world for the better, you also become optimistic while facing the harsh reality we all are facing.

Interview on July 1, 2022, after the Dobbs Decision[2]

Q. I wanted to ask you a follow-up question. We find moral courage very closely related to the values that people hold so deeply these values eventually come to constitute people's core identity. So when events conflict so strongly with these core values, it's something that shakes and disturbs you. The past week [June 24–July 1, 2022] has been a rough one for people who share the values you hold. May I ask how you are reacting to your values being counteracted?

You know, I'll tell you a story that actually happened. It's a little long to explain it, but it affected me quite deeply. I've been doing this [social-political] activism my whole life. I know we need to turn anger into action. I anticipated what was going to happen in the decision on *Roe*. I was ready for it. I have various networks. We needed to mobilize. We needed to move to the elections. We needed to support the centers. I'm on that track. But on Friday night, the day after *Roe* was overturned, I had tickets with a friend to see the play *To Kill a Mockingbird*. I canceled our dinner because I didn't have time, and I told my friend I might leave in the middle of the play. But the tickets were expensive, and she really wanted to go. I didn't want to leave her alone, so I went with her to the play with sort of a bad attitude, the attitude I'm explaining now: "Too much to do. I don't want to be here." Though in part I believe that to do this work, we need to do things that give us love and joy; for me, I'm in three theater groups and two book-club groups because they give me joy. I see friends, I see my grandchildren, and I have other things in my life. But this night I was in a bad mood. I felt, "I've got to get back to work. Why am I watching this play? I don't even want to see this play." I had read the book and seen the movie, which some of you may have seen, but I had sort of forgotten it. The phrase "to kill a mockingbird" is a line in the play: "You can kill jaybirds because they attack others, but it's a sin against nature to kill a mockingbird." The idea is that mockingbirds don't do anything to hurt anyone. Essentially, the story is about the conviction and lynching of a Black man in Alabama, a man who is clearly innocent. That's akin to killing a mockingbird, killing an innocent. As I'm thinking about this during the play, I found it so unbearable to realize this reality that I began weeping in the theater. Intensely. I felt if I didn't get a grip, they were going to remove me from the theater. Literally, people were turning around and looking. I didn't know what was affecting me; it's not my normal reaction. That I'm still affected by it gives you a sense of what my emotional reaction is. It's in part because of *Roe*. It's the feeling that what I've worked on for fifty years is being pushed back. Women will die, especially those without financial resources or family support.

I don't know if people saw the film *The Janes*, but it describes the underground abortion service I had started in Chicago. There were septic abortion wards in hospitals because women had injured themselves or were injured trying to have an abortion. Now it's one in five women of childbearing age who will have an abortion. It was one in three right after *Roe*. One in three! Both because of contraception and because of the rules and restrictions, it became one in four. It's now one in five.

When I watched the play about an innocent Black man who dies, and put that on top of the death of *Roe*, which will result in many innocent women dying, it was too much. Well, it was more even than that. It was the whole thing. Everything. It's the pushback on voting rights. It's the pushback on the murder of innocent people.

When I was in Mississippi during Freedom Summer—if you saw the film on my life, I know that story is told there—I stayed with a family. Four members of the family were lynched. Their house was burned, firebombed twice, and in the second firebombing, a son and two grandchildren were killed. Then later, the mother of the house, Mrs. Hawkins, was killed. Most people don't even know about it. To think if there's one family I happen to know about *only because I lived with them*, who else was affected by this? Now all the advances we made are being pushed back, and at the same time, on this question of how I felt, I also realize that whether it was Andrew and Mary Lou Hawkins and their family, they died in the struggle for freedom. I thought that it was worth that struggle. It was worth the struggle to have the freedom to vote. They fought for a sharecropper's union to increase the wages of sharecroppers. They fought for integrated schools. They thought it was worth that struggle, and within a year there was a Voting Rights Act, but only because people organized.

So, what I think are two things: I was just in a healer's circle (which is trying to deal with trauma), where you start the healer's circle. You were supposed to start with a PIES, which, I didn't really know what it meant; I wasn't familiar with it. You say a number noting where you are spiritually, physically, emotionally, and mentally. It was a new system with which I wasn't familiar. Other people would say a number, and all I could say is "I'm a 9 and a 1 at the same time." So, in part, my heart is deeply affected. At the same time, by God, I am struggling for freedom. This is the time that we need to move forward. When it's easy, our efforts are not needed. *This* is when we need it. *This* is when Andrew and Mary Lou Hawkins were needed. *This* is when we need that childhood education, those trauma centers, those acts of moral courage. We particularly need to drive it now into the elections. There is a path forward.

The last concept I'll say is this: right now we are on a knife's edge in this country, really, between democracy and tyranny. We're not *over* the knife's edge; we're *on* the knife's edge. That means that what we do matters, and there is a path forward. On the one hand, it is the pushback of everything we've cared about, and on the other hand, there are more people in motion on more issues of more concern understanding our interrelation, the interconnectedness, the intersectionality (that some call it), than there's ever been in my lifetime. On every issue, whether it's Asian American, Black Lives Matter, or the Women's March, it's all in motion now. But we haven't moved our social power and our moral conviction into political and organizational power. That is the next move we have to do. In the last election, Biden won with 80 million votes—-more votes than any president has ever had in our history. The difference between Biden and Trump was 7.1 million. With that gap, a year before, people believed that Trump was going to win. It's hard to remember.

I was the outreach director for progressives and seniors for Biden for President, and I am so glad I was. That election was a choice between Joe Biden and Donald Trump. An election is not a referendum on whether we like things as they are. Our hearts are breaking; we have much further to go. But an election is a choice: what's the nature of our power on the day that we have the election? We build up that power every day, we build up moral courage, we build up our message. Then on election day, there's a choice: do you want a candidate for governor in Pennsylvania who was at January 6 and with the Oath Keepers, who've just been declared a terrorist group by the Southern Poverty Law Center? That's who the Republican candidate for governor is; is that who we want for governor? And that's—that's the kind of choice we now need to make. So what we do really matters.

So to return to your answer about how am I now, concerning the values that I hold dear? My values are still strong. In part because I've seen all of you who are carrying on our shared values in different ways; you will find different areas, and we need to find the solidarity to move forward together.

Q: Like you, I actually knew people who went through abortions. In terms of abortion, the question is not, are you in favor of abortion? It's, do you want to have the opportunity for people who need to have an abortion of some kind to be able to obtain one?

We speak a lot about freedom. One of the concepts at the heart of liberalism is the idea of freedom. Now, freedom means a lot of things, of course. But one of them is the freedom to be who you are. One of the things that strikes me about the moral courage of people like you is that, at some level, while your moral courage is often driven by the hope that you can change things, at another, extremely basic, almost primal level lies the idea that if I don't stand up and say what I believe in, then I'm not being the human being that I deserve to be. There's a kind of freedom in standing up and saying, even if the world's falling apart all around you, "This is not right. These are the values that count. And it's part of what it means to be a human being that I can stand up and assert those values, even if I get pilloried for doing so."

I'm going to turn the conversation over to the students and see if they have any questions.

Student: We have a two-party political system in America. We are basically confined to two choices. I know a lot of Americans, including myself, feel we often have to choose between the lesser of the two evils, as opposed to being able to choose to vote for someone we truly support or feel is going to do good for the country. Here's my question: do we compromise our moral courage by supporting someone who is less aligned with our direct beliefs, or is it necessary to support candidates we know are the only obvious ones who have a chance to win?

Here's my perspective: the evil is letting fascism, dictatorship, authoritarianism, racism, and hate win. The question is: at any one point, what power do we have to stop that? What are the best ways to stop it? Is it not doing anything? Which is, in effect, what it means to vote for someone who has no chance at all.

Here's a true story. The first vote I ever cast, when I was eighteen, was for a social-justice [activist and] comedian named Dick Gregory who was running as a write-in candidate against Hubert Humphrey in the Democratic primary. But Richard Nixon was on the other side. Gregory was my write-in because I was so angry at Humphrey over the war in Vietnam, which he supported. But Humphrey was probably the greatest visible liberal in American life on domestic policies. I don't know if he would have changed on foreign policy had he been elected. But supporting LBJ's [President Lyndon Baines Johnson] Vietnam War policy was the price Humphrey paid in order to be vice president.

Now the truth is, no one voted as I did. There were 47,097 votes for Gregory out of the more than 73 million votes cast that election.[3] 47,097 out of over 73 million! I was throwing away my vote. It didn't matter. I chose to do nothing in the face of the rise of an authoritarian right-wing candidate. I was wrong. What I was trying to do was to prove my personal moral credentials. I wanted a gold star in heaven. I don't know what I wanted. I wanted to stand up—I was so angry! But my vote didn't really matter because I wasn't persuasive to others. We only had a few votes.

I am for raising our voice for alternatives that are bolder and more effective if we can win. I started out for Senator Sherrod Brown from Ohio. He decided not to run. I then went for Elizabeth Warren. But when it became obvious that her candidacy wasn't an option, she moved for Biden, so I moved for Biden, and thank God we stopped Donald Trump. It mattered because we organized. So moral action is not the symbolic making of a statement. Those symbols *can* matter. They *can* electrify people. They *can* help us decide we should take action. But symbols that are only for our personal statement and acts of purification are a luxury that . . . it's not even a luxury; I think it's fooling ourselves.

I don't believe it's the lesser of two evils. I think it's a reflection of asking: what power do we have? Elections aren't the only thing worth doing;

many things are: cultural work, teaching, educating, writing, and organizing. Many things matter. Your own work matters. Building organization matters, raising the issues about violence against Asian Americans, against Blacks, against all discrimination. It all matters.

I do want to share one other thing. There's a theory of change that I deeply believe in, and it addresses the question, how do you get there? You want a new world? I want a revolution; I want freedom and justice for all. Yet we find that diminishing our freedom in some ways. How do we get from here to there? So here's my theory of change for these times. Not for every society. This isn't necessarily the theory of change for China or Hong Kong or Russia. Not necessarily. But for the United States, it's a theory of structural reform, what are often called nonreformist reforms. There are three key elements.

The first is based on our values. It all starts with values. We try and work on issues that will improve people's lives. So the values we advocate don't stay as abstractions. It's not that we're for freedom, justice, and democracy. I'm for them, but you know, that and a nickel won't get you much, since the nickel doesn't buy you much anymore. But I'm for a living wage. Is $15 an hour adequate? No. But it's better than starving. I'm for retiring student debt. I'm for long-term care for senior citizens. I'm for capping pollution. It's not everything we need, but it improves lives. We'll be able to breathe; we'll be able to walk safely in our communities. So I'm for improving lives as a standard.

The second is winning by getting people involved. That's a direct-action component. It's not important that I want rights for someone else. Rights can't just be given to people; they have to be desired and earned by the people. People need to feel they won a right because *they* were involved. Then they feel greater confidence in their own power. That's how rights are won.

The third is that we change the relations of power. We have structural reforms that we looked for. Some reforms are more important than others. So, for example, cameras on police are an important reform. It's been transformative. Citizen control of the police and a community review board are structural reforms that start to transfer power into the community. A union is a structural reform because it builds power that's an alternative to the unaccountable power of an employer. That's why I'm so in favor of building an organization. It's why I think elections matter, because you hold offices that have concerted power. That is my theory of change. When we're involved in anything, it's important to have a theory of change; otherwise any action is equal to any other action. Should we have a Twitter storm? Should we throw water balloons at the opposition? Should we practice civil disobedience? Should we do a dine-in? A sit-in? All of those may be good things, but they're tactics. We try and teach strategy.[4]

There's a final lesson here: one struggle leads to another. The first physician I found to provide abortion services for the Jane movement was a doctor I found through the Medical Committee for Human Rights, which my father established. So it all comes around.

6

"I Am Going to Do This. I Am Going to Do This to the End!": Kay Monroe on Caring for the Elderly

> You have to forget about yourself and do what needs to be done and look at life from a very large perspective, from a view above the world, not from just a tiny little selfish "me" town.
>
> KAY MONROE, Winter 2017

How can I even begin to talk about my feelings toward caring for my mother? I think of all the years I cared for her, throughout her long illness, and I'm just overwhelmed. It's a kind of a mishmash of emotions: poignancy, pain, pride, loss, mostly love. People don't know what it's like till it hits you. Being a caregiver, you're stuck inside. Inside the house. Inside the relationship. Inside your own feelings. People give up their jobs to do this. They move. I did. They get smashed financially, and they never get any credit for it, in most cases. It's all done quietly, in private. So yes, I think it's very important for people to be aware of situations in which someone helps a person with dementia get from one moment to the next with as much grace and even enjoyment of life as possible. It does take a form of moral courage if you want to call it that. I just hope others in similar circumstances may feel supported or helped in some small sense by reading my account. That's my fairy-tale wish, that and that perhaps some government reforms may come about in part through what I relate here.

There is an anonymous army of people out there doing caregiving of all kinds, in all sorts of circumstances, some easy, some very harsh and difficult. I'm far from alone in what I did. But then, too, many people *don't* do what I did; otherwise, the nursing homes and retirement communities would not be thriving. *I* don't know who's working on that in Congress. I do know they are talking; there's been quite a bit of movement in at least the direction of giving tax credits, I think, for people who do caregiving and something for people who have to give up their jobs, change their lives, move, et cetera. But nothing's happened. So far.

I'm not at a very good stage of my life right now. I'm not as actively involved in things as I should be and as I used to be. I find myself obsessing about things from the past and having a lot of regrets. It's not good to do that. Not good at all. It's also pointless. It doesn't get you anywhere. But I think that happens to people whose lives have not turned out as they had hoped, and I would certainly put myself in that unappealing category.

Because of all the years I took care of my mother, after that time period, I felt I'd fallen flat. The caregiving took so much out of me. I felt totally depleted. And here's a weird thing: I was so consumed with caregiving and just daily survival for so many years I didn't have time to realize I was aging during those years. It's very odd; I didn't realize during those years that I had aged. I started caregiving during my forties, and it concluded when I was sixty-three. I'm lucky to look young for my age. People usually think I am about twenty years younger than I really am, so that probably contributed to that effect. Anyway, you are still quite youthful in your forties, but by the time the sixties arrive, it's Medicare and AARP, and Social Security. Plus, sagging skin, aches, pains, et cetera. It took me a few years to comprehend I'd gone down the rabbit hole fairly young and come out on the way to old age. That left me feeling like someone punched me in the stomach. There were so many things I couldn't do during those years of caregiving that now I lack the energy or stamina or body strength to do.

After Mother passed away, I was left with having to empty her house, rehab it, and get it on the market. I didn't—I hadn't—prepared myself during the caregiving years for the next daunting tasks. I had psyched myself up only for the caregiving. I had told myself, "No matter what, I will get through to the end with my mother. This is a mission I am on." That's what I felt. Whatever it takes, I'm going to do this. Then, after her passing, I really didn't have the energy—the oomph—for another major project. Renovating and selling Mom's house took me three years to complete. Even after I emptied it out and totally renovated it, it took another year to sell it because the economy tanked at that particular point in time, and there was little interest in real estate because things were so devalued. I did not get the money out of the house I had been anticipating. That was upsetting and continues to haunt me.

So, all those major things are done. My career is over. I haven't really pulled it together since. I wrote a children's book manuscript that I've done nothing with. There's just a few changes and alterations I need to make, but I can't seem to get myself to go back and do it. I'm wasting time and not facing it because I'm not good about approaching people. I found someone looking for children's stories, but I haven't pursued it. I prepared a board game, and I did what I could for that, but there's a final step I haven't done for that also.

The point is, instead of going back to see what I could do with those things, to actively pursue them, I'm just ignoring them and wasting a lot of time. That's not good at all, especially at my age. Then, too, I've hit a time in my life where I've lost several friends. Sometimes they passed away. Another friend moved. Recently I lost a friend over politics. That's another depleting kicker in my life: I'm living in a town I wasn't planning to live in and where I do not, overall, fit politically. It was never my intention to live out my golden years in the town in which I grew up. At least it's quiet and relatively safe here.

So, having said all that . . . I guess . . . I could reflect on some things in my life that I'm pleased with. How about that for a change of pace? I do have to say that in my mind I'm getting a little closer to saying, "Okay, I guess I can do this, do these projects that interest me." But I still haven't done it. I can't say I have a logical reason for my delay.

Q: That's pretty understandable. What do you think is the cause of the initial slump you talk about?

Probably a variety of things. My mother passed away eight years ago, and it took me three years to deal with the rehab and selling of her house because the house was for sale at the worst time in house sales in the century since the Great Depression. It was very time-consuming and a great deal of hard work. Plus stress. All of it took something out of me. I simply haven't entirely pulled it back together since. I was at minus zero when my mother passed away, so dealing with the house put me at double minus zero, I would say. I needed a long time to rest and not do a great deal. Not to push myself quite so much.

I have also had a few health setbacks that necessitated rest and inactivity. For instance, I had macular hole surgery, after which you cannot be jerked or jostled at all in order not to jar the nitrous oxide "splint" placed in your eye. You cannot focus well for about two months due to the blockage from the splint, which necessitates wearing an eye patch. You have to spend eight hours a day with your head totally down for a week afterward. I pretty much stayed inside for two entire months so everything would go as well as it possibly could. After that, I developed cellulitis around my eye, which required hospitalization, and, after recovery, a surgery that revealed a badly infected cyst behind my eye that needed removing.

Recently I had a minor surgical procedure for plantar fasciitis that actually had me in a wheelchair in the house for a couple of months. I would not choose to do that surgery again, but I will say that after about a year, I am doing much better with that.

What I am getting at is that being idle for extended time periods can get to be a habit. I still am quite generally active for a person my age, but I am active in spurts. Some days I go nonstop for hours and hours. But the next day, I feel, "Oh, my God. This is a rest day!" So. There have been "down" times.

Q: You mentioned earlier the passing of your mother. How much time would you say you took care of her for? Do you mind elaborating on that entire process?

How long I took care of her? Over thirteen years. Essentially, my mother did not manifest dementia symptoms until about three years after my father passed away, which was 1993. She immediately became very needy at that point and leaned heavily on me from the day, the very moment, Dad passed away. Things were not good. I stayed in her house for two months after he passed. I slept in bed with her for a week or so. She was just gone. She could barely cope. It was about three years before the dementia started showing up. Then she needed someone constantly at her side, that was the thing. She needed someone twenty-four hours a day, and I was working, so that wasn't possible at that time. I would go directly from work to her house in Collinsville, IL, and leave around ten-thirty or eleven o'clock at night and come over on the weekends. I was living in Missouri then, and St. Louis is about thirty minutes from Collinsville, where Mom was living. It became pretty all-consuming very quickly. I started hiring someone to come in with her during the day while I was at work. Then, finally, I retired. We had an early retirement plan going, and also, I was ill; I simply couldn't keep doing everything and survive. I was diagnosed in 2000 with cardiomyopathy with an 18 percent ejection fraction. The last two years I worked, I was at 18 percent ejection fraction, still going directly to Mother's house after work every day and not leaving until ten-thirty or eleven at night. Not getting to bed until about one, then having to get up at six o'clock to go back to work and do it all over again. This was not good even if had I been 100 percent healthy, and I was not. I needed rest. My heart needed to be rested so I could recover. After I retired, I began to recover, and slowly my ejection fraction increased.

Q: What specifically stands out in your head as the most difficult part of that entire process?

I don't know if I can specify one difficult part. It was physically demanding not because I had to pick her up or anything, but just because of the hours. My mother stayed up late. I'm a night person so, thank God, that really helped. But she also got up early. It just never ended. It was seven days a week. Still, I think the emotional part was harder. When you see your mother not knowing things, eventually not even sure who you are all the time, not remembering things, and not functioning in a competent manner anymore, that's very upsetting to anybody who has to observe that. It's just quite a gruesome thing, and at this point, I don't want to be around situations like that anymore. I'd be happy to advise people, but as far as volunteering in a dementia place, no. I'm not doing that. I can't be around it anymore. It's too much. Maybe some people can do that afterward, but I know I can't. The mother of one of my cousin had all kinds of physical problems, which eventually led to dementia. He said, "Oh, I'm going to go work at her nursing home afterward." But he never did. He didn't go there at all. That didn't surprise me. It's a hard thing to describe to anyone. I think it's hard to be around that situation even if you hadn't known the person before.

Q: It hurts more because you did know that person, I would assume.

That's right. It's pretty devastating. You have to steel yourself for it. You constantly remind yourself that this is still the same person you always knew and loved. I frequently went back in my memory to good experiences and things Mom had done for me when I was a child. I wanted to pay her back, I guess you would say, because she spoiled all of us. So she got her karma back, you know? Perhaps, if a person is dealing with a situation like that and the parent wasn't so good to them when they were young—I can't imagine what that would be like. I'm going to guess that the parent doesn't get so much back. But the overall thing was my life was just totally impacted by Mom's dementia. I did go out and do some things because we did have some hired help, but it was very difficult for me to do anything fun or entertaining at all. For the last couple of years of her life I only got out at night, maybe a few hours a week. One of my aunts, bless her, came once a week and stayed with my mother for about four hours in the evening. Fortunately, Mother was able to go places with me.

Physically, she could get around, so that was good, and she liked being in the car. That was a good thing. I used to drag her around as though she were a kid. She could keep up. She enjoyed getting out. That was a wonderful thing for both of us.

Q: Did reminiscing about the better times when you were younger help you significantly when you were dealing with the hardships?

It did. I would remember different things. She expended quite a bit of time and effort making clothes for me over the years, for one. Also, if I didn't like what she was cooking for dinner, she'd fix me something different on the side. I'm telling you, we were spoiled! For instance, she would take me places. We went shopping and out to eat in downtown St. Louis back in the time when people enjoyed shopping in big-city department stores. We always ate in the tearooms, as they were called back in the day, and we always bought some candy at the candy counters to take home to everyone else. Also, she was an amazing cook. We had a formal table setting every night. My mother could put out a homemade meal so fast, I sometimes wondered if she had food in her pockets! My mother did other special things for me, too. She was one of the Girl Scout leaders; she came up to the University of Illinois Mother's Day weekend. She was super supportive of my musical talent. She always made a birthday request dinner for each of her children, including whatever type of cake we wanted. I always asked her to bake a homemade banana cake with pink icing for my birthday. Wow. I wish I could smell it baking right now! And yes, I did think about those things more often than you would imagine.

Q: When you are looking back at everything in hindsight, do you have any regrets in regard to taking care of your mother?

It became very difficult at times and I did yell at her on a few occasions. I don't like that I lost my temper with her. But, overall, I would say no. I did what needed to be done in spite of the difficulties. Many people around me did not understand why I needed to be with my mother. They just didn't understand why I needed to be with my mother so much. They thought I was, I guess, defective in some way or other. I don't know. I received a lot of criticism. They would ask things like, "Why do you go there so much?" They simply did not understand why I needed to be at her side so frequently. I received a certain amount of criticism, even from family members. People simply did not comprehend the full spectrum of the situation. Of course, whenever anyone saw my mother, she was clean. She was beautifully dressed; her hair was done. She seemed fine. But that's because I micromanaged all of it in the background. I made her appear normal when she was not. In fact, it took a few years to convince one of my brothers that anything was wrong because whenever he visited the house was clean and my mother looked beautiful. The bills were paid, the yard was manicured, everything was done, and it truly appeared that everything was just fine. But it was that way simply because I was seeing to all of it.

The reality hit one of my brothers in a funny way. Funny as in the "you gotta laugh or you gotta cry" way life can be. Mike very generously gave me miles so I could fly and stay for free in Vancouver. I'd long wanted to visit there, and Mike offered to stay with Mom so I could go. Well, one night he heard Mom moving around and got up to check on her. He was in shock when he found her in the TV room wearing nothing but his sunglasses. I'm not sure he ever fully recovered from this! But both of us—as well as the entire family—laughed about this image many times. The sunglasses were the perfect nightcap, I guess you could say.

It's things like this that finally convinced all the family that our mother was no longer *normal*. I think that is typical in many families: some people grasp the problems and others are in denial of them. That is a common thing in situations where a family member has dementia of some variety.

Q: *Definitely. Going back to what you were saying in regard to the criticisms you received, what were some things people said regarding your spending that amount of time with your mother?*

They would say, "What do you have to go there for? Why do you need to go to her house every day?" One of my nephews—who hardly ever saw my mother because he lived in California—commented that I had a codependent relationship with my mother. (He did apologize for this after I reacted negatively.) A friend's daughter said to me, "You need to think more about yourself."

Q: *How would you respond to that?*

Well, I tried to explain it. People didn't say it a whole lot, but I knew they were talking about me behind my back. You know, how you can just sense things. One of my best friends, who wasn't around a lot, simply could not understand and just didn't grasp it. She was down on me for moving back to my hometown, which is where my mother lived. I think she thought I did that because I was losing my independent nature or had lost my courage or something. I valued her opinion, so this was hurtful. A tragic irony of this is that, after she herself passed away, her husband developed the exact condition that destroyed my mother. Her daughter, the one who said I "should think more about myself," began going back and forth from her house to her father's, exactly as I had done the first few years after my mother's condition began to manifest.

We had just assumed my mother had Alzheimer's until I took her to the Washington University Memory Diagnostic Center, where they diagnosed her very quickly with Lewy body [dementia]. Lewy body has similarities to Alzheimer's, though it is actually a much worse condition. But we didn't know what she had until the last year of her life. Until then we did not truly know what the problem was. One of my brothers is still skeptical about the diagnosis, probably because he just wasn't around her much and because he has not read up on Lewy body. It's a horrible condition, and no one wants to acknowledge it may be in their family. After I learned that Robin William's autopsy revealed he had Lewy body, not Parkinson's, I said, "He did the right thing." A person with Lewy body has almost nothing but increasing horror coming his way.

So, overall, no. There were a few times in the last year or so I started losing my temper and I regret that. I was sort of starting to lose it, I guess you might say. She was becoming impossibly difficult at times, especially toward the end.

Q: You said you had hired help, but aside from that, do you feel that there was a lack of support, whether that be emotional or actually being there with your mother? Do you feel that there was a lack of support?

To some extent, yes. People didn't understand it. My aunt was very supportive and took my mother for a few hours every week. My aunt taught preschool children, so she could do some of those activities with my mother, such as various kinds of puzzles. My mother did play Scrabble, and she was able to do that until the last year or so. But by the end, the puzzles my mother struggled to do were for twelve-month-old babies.

I had some support from my brothers. One came in once a month for twenty-four hours [*laughter*]. I know that doesn't sound like much. But it meant that I could have the evening to myself. I could go out at night. I could plan. I could actually do something. I could enjoy one stress-free night. Mom was sleeping at my house by then. I had actually left my place in St. Louis and moved into her neighborhood. My other brother didn't live around here, so he was not able to really do much. But he did send me on a couple of vacations, and he stayed with her while I was gone, so that was great. But things got so bad with my mother that the brother who came once a month stopped coming that frequently. He finally told my other brother he couldn't cope with it anymore. And here's the thing: that brother's a nurse, and he worked in nursing homes during his training. Yet he couldn't deal with it!

Q: *Interesting. You'd think he'd be in a better position to help, if anything, throughout that time. So, when you were talking about the brief periods that you did have—I think you mentioned being able to take a few hours for yourself at night—considering everything you were going through regarding her care, her constantly needing someone there, and you expelling that energy, how valuable were those brief moments of that time you had to yourself?*

Invaluable! Very. I might have totally cracked if I hadn't had some time to myself. You need to get things done. More importantly, you need to get your mind to regroup. You need to relax. When you're with a person like that, where you don't know what they're going to do from second to second and you can't trust what might happen from one moment to the next, it makes you very tense and on edge. So, yes, then I could relax, and that time is very important for a person in a caregiver situation. You need to just be completely away from the experience so you can breathe, so you can relax.

Q: *What would you find yourself doing during those times to yourself?*

During the daytime I would often go grocery shopping. I'd do different projects around the house, things to keep life going. But in the evening I could go out to a movie. Go out to dinner with somebody. There was an episode where I was very sick for a while, and when my mother was gone I'd just rest in bed. You had to do whatever felt right at the moment. It was different things during different times. Thursday evenings, when my aunt was there, I would try to get somebody to go out to eat dinner with, or see a movie, something like that. I couldn't stay out very late, but I could do a little bit. That helped.

What was significantly worse for me during all of this was my chronic illness. I still am ill. I have cardiomyopathy and dilated cardiomyopathy.

I had that the last two years I worked, and I was going directly from my house to my mother's and getting home late. Getting to bed about one. Getting up about six. That was the main reason I realized that if I can retire with full benefits, then I have to do that now. I realized I can't continue to do all this and live. It's just not going to happen. All that stress I'm sure was not good for me, but here's where I made a conscious decision. I was aware of all this, and I said, "Okay, see what you can do. If you die, you die. But you can't just turn and walk away from this. Your mother needs your help." This did not really feel like an option. I could not just say, we're going to throw her in a nursing home. Part of the criticism I received, even from my own family, was, "She needs to be in a nursing home." To give my siblings the credit they deserve, I think they were concerned that my own health was too frail to deal with all of this. But I just didn't want to throw her away, so to speak, by placing her in a nursing home. It's not the same kind of care she was going to get from her loved ones. She was extremely dependent on me. I've read that people in her situation find a person and just cling to that one person. It's like their lifeline. That's just how it was. I took super care of her, and nobody else was going to do that. In the last several months of her life, maybe the last six months of her life, she ended up in different places for different reasons, and it wasn't good. It was not good at all. She fell and got hairline fractures in both her hips and then couldn't walk. I couldn't keep her after that. Her hips did recover, but from then on it was just one place after another. It was awful. I was really upset about it, but I couldn't keep her anymore. It was just beyond hope.

Q: *You were mentioning a cost to your health. I know you were receiving a lot of criticism from many people, pushing you to put her in a nursing home. What made you decide, "No. I'm not going to do that to my mother?"*

I wouldn't say there was any one factor. Rather, it was an overall thing that I just could not bear to do. I felt it would be the end of her; more importantly, nobody was going to do what I did in the way I did it. One example: I got her to take a shower without objecting and, in fact, enjoy it. But I had to do that in a way that no one else would bother to do for her, because it was time-consuming and labor-intensive. Let me explain. Early on in her disease, she began to object to taking a shower. Many people who work with dementia patients claim the clients/people are afraid of water and thus do not want to shower. But my experience with my mother tells me that simply is not the case. When my mother began to object to showering, she expressed herself loudly and angrily. She would stamp her feet and say things such as, "I'm not taking a shower! You can't tell me what to do!" Then she would refuse to shower.

The night before I was going to try to get her to shower, I was so stressed about what I knew would be the impending struggle I was unable to sleep. Finally, I got the idea to warm up the bathroom with a space heater and then ask, "Mom, would you like to come to a warm, cozy room?" She would always follow me to the warm bathroom. Then I placed a shower chair in the shower, and as she sat down, I simply pulled down her pants and underwear and removed the rest of her clothes. I used the handheld shower device to warm up the water at the nearby sink, used a plastic pitcher to transport the shower head over to the shower without getting water all over. Then I tested the water temperature on her feet. When it was to her satisfaction, I slowly began spraying her with the water. So, she was never shocked by water that was too hot or too cold, and she was gradually acclimated to it.

She always seemed to really enjoy her shower and usually took the showerhead and sprayed the water all over herself. At the end, I had her hold on to the grab bar in front of her, stand up and use a washcloth to clean the personal areas, and then, before she sat back down, I quickly dried her chair, placed a folded dry towel on it, and, after turning off the water, placed a folded dry towel under her feet so she could be comfortable and would not slip when she stood up again. She would dry herself, and then I'd wrap another dry towel around her and walk her into her bedroom, where she could dress in clean clothes. I have to say, overall, she enjoyed the experience and never, ever objected to taking a shower again. Did I mention I never once used the word "shower" ever again! She showered at least every other day and often on consecutive days.

Old people—people in my mother's condition, anyway—are often rather bedraggled and unkempt-looking and not very clean. Being clean and sweet-smelling added to her "normal" ambiance. So, unless people were around her for any length of time, they treated her as though she were just like anyone else, and therefore she usually behaved in a "normal" manner. Now, I ask you, who else in the world would go to such effort to shower someone in my mother's condition the way I did it? Especially when it was hot. It could be a hundred degrees out, but we had a space heater going throughout the entire shower! It certainly is not the institutional way of showering. I observed—and tried to intervene in—the shower experience in one nursing home, and it was a horror. If I were tossed onto a rolling toilet seat in the middle of a cold room and hosed down, I would scream, too. It may have been kinder and gentler in the last place Mom stayed because, overall, things were better there. There were only fourteen beds in that Alzheimer's unit.

When she was in my care, I always fixed her favorite foods, and we went out to eat for quite a long time. That became a bit problematic near the end, but if I ordered for her, we were good to go. When we were out and about, we would encounter old friends and relatives. It's a small town and she's lived her whole life here, so she knew a lot of people. She enjoyed chatting with them even when she couldn't recall who they were. At least they were familiar and treated her as someone special. Had my mother been in an institution, she would not have had the opportunity to visit friends and relatives. She would have missed out on birthday celebrations and visits from her children, grandchildren, nephews, and nieces. That was just not going to happen if she lived some other place. So you can see, my decision to keep her at home as long as possible was not determined by a single factor but by a variety of reasons. I just couldn't let myself do it.

Q: Do you think the work you did was appreciated? It sounds like you went through a lot in regard to your own health.

The person who appreciated it the most was my mother, even though she was not cognizant enough about anything to fully comprehend what was happening. She just couldn't. But many people have expressed appreciation for what I did—mainly my extended family. They know. They were greatly relieved there was somebody responsible and caring who was handling everything that was going on. I wouldn't say anyone fully comprehends that my own health may have been impacted because generally I have done well with the cardiomyopathy. I do think my recovery would have been much faster had I not been simultaneously working full-time and trying to take care of my mother almost full-time. I will never really know the ultimate impact that had on my heart. But I survived.

There was a feeling that came over me after a while, though, a sort of cavalier attitude that since I was the single woman with no family, this responsibility belonged to me. Kind of like in previous centuries when single women were relegated to chief cook and bottle washer for the entire family—and, more particularly, the unmarried daughter was responsible for the parents. I found this depressing for two reasons. One, I did not have the family I had expected to have. I was long divorced at this point. And two, it was an unfair situation. But it was an objectively truthful situation in that I had no children to care for and no spouse expecting me to be their companion, cook, whatever. I will say that sensing this depressed me. A very sensitive thing was said to me by my nephew's wife. One day she said to me, "At some level, this is an abusive situation." I appreciated that, but it did not, of course, change the dynamics in any way. It just made me feel more appreciated by at least one person.

My sister, Becky, appreciated what I did because she was entirely unable to assist in any way. She'd had a stroke a number of years before my mother began to deteriorate, and Becky herself needed care. She lived in Ohio, and I drove my mother there a number of times, so my sister got to see her mother and vice versa. We had dual motivations for the eight-hour drive: my nephew (my mother's grandson and my sister's son) is an artistic director of a dance company, and we were prompted to attend the performances. It was very fortunate that riding in the car was calming to my mother. She really enjoyed it, kind of like a little kid does. Children tend to fall asleep when they get into a moving car. It wasn't until the last, I guess, two trips that I realized I had bitten off more than I could chew. We had some horrors on those trips. We ended up driving at night through pouring rain once, and she took off her seatbelt. I managed to get it back on even while driving. But then she took it off again, and I just had to conclude, "Nope. We're not having a seatbelt." It was too dangerous to deal with. That's when I learned that after about fifteen minutes, the annoying beep tone will shut off if you don't put your seatbelt on. She also took off some of her clothing in the car. She was tired, and I think she was simply getting ready for bed. There is usually a skewed logic to what people with these conditions do and say. You just have to look for it. She put her clothes back on when I asked her to. But a really dangerous thing did occur during that drive when she put her hand on the gear shift. That really upset me. I quietly removed her hand, and fortunately she didn't put it back. But I was very concerned she might try to open the car door and just step out onto the highway with the car going seventy-five miles per hour. Thank God that did not happen! So, you see, I pushed my luck taking her on those long trips the last year and a half or so. Of course, I could not go if she did not go. That was just the way it was.

But we survived, and she got to enjoy the visits and that was good. All that stimulation delayed her deterioration. Every time we went to a dance performance, she would ask about the dancer onstage, "Is that Tim [her oldest grandchild]? All the performers recognized her and greeted her warmly afterward. So that was a very nice thing she was able to experience. I'm sure she did not recall it later, but it added to her normalcy and kept her stimulated. You know, you go live in an Alzheimer's unit, there's nothing much normal or special there. Definitely not an excursion to your grandchild's dance performances.

Q: *As a clarification, you mentioned a hairline fracture. Was it you who got the fracture, or your mother?*

No, it was her. Definitely her. She fell. Lewy body causes falling. She did have a number of falls over time, even though she was extremely strong overall. Part of this condition is agitation. People with Lewy body are agitated a lot, so she would walk it off, or at least that's what I think was going on. She would get up at one or two in the morning—after not going to bed until eleven or twelve—then walk through the house without ever sitting down. Just walk, walk, walk, walk, walk. At first she did not take her walker with her, and this scared me. But I got the idea to place it in the doorway so she could not exit the room without it, and then, once she had her hands on the walker, she continued using it. So that made the walking safer for her. But I had hardwood floors, and she slipped and fell getting out of bed a couple of times. I had to phone the fire department a few times to help me get her up, because the floors are too hard and slippery to make rolling over onto the knees and maneuvering around comfortable and safe. One of these rescuers advised me to place a bathmat next to her bed. I did that, and then she never again fell while getting out of bed. But one night she fell at the end of the bed, where I had not thought to place a mat. I don't know what she was doing at the end of the bed, but that is where she fell, and she got hairline fractures in both hips. After that, I could not keep her at home anymore.

During the last six months of her life, it just went from one bad thing to another. It was the deterioration of all kinds. I managed to get her into a high-quality, caring nursing home, but they phoned one day and said, "We're sending your mother to St. Louis University geriatric psych unit because we can't handle her anymore. She may have to go to a place for people with behavior problems." She was very combative. If she was upset, she would scream and yell and fight and hit and wouldn't cooperate. She could be very difficult.

Q: *Would she do that often with you as well?*

No, not often. She didn't do that often with me. Just a few times, because when she was with me, she was calm. She trusted me. Everything was familiar. Everything around her was familiar and she wasn't scared. I let her do pretty much what she wanted if it wasn't going to hurt her or anyone else, like walk around the house at night. I'd get up at night and try to calm her, try to get her to go back to sleep. I even played the piano for her, and that worked for a while; but as her condition progressed, she didn't even seem to notice I was playing. Same thing with the television. She stopped watching television at the end, as though it were not even turned on.

Anyway, this high-quality nursing facility sent her to SLU [St. Louis University] and then things just got worse. She got *C. diff.*, which you probably haven't heard of. *Clostridium difficile*. It's a very bad intestinal illness that people, especially older people, contract in institutional settings. It kills a lot of them. But, oh no! It did not kill my super-strong mother! She didn't even suffer from it very long, but she had to be isolated during that time period. You had to mask up and gown up when you went into her room. That was a terrible thing for her to go through.

At the end of five weeks, they called me and said, "We can't help your mother. We're just going to send her back to the nursing home. There's nothing more we can do." So they sent her back to the nursing home with an order to call hospice. But no one informed me about the order, not even during the exit meeting. My nephew was included on the conference call when we did the exit interview, so I know I didn't just miss the information, because Tim would have heard it, too. It simply was not told to us. I finally contacted hospice on my own. After evaluating her, they said, "She should have been with us a long time ago. She's in the end stage of this illness." So things were bad for the last several months of her life. Definitely bad, generally bad.

Q: As the disease kept progressing, that must have been a tremendous toll on you. Did you see that affect your health as well?

My health? Actually, I've managed to be okay. My heart finally did improve after several years. I was put on some major meds and it took about four years for my heart to show improvement. I'm suspecting that had I not been having to care for my mother and work full-time, as I did the first two years after my diagnosis, I would have bounced back a lot faster. But my heart improved and has pretty much remained stable. So no, it did not seem to profoundly affect it. No. That was a good thing. But the overall effect will never really be known.

Q: It's very touching, what you did. It's super commendable. If you had to do it over again, would you do anything differently?

I would try to maintain all my patience in that last year. Although, oh my, it was really hard. Things were getting very, very, very bad. I will give you a few examples of what I mean by bad, since I have stated and restated it so many times. One, she began to be very frightened and would mutter to herself over and over again, "Please help me, please help me, please help me, please help me." She tended to do this in bed at night, so I would lie next to her to try to ease her mind, but she didn't even seem to realize I was there. If I hugged her, it startled her. It was very hard to witness this.

Her hallucinations were becoming more vivid and more frequent. Remember, Lewy body [dementia] causes hallucinations. Luckily, I don't think hers were frightening, as are those of many Lewy body sufferers. But it was off-putting to other people when she was talking to a bare corner or referring to people who were not there. One time a nurse looked at my mother as though she were a crazy fool when my mother pointed to an empty corner and said, "My family is right there." I hate to think what she said in regard to these hallucinations when I was not around.

One hallucinatory experience near the end was both sad and fascinating. One evening she said to me, "A gentleman caller is coming to take us to a country inn."

"No, Mother. No one is coming."

"Yes, they are. A gentleman caller wants to take us to a country inn."

"Ok. That will be nice," I decided to say. There is no point in arguing with someone in this condition. It accomplishes nothing. It just upsets them, and there is no purpose in trying to set it straight other than your own need to be right.

"Get my makeup. I want to put on my makeup," Mother said.

Now my mother had not worn makeup for decades, so this was unexpected, to say the least. I realized at this point she had been transported about seventy-five years back into the past. She was about ninety-five at the time of this incident. So I rounded up some of my own makeup and brought it to her.

"I need a mirror," she directed.

I brought her a handheld mirror and watched as she spent half an hour applying the first makeup I had seen on her for such a long time. She did a great job of it, too. I had deliberately chosen soft tones so she would not look garish, as though she were Baby Jane. She looked quite pretty when she was done.

The sad thing, of course, is that no one showed up to meet and greet us or to take us anywhere. She didn't get upset at that, thank goodness. I assume she forgot what she was waiting for. But it was just so sad in addition to being weirdly interesting. I said to myself, "Well, you are living entirely too close to Tennessee Williams's niece. (Fran Williams lives a stone's throw from me.) So you have now been plunked down in the middle of *The Glass Menagerie*. She never did ask about putting on makeup again, which I thought was too bad because the doing of it had occupied her nicely for a half hour.

A third example of how bad things got that last year is hard to think about. One night, she went to the bathroom. I saw that her Depends [adult diaper] needed to be changed. She allowed me to remove them but then, she would not lift her foot so that I could pull the clean pair on. Eventually, I managed to slip one foot into them but then she kicked her leg really hard, and the fabric of the Depends tore the fragile, thin skin on her calf pretty badly. Blood was running all over the floor, so much that I feared she would slip and fall in it. She wanted to just walk around the house with her leg bleeding profusely. Thank God I had a chair in that bathroom and managed to get her to sit in it while I applied Band-Aids—really inadequate ones at this point—to stanch the bleeding and hold the skin together. At that point, I was sobbing because it was such an upsetting thing in so many ways. She did not seem to even notice I was crying, and as quickly as she could, she lit out on her walk, just walking around the house. She must have walked for a couple of hours that night, on the bad leg that was still bleeding. The next day I took her to an urgent-care [clinic] to have the wound looked at. They rebandaged it much better than I had been able to, but it was too late for the skin to be reapplied onto the leg. It was a couple of months before I could shower her without an elaborate pre-procedure of encasing her leg in protective plastic. I had to take her back to her doctor several times to have the wound checked, retreated, and rebandaged. In the meantime, I had to dress and treat the wound on a daily basis in addition to the elaborate pre-shower protection procedure of the wound. That was heartbreaking, just devastating to see that happen to someone I loved so much.

I'm telling you these examples just to clarify that when I say things were bad, I am not exaggerating. But other than not maintaining my patience as well as I wish I had that last eight months or so, I also wish I had not caved to pressure to put my mother somewhere. For I did cave to that about eight months before she passed away. My siblings were concerned for my mental and physical health, and that was kind of them. I think that's why they became more and more insistent we move in this direction. I took Mom somewhere for respite care for me, as they say, but I brought her home after only two days. It was a devastating experience for her, that first place. Then I tried another place, one of those glamorous, expensive places promising everything and delivering very little. Another person there hurt her arm pretty badly and that upset Mom. The truth is, Mom was basically just being ignored. She was scared; she was upset. It was terrible, even though I visited every day. After two weeks I brought her home again. The day I went to pick her up, she wouldn't even raise her head or try to make eye contact with me, not even when I told her I was taking her home. She did not look up or say anything at all until we got to her house. Then she sighed, and said, "I'm home." It was so touching and so sad. Just pitiable. So, if I had it to do again, I would stand my ground and not cave to putting her somewhere, even though I definitely needed the respite time, as they call it. That's the main thing I regret: having these couple of times when she was still physically healthy, and I caved in to pressure and tried these places. It was a disaster both times. She had not been incontinent, amazingly enough, but after these traumas, she often was. I think it was just too much unfamiliarity with everyone and everything. She needed to be with family. She needed to be in her own home.

I'm not a religious person anymore. I went through that phase when I was really young, and maybe that's unfortunate. I guess in the worst moments you find yourself offering up some hopeful and desperate prayers and asking for help but . . . I told myself this was one of my purposes in life. This was one of the reasons I was brought to the planet: to serve this purpose for my mother, and I was in a position to do it. I was no longer married. Had I been married I think that would have been a problem because, quite frankly, I don't think most men would have been able to deal with it. It would have just been a lot of criticism and difficulty, and nobody would have wanted to put up with all of it. I saw it as one of my things to do here on Earth. I think I mentioned I felt I was on a mission. "This is what I'm going to do and I'm going to do it." I took it one day at a time, and the last year or so, when things got really bad, it was one hour at a time. "You can get through this hour and then you can get through the next, and then you can get through the next." That became my mantra.

Q: Given all the criticism—obviously you were aware of the alternative of putting your mother in a home. Did you ever doubt yourself? Was there ever a point where you said, "This is just too much! This is ridiculously stressful!" Did you ever at any point say or think that to yourself?

No, actually I didn't. No, I did not. I said, "Whatever happens, I can do it." Until that last year, when I started caving to people's pressure. After my mother fell and fractured her hips, I had to face the fact that I couldn't keep her at home. Because I couldn't handle her. I was too small. I couldn't deal with it physically anymore. She simply needed some physical care that I couldn't give her. Although she did recover from the hip break—even though an extraordinarily rude doctor told me in no uncertain terms that she would never walk again—but she sure did, and it didn't take her long, either.

Q: After her passing, you spent nearly three years dealing with her estate, is that correct?

Yes, unfortunately. That was more of a burden than taking care of my mother. I had just geared myself to take care of my mother till the end. Then I didn't have any other big projects left in me. It took about six months of not doing much other than rest and relaxation for a while, except writing thank-you notes. To handle her estate, I had to get into the house, which had more than its share of memorabilia—photos, albums, old things. You can't imagine all the stuff in that house! My mother wasn't exactly a hoarder, but she wasn't exactly not a hoarder, either. We had everything back to the '30s and '40s in that house. Oh, my God, I can't even tell you! Somebody had to deal with all of that, and I'm the one who did it. I just didn't have it in me at the time. I was pretty worn down. We lost a lot of money in the stock market at that time, also. Thank you, George Bush! There had been all this bad economic stuff. My siblings agreed I could have the house as a way of paying me back for all I'd done for my mother. The way things turned out, though, financially, I would have been better off to have taken the money we had left from the stock market and had my siblings take the house and then hire somebody to go through things.

But then I imagine that scenario. What if somebody else goes through Mother's things? They are going to throw away the meaningful, sentimental things. They're just going to toss the precious, sentimental thing as fast as possible. If someone from the family goes through things, they'll realize the value of what they find. Bottom line, you have to do the sorting yourself. Here's an example. My mother had saved all of our ugly art projects and cookbooks from our elementary school days. She had saved all of those, from each of us! I gave those to my siblings because I was able to figure out which ones each had created. Somebody else, if you hire someone, they are just going to throw the junk away.

In one of the drawers I found our jacks and our marbles from when we were kids. When I came across those, boy, I teared up. That night I sat down on my hardwood floor and played jacks for the first time since the 1950s. I found so many pictures and, oh God, so much stuff. My parents had their family's pictures as well as their own family's. So I now have three generations of pictures and documents. I redid the house beautifully. Partly because I thought that would help it sell quickly, but more because it was my last labor of love, so to speak. The last way to honor both my parents.

Q: *When you were going through all the possessions in the house, was it hard for you?*

Oh, yes. There were many times that I would tear up with what I would find, as with the jacks and marbles. Some article of clothing or personal things—my wedding dress, my prom dress—she had saved all that! Different letters my dad had written.

Q: *Do you value that time, seeing those possessions one last time?*

Oh, yes. That was well worth doing. Going through all that was a valuable experience.

Q: *What I took from your initial interview is that throughout life we're going to have these moments where life is going to be difficult. In that difficulty, you have to force yourself to have courage and keep going. Even though it's not a great period of time, you have to overcome the obstacles in front of you and keep moving on just because you simply have to keep moving on. Is there any type of advice you would give to someone going through that type of period?*

You have to forget about yourself and do what needs to be done. Look at life from a very large perspective, not a tiny little keyhole perspective like, "I want to go on vacation. I want to do X or Y. Blah, blah, blah." You just have to look at things in a much broader way, from a view above the world, not from just a tiny little selfish "me" town.

Then, too, I have read some of the great literature of the world, and most of the time people in great literature are suffering through something. That's just the way things are in great works. There's not a lot of comedy out there. That's one reason kids don't like to read great literature sometimes, because there's a lot of sadness and people are struggling. I thought back on some of those works and used them as a guidepost. I remembered Hester Prynne [the heroine of Nathaniel Hawthorne's *The Scarlet Letter*] struggling, and after everybody rejected her, even as life went on for her, she began doing things for other people and growing and maturing as a person. She struggled and struggled and did her best to stay on top in spite of how badly she had been treated by [Arthur] Dimmesdale and the townspeople. Tess, of [Thomas Hardy's] *Tess of the d'Urbervilles*, did the same thing. She just survived each day and tried her hardest to do what was right, what was best for everyone. Maybe this sounds goofy, but remember, I have a master's in English literature, so the guidance and inspiration from books I've read is very meaningful to me. It has been ever since I was a kid. All of that helped. While religion might help some people, literature helped me.

Q: *Did you see literature as a guiding force?*

Yes, sure. But when you're in a situation like the one I was in, you don't have much time even for contemplation. You're just surviving, trying to make the best of each day, each hour. Once I made the decision to care for my mother, I said, "I'm just gonna step up to this." You have only two choices: you do it or you don't do it. There aren't any other choices. You can't do something like that halfway.

When you have a conflict in your life, when you have something that's difficult, you either step up or you don't. There's nothing else. Once you decide you're going to do it, you have to follow through. I never found myself saying, "Oh no, you shouldn't do this. This is too hard."

I said, "I am going to do this. I am going to do this to the end!" And I did.

*

Postscript. As this book went to press, I asked Kay if she wanted to update her story in any way, since I knew her life had changed dramatically for the better when she bonded with a kind man who had also been a caregiver. She agreed and asked me to convey "a touch of hope for people needing to be uplifted during difficult times."

7

"The Courage You Have . . . It's Not Something You Consciously Think About": Amal on Anti-Muslim Bullying

> If I can change just one person's opinion or make that person feel more connected to a good cause or making a difference, then that's what I want to do.
>
> AMAL, February 25, 2017

My name is Amal.[1] I was born in Beirut in 1983. My family and I moved to California in 1988. My parents are both originally Lebanese and I come from a Muslim background, so I consider myself a Muslim today. Today I live in Abu Dhabi. When I told my parents I wanted to try out Abu Dhabi, I remember my dad asking me, "Who leaves Southern California to go live in the middle of the desert?" He didn't fully agree, but he encouraged me. "You are young and this is the time to make these crazy moves. See what's out there and get in touch with your passion. Figure out what you want to do." So I did it. I took the leave. I stayed out here for about two and a half years. Toward the end of 2010 I decided to get my MBA [master's of business administration] in Beirut. It was a great experience for many reasons. It rooted me and taught me what being Lebanese was all about. It was really exciting in that sense. When you come to these countries that are a little bit smaller, yet inundated with social issues, you can see and feel the impact you make. During that time, I met my husband, also Lebanese but he grew up in Canada, so similar to me since we both had Western upbringings but origins in the Middle East. We married in 2013 and lived in Lebanon for a year, then his family business took us to Africa for a couple of years. We lived in Cameroon—in Douala, a French-speaking city.[2] That simplicity of life there was charming and challenging. We left a year later and came to Abu Dhabi, where we are now. Life here is a story on its own. I now work for a non-profit company called Fashion Forward. We promote, celebrate, and develop the regional fashion industry. We work with emerging fashion designers from the Middle East.

Q: You mention your Muslim background. What does that mean to you?

I was born in Lebanon and my parents are Muslim, so initially it was natural, just something I was born into, therefore, that was my identity. Growing up, my parents would teach us about religion a little bit. They wouldn't overdo it. We went to classes once in a while on the weekends. Even in California, there was a mosque offering courses on the Quran that would teach us different verses—what they meant and how they could help in life. It felt comfortable for me. It was a sense of belonging. It was never something forced upon me, but rather something that in a way simply resonated. I was taught to believe in one God and to be kind. It was really simple, to be honest.

When we moved to the US my parents automatically put my sister and me in a private Christian school. A lot of people were asking, "Why would you do that?" My parents from the get-go said, "We want them to learn about other religions. We want them to be around people of all faiths. Tolerance is something our religion teaches. We are taught to love everyone and get along with all types of people. Putting them in this environment will make them more well-rounded." At the end of the day, if Christianity made more sense to us, my parents were open to it. They never forced anything on us. They presented different options—Christianity, Islam, Judaism—we learned about all of them, and they left it up to us. By doing that they made our religion that much more enticing.

Q: *Did they practice the Muslim religion themselves? Did they go to mosque, your parents?*

No. It wasn't like that.

Q: *Were they what we might call assimilated Muslims? Similar to people who are nominally Christians but don't ever go to church? Would it be accurate to describe them as assimilated Muslims?*

Exactly. Yes. We would fast during Ramadan and there was Eid al-Fitr.[3] During our holidays we would have a nice big dinner together. They would give us gifts on the Muslim holidays when you are supposed to give gifts. But we also did Christmas, and that was fun. We had a Christmas tree in our house. We did Easter stuff. At school all of my best friends were Christian. My greatest childhood memories were with my Christian friends. I did so many fun things with them. They would come to our house and celebrate and eat our food with us, and they loved it. It was so normal. All of this was before 2001, when the media started getting more vocal about antiterrorism and began to teach people to connect Islam with terrorism, when in reality Islam had nothing to do with 9/11.

Q: What kind of bullying did you encounter? You had an incident with bullying, right?

Yes. I had two incidents growing up in my school. I went to a Baptist Christian school. For the first few years, up until junior high, we had a great administration, very open-minded. We were young and the kids were young, and no one really knew the difference. It changed as we started getting a little older. I actually had this boyfriend. We were in love, or whatever. It was very eighth-grade. He was convinced he needed to make me a Christian so in case we died we would go to heaven together. It started to get a little more serious, these conversations about how I wasn't going to heaven. It started with him having the idea that I wouldn't go to heaven. I was going to go to hell because I wasn't Christian. We wouldn't be together. The conversations started like that. He got to the point where he told me we couldn't be together anymore if I didn't change my religion. I also had friends—not friends so much as a couple of people in my class—who started to give me a hard time. We had a new pastor who started with us, and that became a little bit intense. There were a few of us who were not Christian in the school. The pastor would take us into a room and talk to us about how we needed to change our religion, saying we would go to hell if we didn't. I would go home crying sometimes, thinking, "Mom and Dad, I don't want to go to hell." It was a fear tactic, and when you are young, those things can really affect you, of course. This is in junior high school, so 1997. I don't want to stereotype or generalize, but this specific group of people was a little more proselytizing. They sincerely believed the more people they made Christian, the better. You can't blame them. It was what they believed. However, the way it was being done was a little scary for a young kid.

They would make us watch these movies, like *Left Behind*, which talked about the end of the world. The movies showed that when the world ended, Jesus Christ would come back to the earth and all the Christians would disappear and everyone else would be left behind. The people left behind would have to live in this horrible world. It painted this really scary picture of what it would be like if you were not Christian. Thankfully, I had a very strong foundation at home, and when I would talk about my feelings to my parents, they always told me, "This is not what we believe.

We believe that all monotheistic religions will go to heaven." They taught me the other perspective, and I preferred to believe we were all going to heaven. Not just one of us. That was my driving force. As a result of the way the people at school approached me with religion, I was never that enticed by it. It wasn't something I thought I wanted to be a part of. I couldn't see myself being like that.

Eventually, I had a couple of people who were not really nice to me because of that, but I never really felt the need to fight them back. I would say okay and move forward. I would tell people, "I believe we are all going to heaven." That was never really a big fight.

Then we went to high school and I ran for class president. I ran against this girl who was the token goody-goody girl. I was a good girl, too, of course. I had straight A's just like her. I was doing very well. We ran our campaigns, and I won the popular vote. The electoral college was our administration. The administration invented something, like I passed out cookies and that was against one of our bylaws. Which doesn't make any sense, because my opponent, Elizabeth, did it too. Anyway, the upshot is that they took it away from me, the class presidency. It was because they didn't want a non-Christian girl as the president of the high school. I was a senior at this time. Basically, they took it away and told me I couldn't be class president. Instead, they gave it to Elizabeth. I had an option at that point. I spoke with my parents, and we talked about getting a lawyer, because we felt it was becoming very discriminatory. We started speaking to some people. My parents really did more than I did. I was in high school and didn't want to cause too many problems, especially because I was graduating soon. I felt like somehow being humble about it and allowing her to take the position would make my life easier. We did seek some legal counsel and they told us, "You are in a private school so essentially they can do whatever they want." They basically told us, "You can't file a lawsuit." If we did go that route, it would be long and drawn-out and cost money, and they discouraged us from doing it. From the beginning, I was a little hesitant. I don't know why. I was just resigned, like, this girl is going to take the presidency. I even ended up telling her, "If you need help, I will be able to help. Best of luck." I wished her the best. My friends, the people I was in school with, were totally against my acting that way. They were protesting, "No, Amal should be president." So there were two parties at that school: the ones that were against me and the ones for me. Everyone knew it was related to religion. This was 2000, so it was before any 9/11 conversations that were anti-Muslim.

Q: How did this make you feel when they took away the class presidency? Did the headmaster call you in? Can you walk me through that?

They called me in to the principal's office and basically told me, "You broke one of the school regulations in your campaign, and for that reason we are disqualifying you."

I was shattered, because I had worked so hard. It takes a lot to run a campaign. You are in school at the same time and you are trying to get good grades. I knew from that moment there was something going on behind it. I knew it was because they wanted Elizabeth. It was their agenda to have her. They never thought I would make it. I don't know. It hurt me a lot. I felt like an outsider.

Q: What did you say to the principal when he told you this?

I said, "You ate the cookie." It was something related to the cookies I made. Which was really just outrageous. I said, "I walked around the hallway and I gave you a cookie and you ate it and you said, 'Thank you.'" The reason you are giving me now, for not letting me have the presidency, is not enough and it is not fair."

They didn't say much after that. There was nothing that could be done at that moment. I didn't feel empowered enough to say or do much because they didn't give me a chance. There was no fighting it. They decided it, and that was it. It was tough, and for the rest of the year this girl was making decisions and running the class events. I was available to help her out. Sometimes it hurt my ego a bit and I felt uncomfortable, but at the end of the day what was really helpful was that I still had my close friends around me. They never let that be something that defined our friendship or that defined who I was.

Instead, it was the exact opposite. They appreciated me for who I was. The whole situation with her kind of disrespecting me, with the school disrespecting me for who I was, affected the way teachers saw me too. To be honest, I liked school. I enjoyed chapel. I would go sometimes to youth groups with my friends because it was fun and social. It was never . . . I don't know. I kind of assimilated as much as I could. Not because I felt like I had to but because it just felt natural. Yet the fact that I was from a different religion made a lot of teachers look at me differently. Not all of them looked at me differently. Please don't get me wrong. There were some teachers that until today I am in touch with. I have an amazing relationship with those teachers, and they never saw me differently. But there were some that weren't as kind. You can tell sometimes how people treat each other. In some of my classes I was looked at differently, and that scenario made me feel it even more. It kind of makes you feel a little like an outsider. I never did anything crazy to fight it; I didn't feel the need to. It has worked to my benefit so much.

Just recently, after Trump was elected, Elizabeth—the girl who was elected class president after I was disqualified—messaged me. I can actually read the message to you because it touched me. "Hey, Amal, it has been forever. I know this is super random but all this nasty stuff with Trump and his treatment of Muslims reminded me of my own behavior back in junior high and high school. I wanted to say I am so sorry if I ever made you feel like your religion was wrong or that you needed to change. I am honestly so mortified looking back. That must have been so tough holding unique views in a place that wasn't tolerant of other faiths but you handled it all so gracefully. You never swayed in your beliefs and I really admire you for that."

She sent the letter to me on January 29, 2017. I feel like we could have made a huge deal out of it at the time. We could have been more vocal. But at the end of the day, that was where I went to school. Those were the people I was going to be around. Had I made it even more uncomfortable by creating more tension, it would have been worse. So we decided to just stay humble and stay a little quiet and peaceful about it, and it turned out for the best.

Q: I am just thinking, as I am listening to you talk, about Michelle Obama's statement "When they go low, we go high." That's what I think I am hearing you say. Correct me if I am wrong, but—you had a decision to make. You were basically faced with unfair discrimination. You could have fought it and made an ugly scene, but you decided to find the inner strength to carry yourself with dignity and integrity and show how people can live their lives without being angry and bitter about something that is unfair. Is that right?

Absolutely. Yes.

Q: That takes a certain kind of moral courage, to do that kind of thing. I'm just wondering if the fact that you found whatever strength you did to do this then opened the door for Elizabeth to respond the way she did later, when Trump was elected. You showed her how to be gracious about things and showed her how people could have integrity even in the face of discrimination. That may have helped her in the current situation, where she realized that what was happening in the country, as a whole, was something that had happened to her, that in some ways she benefited from it and that she now felt sorry about that. And she was able to write you a very nice letter.

It *was* very nice. It touched me so much. I think we could have a renewed friendship because of this, and I hope I will be able to see her when I come back to the US and catch up with her. Right now our friendship would be so much more meaningful, and we could learn a lot from each other.

After high school, I went to Berkeley. It was a great atmosphere. You know how it is up there; people are very open-minded. Up north, I didn't feel different being an Arab or a Muslim.

Q: Interesting. I want to raise an issue about a different kind of courage. Not moral courage per so, but perhaps not unrelated. Can you tell me about the tsunami?

You know, it is funny because when you are in these scenarios, even my high school scenarios, the courage you have and the decisions you make, it's not something you consciously think about. It's something that just happens. Maybe it is upbringing. I don't know why I decided to deal with that situation in high school the way I did. I credit my parents for teaching me various moral values growing up. Even in the case of a tsunami—if you don't go through it you would never think you could handle so much stress and tension.

I'll tell you about the tsunami; then maybe it will be a little clearer about how these different events—the bullying and the tsunami—are related. The tsunami was in 2004, so I was in college. I went on vacation with my best friend, Rebecca, to Thailand, where we were going to do scuba diving courses and get our licenses.[4] We landed in Thailand on Christmas Eve. We got settled in our hotel and had our first dive on Christmas Day. We went out for Christmas dinner, had a great time, and met some lovely people, and then her parents said, "Okay, guys. Time to head back home since we're getting up at eight tomorrow morning for our dive."

We were like, "No. It is so early! We don't want to go at eight."

Her parents insisted. So long story short, we ended up waking super early to go to the dive shop, get all of our gear, and head to the boat. We got on the boat around eight-thirty and headed out into the ocean. If we had left at ten, we would have met the big wave when it hit the island. But we were under water by nine forty-five. Something like that. We were practicing things you need for your license. A few minutes in, it felt strange underwater. There weren't that many fish. I remember thinking, "Why did we fly a million miles to go scuba diving in Thailand and there are no fish? I don't understand."

I looked at the scuba diving teacher underwater and signed this thing you do underwater so you can communicate, like, "Is everything okay?" He signaled, "Yes everything is fine." But within five seconds of that exchange, a very strong current took us with it, for fifteen, twenty seconds. It was really strong, but you couldn't swim against it. You just had to go with it. There was nothing you could do. It was an enormously powerful current. All I was thinking at that moment was, "What did the book say to do?" The most important thing they remind you in the scuba diving course is just to keep breathing, so I said, "Okay, Amal, just keep breathing." Ignorance was bliss, because I had no idea what was going on. I just thought maybe it was something normal that happened underwater in Thailand. I didn't panic because I didn't know what it could be.

About fifteen or twenty seconds passed, and eventually the wave passed us. We had all grabbed each other, which was great. It was our reflex to grab whoever was next to us. We were all together. The teacher told us to go to the surface slowly. We were still a little bit confused. We were looking for our boat and it wasn't there, so we had to inflate this emergency buoy the teacher had. It's big and long, and the boat will find you if you inflate it. Eventually our boat found us and we went to find Rebecca's parents, since they were diving in a different area because they were more professional than we were.

When we found them, Rebecca's dad was quite pale, yellow-looking. When the tsunami hit, Rebecca and I couldn't get pulled any lower because we were at the ocean floor. Rebecca's dad was in a much deeper area so he got pulled down extremely fast and got disorientated when he was underwater. Thankfully, he was able to make it up to the surface, so we got everyone on that boat. At that point the dive master—the head teacher—said there had been some kind of seismic activity, some kind of earthquake, and we couldn't scuba dive anymore today. We were like, "Okay. Let's just go back to the island so we can enjoy the weather." We didn't grasp the significance of what the instructor had said about seismic activity. We picked up two men in a smaller boat and they told us two waves, twenty-five-foot waves, had hit the island! Everything was destroyed. Everything was gone. The people were all dead. Two tsunamis hit the island, and that was what we felt this morning when we were swimming. That's when we learned about it. But we still had not grasped the magnitude of how horrible it actually was. We had no idea it was not one island; it was actually nine islands, and already at that point 35,000 people had been killed.

As we started getting closer to the island, the water was getting darker, almost like soot. What was on the island was now in the water. Furniture, chairs, cabinets, everything. Still, somehow, we were still in denial. We got closer and closer. Once we got ten minutes from the shore, the boat crew asked us to go down below. They made something up, so we went below. I realized afterward that the captain asked us to go inside because bodies had started to wash up to the shore; they wanted to spare us as much trauma as possible. By asking us to go inside, they would at least spare us from seeing the contorted dead bodies that washed up. When we got to the island, everything had been destroyed. There was no electricity. Nothing.

We didn't know if another wave was coming. If there is another wave coming the best place to be is somewhere out in the ocean and not on the island. It finally started to sink in that this massive wave had destroyed the island. We were sitting in one of the most dangerous places possible. We were starting to understand we were part of a larger situation, that other islands were involved. We realized there were many people dead and the media was covering it. At that stage I started to freak out. My parents don't know I'm safe. My mom was in California and my dad in Lebanon. Mom knew exactly where I was, and my dad knew I was on vacation with Rebecca somewhere in Thailand. Given the time difference, I knew my father would find out before Mom. I just knew my parents would find out and probably panic. Essentially, my parents lost their minds. It was then that reality and fear and anxiety set in. We are sitting here and another wave could hit any minute. Literally, the thoughts that were coming in my head were, "I'm not ready to die. I'm still young. I have so much I want to do with my life and I really want to see my parents again." That's what I was thinking.

Then I thought, maybe it was going to be over, and we had made it through the hardest part. I was confused. There is not much you can do when you have no access to phones or the ability to get in touch with anyone. We just tried to support each other. We just sat there and had our thoughts going through our heads and prayed to whatever gods we believed in to keep us safe so we could get out of there.

Oddly, there was a Japanese family with us, and I was watching them; they were so quiet the entire time. I started to realize there are cultural differences in how people accept their fate. They just sat there and didn't say much, maybe thinking, "This is how it is." While we were talking, trying to think of solutions and rationalizing, trying to figure out what to do, they were just quiet. It was interesting to see how other people were doing in the same situation. Ultimately, we became very quiet and lay there, waiting for the captain to come back. When he came back a couple of hours later, he told us we didn't have enough fuel to get to Phuket, which is where the airport is, so he would take us to another island that wasn't affected by the tsunami. He was going to take us there to spend the night, and he would pick us up the next day.

We got to this small island, not populated at all. It's one of those islands where you go to the restroom and it's a hole in the ground. It was primitive. The people were so kind! I'm sure they had heard what happened so they opened their homes to us and put blankets on the floor. We went into the houses and lay down. I did not sleep a wink. With every wave that crashed, I became worried about what was going to happen. The island was safe because of its location, but after a tsunami you aren't really in a rational mindset. Even today the sound of waves crashing is not the most comfortable scenario for me if I'm half asleep at night. It's something that stays with you for a long time.

Once I saw the sun starting to rise, I got up and started looking for a phone, because that was my main priority at this point. I was no longer concerned for myself. I was concerned about getting through to my parents before something happened to them. I started to walk around the island. Rebecca's dad came with me to make sure I was okay. We found this lady with a phone. I asked her if it would be possible to call my mom, to let her know I was okay. I told the lady I had no money and the phone call is international. I was still in my bathing suit. That's all I had when I left the morning of the day before. She let me call. I tried to dial but my hand was shaking so Rebecca's father helped me dial. It rang a couple times and I heard my mom's voice. I cried, "Hi, Momma!" Then I got a little bit emotional.

She cried out, "Amal!"

I was like, "I'm fine." After that, I couldn't hear anything. I think she fainted. Dad had learned of the tsunami and called Mom at four in the morning California time. That's never a good sign. My mom picked up the phone and heard Dad say, "Where is Amal exactly?" Mom told him I was in Thailand. So that's how they learned I might be involved in the tsunami. I told them where I was at the moment and that we were going to be leaving in a couple of hours. I told her, "I'll basically get in contact with you as soon as I can again. But I'm fine, I'm alive, everything is good."

That was that. The boat came back to get us and took us to a crisis center. The Thai government gave us clothes. They made identity cards for us because we didn't have passports. They gave us hotel rooms for the night and free flights to Bangkok, where we could visit our respective embassies and get passports. The next day we left.

To be honest, the emotions there, well, there were so many small emotions you feel during this whole experience. But this is why the tsunami experience relates to the bullying, you know, and to moral courage generally. Some of the most interesting emotional times requiring a lot of courage are really scary, something you wouldn't think you would know how to handle and get through until you are there and you *have* to get through it and survive it. What I learned from this experience was that all we had was each other, and as much as it was important for each of us to survive on our own, we all really stuck together and functioned like a family. All the people with us, we saw humanity at its best. It didn't matter who you were, it didn't matter where you came from or what your background was. It was all of us being together, being safe, and making it out alive. We became so close. As difficult as it was, it was so beautiful seeing people help each other so much. The way the Thai government handled it, the way they created the crisis center out of thin air in twenty-four hours. They had clothes ready to give us, and they were offering us free tickets and giving us places to stay. It was all beautiful to see. Not just the courage of the victims, but the strength of the city to come together; a city you wouldn't think had that many resources in the first place still was able to come together.

Q: It's interesting that when you were talking about being in the water, your first instinct is to hold onto each other because you don't know where the current is taking you and you don't have any idea what's going on at that point. What do you think it was that got you through that? Was it the desire to be back with your parents? Was it just raw instinct for survival? Was it because you were with other people whom you wanted to help? What was it that helped you get through this without getting hysterical or falling apart in a situation when you basically are all on your own?

It was a combination of all those things together. No one has actually ever asked me that question before—and I've told this story many times. Of course, it is your internal desire to want to survive and make it. I just didn't feel it was my time. I wasn't ready for it to be over. Just wanting all of us, whoever was still alive, to stay alive. Something that goes through your head when you survive is this sense of guilt. How come all these people died? These kids lost their parents, and other parents lost their kids. They're going to suffer for the rest of their lives. What did they do wrong? What did I do right? It wasn't fair. It was a feeling I struggled with; even Rebecca spoke to me about this. We both have it. It comes with the territory of living through this sort of trauma. What makes you want to get through it is wanting to stay alive, wanting to be with your parents again. Wanting to do more.

Q: Did you ever come up with an answer as to why you think you survived and others didn't? Was it just chance or luck?

The way that I would explain it now was that it wasn't my time. Fate. God had another plan. I made it through because I'm meant to do something more with my life, create some impact in some way. What got me through it was fate and the belief that I am meant to be here to do something with my life to help others. I am meant to have a more meaningful life. What you learn in scenarios like this is how quickly life can go. You don't realize, at the snap of your finger, that in an instant you could be gone. That's actually how it is. It's such a gift to be alive. That's one of the biggest lessons that came out of the experience for me.

Q: What do you want to do with your life, Amal?

I became passionate about working for social businesses, businesses that can be sustainable and do good, because of those experiences. That's why I'm doing what I'm doing today. I feel I'm making an impact by helping these small businesses grow and be better and contribute to economies and create jobs. And to have a family; I want to raise kids.

Everything I do, I see it through that lens. I ask how it is contributing to a greater good, and if it's not, then I don't do it. That's the lens I see my life through, even in relationships. The reason I talk freely about my different experiences is that I sincerely believe that if I can change just one person's opinion or make that person feel just that much more connected to a good cause or make a difference, then that's what I want to do.

Ideally one day I will be making very large-scale impacts, but for me, it starts with the individual. If you can do it in your own way on an individual basis, then eventually it starts to have a more exponential impact.

8

"It Would Be a Violation of the Public Trust to Not Do All I Could to Stop the Wrongdoing": Loretta Lynch on Speaking Truth to Power during the Enron Crisis

> A person is only as good as their character and their word. Why go into government if you're not going to try to do the right thing?
> LORETTA LYNCH, Summer 2017

I was born in Independence, Missouri, into a large Catholic working-class family. I was a debater in high school, so I went to the University of Southern California for college because they had the number-one debate team in the nation. I debated for only three months because in the fall of my freshman year the *Los Angeles Times* broke the story that the debate team coaches were signing off on nonexistent courses for football team members to allow them to keep their NCAA eligibility. The debate team's travel budget was funded by the athletic department, so they fired all the debate coaches and the debate team fell apart. That was one of my first big moments of cynicism about how the world really works, and I then had to scramble to get scholarships and loans to stay in college.

After college I worked for the California state legislature in a fellowship program. On my first day on the job this long-term legislative secretary told me, "Okay, I like you so I will tell you all of the members who you should not be in an elevator alone with; if you do let yourself be alone with them, then it is your fault." This was 1983, and I did not realize just how pervasive sexual harassment in a workplace was. So that prompted me to go to law school. Well, that and other things.

There are three kinds of jobs for women in the legislature: secretary, fundraiser, and lawyer. That pretty much is what women in the legislature did. They were staffers. So, I went to Yale Law School and then clerked for a woman judge on the 9th Circuit Court of Appeals in Los Angeles. She was part of the "Carter dozen." President Jimmy Carter appointed

---

Loretta Lynch was former head of the California Public Utilities Commission during the Enron crisis.

twelve women to the United States Appeals Court. She told me about how she charmed Senator Hayakawa, who was not initially for her, very interestingly, by inviting him over to her house for dinner. He admired her cooking skills [*laughing*]! She was one of the last people confirmed by the Senate during the Carter administration. She also was head of the Bahá'í of America. She was a convert to the Bahá'í religion, so when I clerked for her, she was the president of the Bahá'ís. All sorts of people from around the world would call to have her intercede on the Bahá'í's behalf. I remember that at one point Mrs. S—— called to tell her that there were Bahá'ís facing execution and asked if she could intervene and perhaps save their lives. So she went to Egypt and did that. I learned a lot from Dorothy Nelson about doing the right thing.[1] Obviously, she was a federal judge for life, but even so, there were a lot of political pressures within the group of judges to kind of go along, to not dissent, and to work it out behind the scenes. Dorothy was very good about taking a stand when she felt it was necessary; that was a helpful lesson. She was an important role model for me, but she also told me I needed to learn how to pick my fights, because there is a lot of injustice in the world and there is only so much an individual can do. It's advice I am still trying to follow. It is hard to follow the advice.

I then became a lawyer and moved back to D.C. and worked in an appellate law firm, which did not suit me, as it was very staid and white-shoe and slow. Appellate work is not trial work, and you are not in court much. But what I did learn from the appellate group is that most of their work, or a good half of their work, was energy work of FERC [Federal Energy Regulatory Commission], and they represented a ton of coal companies.[2] I was determined that I was never going to do any of that work. It was dirty work, and I didn't want to work for FERC or know anything about that. I left within a year to go on the Van de Kamp campaign.[3]

I moved back to Los Angeles and worked for John Van de Kamp, and it was a fabulous campaign. He lost to Dianne Feinstein. I played Dianne in our mock debates and was devastated when he lost, although, sadly, I knew it was coming. I worked for Los Angeles Legal Aid after that until we won a big case that had to do with stopping discriminatory rules regarding trying to kick people off general assistance. We won that case in some sense through politics, because the Los Angeles Board of Supervisors at that time—this was the early '90s—was two to three, Democrat to Republican, and there was a lawsuit based on the Voting Rights Act, based on a case that I had worked for with Judge Nelson. Judge Nelson was the author of this voting rights case, which said, "Hey, we can't discriminate against Latinos so you need to draw the district in the right way." Los Angeles had redrawn their district in 1990 in accordance with this case that I worked on, and that led to Gloria Molina being elected supervisor in Los Angeles and the county shifting to three to two in favor of the Democrats. So the county settled this case and stopped the very discriminatory rules that were designed to kick people off assistance. Legal Aid then responded by disbanding my unit [*laughs*]. They gave me six weeks to learn Spanish and go into a neighborhood legal services office or I was out. Sadly, I didn't think I could learn Spanish in six weeks, so I needed to find another job. I moved to Northern California and worked for Keker and Brooke law firm. John Keker had come to fame by prosecuting Oliver North; he had received a Purple Heart in Vietnam, and they wanted somebody of that type to prosecute Oliver North for his Iran-contra war crimes.

I learned a lot about working at a law firm, but my heart was in politics after working for Van de Kamp, so at the end of 1991 I interviewed with a bunch of political campaigns for the 1992 presidential election. I wanted to work with Tom Harkin. I thought, "He is from Iowa; I am from Missouri, I am also from the heartland." He was seen as more progressive, which was great. I had an in because Van de Kamp's pollster was then polling for Harkin. So I got a job interview and I showed up and they said, "Oh, well, before you can interview with the policy people you have to come over here." They gave me a typing test.

Q: Are you serious?

I am serious. This is November 1991 and I noticed that all of the people who were given the typing test were girls! I was a Yale lawyer and I was there to interview as a policy consultant for a presidential candidate. I had worked on the California governor's race, which was the next best thing to the presidential one. I had never learned how to type because I never needed to. I took accounting in high school instead of typing, and I was proud of the fact that I couldn't type at all because I knew that if I learned how to type I would be the one taking all the notes, right? So I walked out and I then went to interview with some people I knew through my first job in Washington, with Bruce Reid, who became Clinton's campaign policy director. He said, "Loretta, if you want to come to Arkansas, come on down." So I did. I worked in Newark, Arkansas, until the start of the Quick Response Team in Arkansas. My issues were Whitewater, the draft, and then Hilary's clients.

It was the best of times and the worst of times! Amazing, is all I can say. After successfully steering through the debate work in the primaries I was told I did such a good job on defense that my job for the general election would be to keep the lid on Whitewater. I had thought I would get a better job than the mucky job I had during the primary [*laughing*] precisely because I had killed myself to stay one step ahead of the press. I did not want to keep the lid on Whitewater, and frankly, I didn't think I could. The Republicans had more than the Democrats did on Whitewater. So I quit. I then went to work for Dianne Feinstein as her assistant campaign manager for her 1992 campaign. Dianne asked me in my interview why I didn't continue working for Van de Kamp, and I said, "Well, I intended to continue working for Van de Kamp but you put a stop to that so here I am" [*laughing*].

I moved back to San Francisco as her assistant campaign manager. I wrote the speeches and the policy papers and things like that. When she won, she was interviewing people to go to Washington, but she had made a campaign promise to cut her staff salary by 10 percent and she decided to cut the salaries by more, and I didn't think this was fair. Although she had offered me a job in Washington, I did not take it and went back to my law firm in 1993. In 1994, I left again and ran a California statewide race for Delaine Eastin to become California Superintendent of Public Instruction.[4] She won. We were one of three Democratic races that won in 1994. We thought that California was blue, but as recently as 1994 California was majorly red. We won with one-tenth the money of any of the other successful Democratic candidates, and I learned a lot about winning in that race. In 1995 I went back to my law firm and stayed until I made partner in 1996.

I then was looking for a race to work on in 1998. I hooked up with Gray Davis and essentially worked as a chair on Davis's Earth ad as campaign manager, scheduling and attending meetings. After the campaign they offered me a job as the Office of Planning and Research (OPR) director, which does land-use planning and development for the governor. It has a niche within the governor's office. I came to realize, more importantly, that it had fifty exempt positions, meaning it was a political position, not filled with public servants, so a lot of the governor's political folks were housed at OPR. I dove into policy and did as much policy as I could in the governor's office. One of the policy areas I had was primarily because no one else wanted it. Gray Davis wanted someone within his office to be a liaison to every agency. He wanted a corresponding governor's-office person to essentially know what was going on in every agency rather than using his cabinet secretaries for that. One of the offices I became a liaison with was the California Public Utilities Commission [PUC]. When Davis's PUC commissioner quit to become the financial advisor for Al Gore, this guy famously told Gray Davis that nothing is going on in the PUC and Loretta knows it all, why don't you appoint her? The guy who recommended me was Joel Hyatt,[5] Howard Metzenbaum's son-in-law.[6] He was the one who started Hyatt Legal Services and is also apparently the guy on whom the movie *Philadelphia* is based. Joel had taken the job thinking it was the springboard for running for office but found out it was an intensely technical, bureaucratic, five-days-a-week job, so if you're not interested in the subject matter it can be kind of boring. Also, you're going to make somebody mad, either the company or the consumers. It is hard to reconcile, to make everybody happy, if you are going to be on the PUC.

I was looking for a way to come back to San Francisco, because it turns out that commuting to Sacramento is tough when you are working fourteen hours a day, so I took the job. In January of 2000 I moved back to San Francisco, thinking, I will learn this job and work hard for six months and then I will be able to take weekends off. Won't that be different? Six months later we had our first blackout, on June 14. I knew as of May that something was wrong. California had passed the Deregulation Bill of 1996, which had a delay in it. These legal steps had to happen between 1996 and 2001 or 2002, so the market wouldn't open until 2000 or 2001. In the meantime, we sold off all the power plants and took legal steps to take away California's control over the market. That all happened not on Gray Davis's watch. He inherited this rumbling volcano, but because he put people in charge of the PUC who didn't know anything about the PUC, the warning signs were not seen properly. The people who were still on the PUC knew what was happening, but as free marketers they believed it was going to be okay. The problem was, I was a part of the minority. There were still three Pete Wilson appointees who were very antideregulation, and they formed the majority of the commission.

By May I knew something was wrong, so I began digging into these markets and learned that the California government did not have the right to the information. This new nongovernmental entity called the Independent System Operator controlled the information of the market, and they refused to give it to California. In addition, the PUC had been starved of so many regulatory agencies that the budget had been cut; it had gone from 1350 employees to 850 employees. That's a lot of people to lose in just ten years. The people who stayed were by and large pioneers who had drunk the deregulation Kool-Aid. There were not that many people who were critics of deregulation. So, when I was trying to figure out why this works, why won't prices go down, and why won't people go into the market, people didn't think I had intellectual capacity, because they thought, "Who would ask those kinds of questions?" By June I was scrambling to get in the minds of legislators to get a handle on it. But then the first blackout happened on June 14, and the second happened on June 15. So I convinced the governor to appoint me to do a report on the causes of the blackout. He said, in a very Trumpian way, "I want it in thirty days!"

I was thinking, "Yeah, right!"

Forty days later, I got him a report that alleged market manipulation, but I couldn't prove it because we couldn't get any documents. Well, that created a firestorm of political hell raining down on me. Certainly lots of people complained to Gray Davis, "Who is this idiot girl you put in as the head of the PUC? She doesn't even understand deregulation."

I decided this is wrong that we can't get the information. I had read the Public Utilities Code before Davis appointed me. He had told me in November he was going to appoint me. He didn't do it until December, but I spent Christmas of 1999 reading the statutes because, as a lawyer, I thought you start with the statute to find out what the governing law is. I read pretty much every single case having to do with the PUC. It was a lot less daunting than it sounds, because the PUC at that time had only appealed to the California Supreme Court, so there were only about a hundred cases to read since the inception of the PUC.

With only a rudimentary understanding of the law, I realized we had subpoena power. I spent the month of September figuring out what to do because (1) my lawyers had never issued a subpoena and (2) many of the lawyers were too scared to do it. So I worked with a couple of legal advisors who were our political appointees, a band of four people, writing 127 subpoenas to all of the companies in the market for information, subpoenas which I then promptly issued at the end of September. No one at the PUC would sign the subpoenas because they were too afraid the companies would come after them, so I signed them all. Technically, it was supposed to be someone from the legal department, but I realized I had the authority as a California lawyer and president of the PUC to sign, and so I did.

Immediately, the companies lawyered up; I knew what that meant. My law firm was known for dealing with white-collar criminal offenses. I had done some work with white-collar criminal offenses working as a criminal defense lawyer at the Keker firm. I understood the behavior of corporations when they get a government subpoena. Folks who think they don't have anything to hide cooperate because they want the subpoena to end, and then they can go back to their business. The folks who don't cooperate, well, there is smoke at least. So when I learned all the companies had lawyered up, I knew it was time to go dig. We opened an investigation, and I began going to Washington to talk to FERC (the Federal Regulatory Commission). The companies had run to FERC to quash my subpoena, but FERC neither crushed the subpoenas nor allowed them to go through. They just sat on them. That to me was another huge red flag. In the meantime, the California energy market was melting down. Prices were exponential, ten to fifteen times higher than the year before, and manipulation and fraud were in full flower. We were forced to go to FERC to plead to give us price caps on our market that we now no longer controlled. On November 1, instead of granting our petitions for price caps, they completely denied price caps and opened our market to any price. Within one week the price of power quadrupled in California. It went up 400 percent. Utilities came to the governor and said, "We can't pay these prices. We need a price increase immediately." We were in a real energy crisis of California from November 2000 to February 2001. Gray Davis had been going to the Clinton administration asking for help, and Bill Clinton just kept saying, "Wait until after the election. How bad can it get?"

Then Bush beat Gore and they all became consumed with that while California was melting down. Bill Clinton and FERC were doing Enron's and Wall Street's bidding and our utilities were falling apart, so I decided to institute an emergency rate increase proceeding. At the time Gray Davis had told me privately to do no more than 10 percent, and that is what I did in December. Well, that wasn't half enough to cover the 400 percent increase. So I opened an investigation into how the utilities had been spending the excess money they had been getting for five years, because under the deregulation deal they got a lot of money in advance to prepare them for market shifts. So I began looking for the stockpiles. This was also a time with the lowest reported power usage in California. Summertime is the highest because we use air conditioning, and we use less electricity in the winter because a lot of people use gas to heat their homes. So the power usage curve goes way down in November. Nonetheless, we had blackouts in November. That's when I knew the energy companies were in control of our markets and power supply. They were manipulating the power supply, because we had plenty of power. We instituted programs where the state would drop power. If one were to go to a state building in

November or December, only one out of three light bulbs would be on. Not everything would be working, because we could drop 2000 megawatts within twenty minutes through state coordination, which was a great feat. On the first two days, we dropped 2000 megawatts, and on the third day, California was short by 2500 megawatts. The power companies responded and withheld more power. So I convinced Gray Davis in his State of the State Address to threaten to take over the power plants, kind of like how Kennedy took over the steel mills. When there is a national emergency, the government can come in and take over the means of an essential good. But unbeknownst to me, Gray Davis had met with Kenneth Lay, the head of Enron, who asked for more time to sort it out.[7]

"Yeah, right," I thought when Davis told me this. "Just give us a little bit more time to rape and pillage in your state," was what I was hearing.

Nonetheless, Gray Davis said, "If the companies don't come to the table, I will take over a power plant."

In the meantime, I was preparing at the PUC to do exactly that. I was looking at our legal authority to literally go send inspectors with guns to take over a power plant. We also realized we were close to the union, who had a bunch of laid-off power utility workers who knew those plants and could go march in with us to take over those power plants.

After the State of the State Address, the next day the Clinton administration and Lawrence Summers called Gray Davis. By this time we knew we would have the Bush administration in a couple of weeks. We called a meeting with Gray Davis, his people, and the power plant companies to fix this problem, and we walked into an ambush. It was the Clinton administration telling us to do what the power plant companies wanted.

Q: *Why did they do that?*

Well, one could argue that the Clinton administration was a corporate shield for the deregulation movement. One also could argue that Bill Clinton was as close to Kenneth Lay as George Bush was. And Jim Hecker, the Clinton administration's head of FERC told me he was going to be fine either with Bush or Gore because he understood how his bread was buttered. I took this to mean he was going to do what the companies wanted because no matter which administration held power in Washington, they were going to do what the companies wanted. Gray Davis, to his credit, said no, and walked out of the Clinton meeting. At this time, in January, the month with the lowest energy demand, California experienced two blackouts.

I knew they had us over a barrel; they could black us out whenever they wanted because they coordinated in an organized conspiracy to withhold power from California no matter the human cost. After the two blackouts, Gray Davis caved, and I must say I don't blame him for doing this because we had very few levers left. I think if he had acted earlier or taken over a power plant, we would have had many levers. I also understood, from being a corporate defense lawyer, that the companies had a fiduciary duty to safeguard their assets for their shareholders, so if the government acted to take over one power plant, the second power plant would need to play ball with the government instead of being taken over. Otherwise, they would be subject to shareholder lawsuits for acting unreasonably. That is why I was advocating taking over at least one power plant: to force the companies to comply, to make a deal. Gray Davis did not do that, and therefore California was on the hook of the energy crisis.

I decided to break with Gray Davis. I did not believe he was doing enough to fix the problem. He was listening to the companies and Robert Rubin, who I understood went back to Citibank after leaving office, which was a part of the problem.[8] So on Rubin's behalf they were calling the governor, saying, "There isn't a problem. Not to worry. It is only a temporary blip."

I kept saying, "No! That is not true!"

I later embarrassed the governor on a conference call by saying to Secretary Rubin, "Excuse me, are you not the head of Citigroup now, and doesn't Citibank have investment in our market? In fact, aren't you playing directly in our market?"[9]

There was a long pause, and Bob Rubin said, "Governor, I think I can't be on these conference calls anymore," and hung up [*laughing*]. He was conflicted. Some of the folks Gray Davis was consulting with were using the information they gained from him against the California market! I spilled that out and no one believed me, so here we were.

I decided in 2001 I needed to do my job as president of PUC to contain this crisis. I started issuing emergency orders. We continued going after the companies. We started going to court for the documents, and finally I did another emergency rate increase in March. It was a lot more than would keep the companies on the hook to provide power to their customers. In response PGE [Pacific Gas and Electric], decided to declare bankruptcy. They were sitting on over $2 billion of cash, repair money, but they didn't like the conditions I put on the rate increase. Gray Davis began to really pressure me to concede to the companies. I said, "No. That is not lawful and that is not my job." Given that the summer before the governor had told the legislature that it was their job to implement his vision, you can imagine how he felt when a political appointee of his told him no [*laughing*].

Well, I had read the law and thought we were not taking sufficient steps to safeguard our economy or our ratepayers. We were receiving thousands of letters from people saying they couldn't pay the light bill. People saying they had to choose between shoes and the light bill, between food and the light bill. I had grown up in a family where there wasn't enough money generally, and so, often, to pay the light bill, we ate macaroni and cheese. I understood that basic, human, family decision, and I also understood that the only reason it was happening was because of corporate greed. I saw this happening to so many families across California, so I started to move forward to exercise the power of the PUC without having the governor's approval.

Q: *How did that play?*

Well, he eventually kicked me out of the PUC president position. But not before the election, because they had polls that said I was popular, so he wasn't going to take me out until after he was reelected. Also, in February I challenged Bob Rubin and exercised the power of the PUC in a creative pro-consumer way. The legislature instituted oversight proceedings to determine whether to impeach me for incompetence. I think there were two weeks of public hearings about my incompetence as a PUC president for questioning deregulation and for not doing what the companies wanted. Remember, this is a Democratic assembly trying to impeach me. The only way to get me out of office was for me to resign or for me to be impeached for corruption or incompetence. They decided I was incompetent for not understanding the benefits of deregulation [*laughing*].

One of my other personal heroes, Sheila Kuehl, took me to dinner the night before my first hearing and said, "Look, Loretta, everyone wants to see you crack. They all think you are a hard bitch, and so it is your job tomorrow to go in wearing makeup and pearls in a very modest suit and say, 'Yes ma'am,' and, 'No sir.' Smile and be as polite and as slow as you can and make sure you do not crack and are perceived as a nice girl."[10]

I said, "Sheila, I don't think I can do that." So she told me what she does. She said to dig your fingernails so deep into your palms that you begin to bleed, and then you'll be ready to play calm. So I did exactly that. I dug in my fingernails the entire first day, but I also did something else. I marshaled my political friend, the union, and I asked everybody to come to the first hearing and sit in the front row. I picked the people to come judiciously, because I understood the legislators who were on this oversight committee and especially the guy who was heading it. I picked union guys who had been their champions. Six of them came and sat in the front row, and before the hearing the legislators were really wondering why the union guys were at Loretta's hearing. They were being very nice to everyone, and the union guys told the legislators they were there to make sure their girl was being treated fairly.

At the first break, for the first time the assembly staff came over and said, "Hey, Loretta, are there any questions you would like us to ask you?" [*laughing*]. Anyway, so I survived those hearings and I felt like I tried to do the right thing in spite of suffering the imminent political consequences.

Q: *The consequences must have been significant; what were they?*

Well, I was cut off from the governor's office, called a traitor. The chief of staff told me I was the worst hire Gray Davis or she had ever done. The deputy chief of staff told one of the legislators that when they passed me on the street in Sacramento, if she had a gun and nobody saw her, she would clip my head right off. Eventually, that same person was put on the PUC after Gray Davis was recalled; he put her on the PUC for the express purpose of making my life so miserable I would quit. Oh, and Gray Davis offered me a judgeship if I were to quit. First it was a carrot and then it was sticks. I was not perceived as a "go-along, get-along girl," which, let us just say, was unusual at the PUC. I wouldn't play those games, take those trips, dinners, or gifts. I also wouldn't take private meetings. They all had to be noted, and I would give both sides the same amount of time. The companies hated me because I wouldn't go along. When I left PUC, the senior lobbyist, the senior vice president for Pacific Gas and Electric, told me, "You know, Loretta, if you ever thought about running for dogcatcher, PGE would put in a million dollars in an independent expenditure against you, and we are not the only ones. Every single company will follow with pleasure."

I just told him, "Well, good thing I am not thinking about running for dogcatcher."

Q: *I would think, though, that at a certain point it would be very hurtful to feel that people don't like you that much. Who did you lean on?*

I had my then-boyfriend, my now-husband, who has been my strongest defender.

Q: *That helps, that helps a lot, I am sure.*

Yes, it does. I also had longtime friends and allies who knew my character despite what people were telling them, saying I was a liar and disloyal, which are bad things politically, saying I had betrayed Gray Davis and whoever. They said my word was not good; things like that were very painful. The first person I worked for in the Van de Kamp campaign, when I was the assistant campaign manager, the campaign manager—who was a wonderful woman and lawyer in Los Angeles—she told me my first week on the job, "If you are a woman in politics you have two choices: to be liked or respected. Choose now." I laughed and looked at her and told her I would rather be respected, and she said, "Great! Go fire this consultant." And I did. I understood that concept. My uncle was also a fifty-year member of the IBEW [International Brotherhood of Electrical Workers], which was for electricians. When I was on the PUC, he gave me his fifty-year pin and told me, "Remember working people."

Q: *That was very nice.*

Ultimately, you had to decide whether you could sleep at night. I made sure I read a bunch of those letters; you know how President Obama had penned letters given to him daily, or weekly? I forget. Well, I read a bunch of those letters all the time to remember who I was working for and why the law was written the way it was. It wasn't written—well, actually, sadly some of it is written for the companies, but a lot of the laws were written during the Progressive Era, the reform era, of the 1910s. Certainly during the Depression of the 1930s it was written for the consumers. Those consumers included businesses that were getting reamed by those prices. So from my perspective, I was following the law, and that helped a lot. The hard part was that people don't typically follow the law in my job. I guess I was a bit naive to think that when you take the oath of office to uphold the constitution of the state of California, you follow those laws in your job setting. People just don't fulfill that oath on a routine basis.

Q: *Can you tell me more about what you said about how you wanted to sleep at night? Was it really a decision? Or was it more "This is the kind of person I am and I really don't have a choice unless I want to change who I am and sell myself out"?*

Well, I did have a choice. I could continue to try and convince Gray Davis to do the right thing. However, things had spiraled out of control so much and I guess by that time I had worked with him long enough to see his choices through 2000 and to understand he wasn't going to do the right thing from my perspective, which was to do what had to be done to stem the crisis. He continued to make person-rich choices, choices that were compounding the expense of the problem without going after the wrongdoers. Davis was trying to make a deal with the wrongdoers, and I understand why; he thought we were operating from a position of weakness, so he had to make a deal with the wrongdoers to get them to stop doing wrong. My view was a prosecutorial view: "No, you do need to go after the wrongdoers and get them to stop. You can't make a deal with them. You need to call them out and bring them to justice." Interestingly, we brought a lot of lawsuits at the PUC, which we very wonderfully handed off to Bill Lockyer, who was attorney general at the time I was leaving. I had no confidence that my successor, the vice president at the PUC, wouldn't settle those lawsuits out and make a deal, and frankly, for every possible lawsuit he could, he did settle those out, and for pennies on the dollar. The key lawsuits were then transferred to the AG [attorney general's] office, and Lockyer ran with them. Just last year, this is 2016 we're talking about, based on the lawsuits we filed in 2000 and 2001, the 9th Circuit [Court] held that yes, California's market was manipulated and yes, the energy companies must provide restitution. Fifteen years later we finally got the decision I knew was true. But it took that long in the courts. The problem with courts is the way justice is denied and, on the side, they'd been settling out of court with those wrongdoers, so there were just a couple of companies left that hadn't settled.

Q: *I see. This is all a little late, yes?*

Right. But am I proud we went after those wrongdoers and we eventually proved their wrongdoing, legally as well as morally and factually? Yes, I am proud we did that. Did it cost me a lot of relationships and jobs and reputational slights? Yes, it did. Am I a stronger person for it? Yes, I am.

Q: *How did you leave things with Davis? How did that play out?*

Well, for a long time after I said no to the judgeship [*laughing*]—he made a deal with my vice president, David Freeman, who was cut from the same cloth in my perspective, for them to go and negotiate deals with the energy companies. Instead of signing one-year contracts, they signed twelve- to thirteen-year contracts for top-of-the-market power. It was criminal capitalism at its worst. Those deals are still in effect.

But later, I did see the governor in an odd way: we were both invited to the same wedding. I hadn't seen him personally, outside of the crowd for probably a year at this point. I used this opportunity of seeing him at the wedding to say, "Hey, you know, Governor, we really need to renegotiate these deals. I can prove, and you can see that I can prove, manipulation eventually, so let us renegotiate and stop these thirteen-year deals."

He talked to me in the middle of this reception. He pulled me aside, and his bodyguards made a circle around us. So in the middle of this guy's reception there was the governor, talking to his then current PUC head. We all knew my head was on the chopping block, but for the moment I was still PUC president. He talked with me for twenty minutes about how to make the deal. He had somebody call me up the next day and we started to renegotiate the contract, so we got a slightly less bad deal. However, to this day I bet you he would say I was his worst hire because I did not do what he told me to do. I read the constitution and I read the history of the PUC and yes, I was a political appointee of Gray Davis, and I am very grateful that he gave me that opportunity because I do think I was the right person at the right time for that job. Otherwise, it would have all been slipped underneath the rug and we would be paying even more today. Again, we still have manipulators in the market among us without its being proven that they manipulated. But I do not believe Gray Davis ever will get over the fact that I did not do what he told me to do. By not doing what he said and by going after these guys legally, the ones Davis was trying to make a deal with, I made it harder for him to make the deals, and it kind of showed publicly what was happening, eventually.

Q: *You called for the investigation. Is that the one Senator Joe —— headed?*

No. The legislature also investigated and they formed a special committee that Joe —— headed.[11] Joe and I worked together well on this. What I understood was that I had subpoena power, but my subpoenas were caught up in FERC. The legislature had independent subpoena power, and by that time Enron had gone under. Joe and I discussed a lot about how we should go after these guys. As the PUC, we were suing them. They were suing us. We then were countersuing as well and we were investigating them. So I said to Joe, "You have subpoena power, why don't you go and use it?" And he did. He ran with it, and he was brilliant. Joe was a claims lawyer and understood the duties of the board of directors of a corporation, so he went to the board of the bankrupt Enron corporation and individually told them if they did not give him the documents personally, he would sue them criminally and he would also get their insurance and bankruptcy corporation. So, he got the Enron board—after Enron went bankrupt—to give the legislature of California documents that damn them and showed that Joe was the one who discovered the Enron memos. After I issued the subpoenas, Enron lawyered up, and the Enron lawyers wrote memos about Enron's exposure to my subpoenas; that's why they had to go to FERC, to make sure that they would never comply with my subpoenas. Those were the infamous Enron memos written in response to my subpoenas that Joe got. Once those were public, it was pretty clear there had been a conspiracy. So yes, Joe was fantastic and really showed in creative ways the power of the legislature. They have subpoena power over anybody or any entity that does wrong in California.

Q: Did Joe's action also end his friendship with Gray Davis?

I am sure it did. If you have somebody whose entire political advancement has been about being a corporate Democrat and getting along with corporations and then you have colleagues (like Joe) or you have minions in the form of political appointees (as in me), and those colleagues and those minions are not going along with those corporations, well, wow! That kind of goes against your sense of being, I get that. Frankly, Gray Davis didn't cause this crisis; Governor Pete Wilson did. It was Wilson who put all the wheels into motion. Gray Davis became governor just as the crisis was about to blow, but it is in crisis that you see the true character of people. It is in crisis that you have to choose between companies—or, I would argue in this case, the economy, or companies and consumers. I know who I choose! Reflexively I choose consumers, the people of California. But perhaps Davis did not see it the way I did.

Q: Do you have any contact with Davis now?

I do not and that is sad. I wish I did. I think that Davis was doing the best he could with the tools he had, and I do not think he was corrupt. I think other people were corrupt, but not him. I do not think he was paid off or anything like that. I think it is in his nature to try and make a deal.

Q: *What is he doing now?*

After the governorship, he went to Loeb and Loeb as a rainmaker. Rainmakers are well-known people who join law firms and bring in clients. It is an L.A. firm. I don't know if he is still there. I know he is giving a lot of speeches.[12]

Q: *What are you doing now?*

I have been consulting behind the scenes. My successor put out a fatwa against me, told everybody when I left the commission that if anyone used me to do anything PUC-related then they would lose whatever they had from the PUC. I wasn't going to do anything for a while anyway because there is an ethical ban for a year, which I presumed was longer. However, there are a lot of commissioners who go out and work for companies or become consultants for companies and lobby the PUC. So in retrospect my successor gave me the chance to not go out and do that [*laughing*]. I went to UC Berkeley and I was an executive fellow of the Institute of Governmental Studies, and then I was an adjunct at the Public Policy School. Since then I have been working with community and environmental groups to try and get clean energy in California. This year I decided to write a book on energy markets and why they don't work, because the California experiment got exported pretty much nationwide in slightly different forms. It is no longer the boiling frog of the economy; it is simmering. But in most other states electricity prices have gone up 40 percent to double for no reason other than there are extra profits being reaped by marketers in the system. I decided I needed to show that more systematically. I now live in San Francisco. I left Berkeley in 2013.

Q: *What did you learn from this experience?*

My dad always used this expression, I must have heard it a million times growing up: "Keep your nose clean." You know, we would be going out of the door and he would be saying, "You keep your nose clean." I never really understood what that meant until I was very softly solicited for bribes. It's very clear now, I tell you. I mean, my God! I now have lived what it means to keep your nose clean.

Q: When Davis offered you the judgeship, how was that done? Was it done subtly or was it, "Hey, look. I need to get you out of here." Or "I am going to bump you upstairs." I mean, how does someone do something like that?

Oh, it was [*laughing*]... subtlety is not his forte. It was very clear. "The governor wants to see you and needs to talk to you about your continuation on the PUC."

He sat me down and said, "We have had our differences. it just doesn't work for me for you to continue."

I said, "Well, Governor, I have a term appointment and I intend to see it out."

He said, "Well, I have been thinking about it and I think you would be a good judge so I am going to appoint you to be a judge."

I then said something to him that I knew would be a disqualifying event. I said, "Well, Governor, don't you want to know my position on things? For instance, I am anti–death penalty and I would not enforce the death penalty." I said this knowing that when I was on his campaign, he made a campaign promise to never appoint a judge who would not enforce the death penalty [*laughing*]. He threw his pen at me, he was so mad. He was sitting behind his desk and I was sitting across the desk from him in his private office.

He looked at me and said, "I didn't ask for your opinion. I am not asking your opinion on anything. I don't want to hear where you stand! You are taking this judgeship!"

I said, "Governor, I will have to respectfully decline."

Q: Wow. What did he say then?

Ah, I do not choose to share that.

Q: Okay, got it. What do you think caused you to have the courage to stand up to what was a lot of political pressure from people, people whom you had respected and worked with, or were still having to work with?

And who were Democrats. I was being told I would hurt the Democrats of California. My answer? It was the right thing to do. I had taken an oath at the Oval Office to uphold the constitution of the state of California, and those laws under the constitution were under attack. Our economy was under attack by wrongdoers. From my prior experience as a criminal defense lawyer, I could see they were criminal conspirators. It was just going to take some time and effort to prove that. If you know that and have seen what is happening enough to know there is no possible way in a working market that these prices and power outages could occur, how do you then turn a blind eye to that? How do you sit down and deal with those people? I saw no possible way to do that and fulfill my oath of office. I understand other people saw it differently. But I had taken a personal oath of office and I was tenfold fulfilling that. I worked to uncover, denounce, and untangle the wrongdoing.

Q: So it wasn't a choice for you; it was something you had to do, given that you had taken an oath and what that oath meant to you.

Yes, but also, politically, a person is only as good as their character and their word. How could I face the people who were my friends and family if I made a deal? And a secret deal it would have to be. Ugh. Why go into government if you are not going to try to do the right thing? I do not see the government as pigs at the trough. I don't believe you should eat the spoils, as the Trump administration clearly does. Even after what I have seen, government can be a force for good. It can also be a force for immense cynicism, and [things can] devolve into a banana republic. But I was never going to go down that path. Shoot, I could make more money in a law firm; why not just go back there? From that perspective, when you are in a public office there is public trust, and to me that was a real thing. Gray Davis was the fourth Democratic governor in the twentieth century. The other three were Culbert Olson, Jerry Brown, and Pat Brown, so I understood this was a special opportunity and responsibility to be able to be in government.[13] It would be a violation of the public trust to not do all I could to stop the wrongdoing.

Q: That was important to you?

Absolutely.

Q: You mentioned the Trump administration. What are your reactions, what are your thoughts as someone who does seem to take very seriously oaths of office and the idea that being a public servant is a noble profession? How does it make someone like you feel when you look at the Trump administration today [summer 2017]?

Well, it was a travesty. We knew what was going to happen, right? This man was going to become a tin-pot banana-republic dictator if he possibly could. He was going to unleash his people to be pigs at the trough. I don't think he made any bones about that. He said during the Forum, out of the other side of his mouth, "I am going to keep her out of my business, I am going to bring in all of these people from Goldman Sachs." From that perspective, it is not surprising what Trump is doing. But does it tear the fundamental contract we all made as citizens of this great United States of America? Yes, it does. We are at a fundamental point of taking a stand because it is so clear the Trump administration is destroying that public trust. So are we going to protest? Are we going to fight them? The Republicans essentially did a good thing with Nixon, and when you look at that situation versus this, Nixon is a schoolboy compared to Trump, which is something scary to say.

Q: *Are you happy about how the Democrats are responding to Trump?*

I guess we have to define the word Democrats, don't we? It is not one monolithic source.

Q: *Let me rephrase the question: who do you see who is standing up and exerting the kind of political leadership you like in terms of what is going on today?*

Both Minority Leader [Charles] Schumer and Minority Leader [Nancy] Pelosi are doing a good job of maneuvering the levers against Trump where they can. It is a complex procedural process, and they are working that process to get answers where they can, which is great. We need more of that; we need more leadership. And I have to say, where is President Obama? He has the moral authority so many people crave. Where is he at this moment of crisis? I understand he must be at least bummed or bitter, but it's time for him to come back into the fold in a very forceful way.

Q: *Would you think about going into politics yourself? I mean, going back into it, I suppose?*

I have worked for a bunch of corporate Democrats and I consciously chose Bill Clinton and Gray Davis to work for, knowing their records. I did it because I thought they could win. It had been a long time since we had won the presidency, and it had been a long time since the Democrats had captured the California governorship. I felt it was important to win those offices because of the kinds of political appointments that are made and how that shifts the government, and how that shifts the economy even for a corporation. However, I knew these two particular politicians were corporate, and I picked them because I thought they could win. And because Bill Clinton didn't give me a typing test [*laughing*]. Actually, the Bill Clinton campaign was one of the least sexist campaigns I have been on, surprisingly. That was great. Individually there was sexism, but the general campaign was not. I personally think Hilary Clinton had a lot to do with that. I also saw the limitations of what it means to govern as a corporate Democrat, and I disagreed with a lot of that governance.

So would I go back in? Only for the right person. I now realize even more than ever that character matters. My father did not vote for Bill Clinton. My father was a Democrat, and he was furious because I worked on the Clinton campaign. He said, "He lied. I can't vote for a president I know has lied because character does matter in a president. The man also cheated on his wife. I can't vote for that either." I really discounted that. In 1992 I was a true believer, but now I think my father was exactly right: keep your nose clean, and character matters in a leader. So I would go back into politics only if it was for the right leader.

Q: *You would never run yourself?*

I wouldn't say never, but I do not think I have a record that draws political contributions to me [*laughing*]. I am not an independently wealthy individual, and I know well the demands, the requirements, of a campaign.

9

"Nothing Else . . . Would Enable Me to Look in the Mirror the Next Day": Vikram Tej on Fighting Caste in India

Parenting isn't always about giving your children money. Parenting is about leading your life in a way you would want your kids to lead.
VIKRAM TEJ, August 2017[1]

I have worked for the Indian government, and that was the proudest time of my life. I served on the Foreign Council [Council on Foreign Relations], and my responsibilities included research, talking to foreign ministers, and drafting policy. But really, I enjoyed the job because I came from a household that greatly respected the country. I came from a family that always wanted to do better for everyone else, and at this point, India was going through a time where foreign relations would be extremely important for its growth. It was an acute time in Indian history, which demanded we have good relations in terms of trade and agriculture and exports with other countries.

Q: *But then?*

I was working under someone who believed in the caste system very strongly, and I had disagreed with him very, very much. But I wanted to make sure I completed my job properly. So I did as any other employee would do. I just focused on my job, and I delivered very well. I had meetings with top officials in other countries, and I was appreciated at high levels of government. I thought everything was good as far as I was concerned, but I routinely saw people in the office get discriminated against because of their family's caste. That was wrong. The official—I don't want to name him—continued to threaten to fire people. He called them derogatory names and told them they didn't deserve their position. So I decided to stand up to him. I nearly got fired, but there was nothing else I could do that would enable me to look in the mirror the next day.

Q: *So what did you do?*

My higher official was threatening and repeatedly bullying my subordinates. I tried to talk to him about it, but he repeatedly denied it and threatened to fire me if I took it up to higher counsel. I decided enough was enough. It was important to take this to higher officials because it not only violated my beliefs about how society should be, it also violated the Indian constitution, which I had pledged to protect. Indian democracy is beautiful, and it was designed so it works for all people, regardless of their caste, their color, or anything like that. It's designed to work for them. When I heard people in the government being threatened, I decided it was important to take it up to counsel and the courts. The courts decided against the discrimination that was going on, and they fired my superior. Everything was good. But I still have to say it was not easy for me to do that. I had two children I was addressable to, and their futures depended on their father working. In India, once you get fired from the government, no one else will hire you. But I decided this was the type of case that was so wrong that if I didn't say anything, I couldn't go to work. So I spoke out and tried my best, and thankfully the system worked.

Q: *So you were never scared you would get fired? Fearful of what would happen to your children?*

Parenting isn't always about giving your children money. Parenting is about leading your life in a way you would want your kids to lead [theirs]. If my children encountered the same problem when they were working, I would expect them to do as I did, and I would chide them if they didn't do anything. I wanted my children to grow up strong, to understand that fighting for good will always enable you to live a happier life. Even if you don't have all the material wealth in the world, if you're a good person you'll always be one of the happiest people in the world for following your moral compass. I've known people who are a lot more successful than I am, but they always wanted more. They never paid attention to what they had. They never knew the value of family. They could never appreciate anything, because all they could think of was climbing another mountain and expecting praise for doing so. Career goals are great, but if your career is not based on the need to serve a purpose, then you don't know the value of community.

Q: *What is the value of community?*

Community is everything. The worth of an action is measured in terms of contribution to community and not to self. We live in a time, especially in your country [2017 in the United States], in which people like to fight against each other for resources, promotions, college, and everything you can do to elevate yourself. Selfishness is the death of one's soul. I tried, when I was very young, to do the best I could to join the best college, to get the most money, to get the highest promotions, and I got all of those. I thought I was very lucky. But I realized all I was doing was subscribing myself to an eternal form of torture. People don't realize that selfishness never ends. There is absolutely no end to wanting, but there is a stability to peace and inner strength. So I chose to live my life peacefully and without the need to climb the steps society wants me to climb. While I was still thinking in that mindset, I found meaningful work, married a woman I loved, and had beautiful children who still teach me new things: your mother and aunt.[2]

Q: What does moral courage mean to you?

Moral courage to me means doing what you would do if there were no negative repercussions to yourself. Moral courage to me just means doing the types of actions that can help other people without regard to how it will benefit me. To be honest, I don't like to think or talk a lot about what I've done. Obviously, I'm talking to you because you are my granddaughter, but I don't think that one should talk about what they've done. It sets the wrong tone for goodness. People who are good don't usually announce they are good, because then they would be doing it to elevate themselves and not others. There's a fine distinction between being good for selfish reasons and being good for other people. It gives me no satisfaction to talk about what things I have done because I don't think I have done any great things. One should act in a manner they would expect someone else to act toward them. I wasn't of lower caste, so I never had to deal with that problem [discrimination], but if I was of a lower caste, I would expect my officials to stand up for the Indian constitution. So that's exactly what I did.

Q: Did you tell your children about the story?

Yes, I told the children about my story. But I told them very specifically that this is what I expect everyone to do, and this is what everyone should do. When they said, "Papa, you're a great man," I yelled at them and said you should never praise someone for doing what they should do. If I take out the trash, no one's going to say congratulations or throw me a party. It's what you do to keep your house clean. So why would anyone—why should anyone—praise me for defending a constitution I had pledged to defend? I was following what I said I would do. That's what every human being with a sense of self should do.

Q: *Did your perception of yourself change after the incident?*

No, it did not. I didn't want my perception of myself to change; otherwise, if I felt any sense of elevation by doing what I did, then I would immediately feel guilty for having done something to elevate my image of myself. I did it and I never thought about it, or at least about how I would look to the rest of the world. It didn't matter to me what other people would think of what I had done, so I didn't share it with anyone besides my own family.

Q: *People might have learned from you if you talked about it, though.*

People don't fundamentally change their mindset just because somebody does something. If I had told people about what I had done or what the Indian government had done because of my complaint, then people would think committing good acts gives you a right to boast. I didn't want people to think defending people of lower castes is a heroic act. It makes me seem like a hero and it makes them seem like poor victims, and they are not. They're just like anyone else, and they are human. So painting the story of moral elevation makes them subhuman, and I didn't want to do that.

Q: *Did you see the caste discrimination in your workplace as a microreflection of the rest of society?*

Absolutely. Your grandmother's family was very caste biased. But that's family, and in family, you can't necessarily yell at people with different views from yours, especially in an Indian family. But the Indian government specifically said in its constitution it would never discriminate, I found it wrong for the government itself then to discriminate against its workers based on caste. You can't run an entire country based on irony and hypocrisy. Intellectually, it just did not make sense to me. The caste system is so outdated; it doesn't make sense for society anymore. It doesn't matter what somebody's job is these days. We can't say some people deserve high positions and other people don't deserve them just because of the way they were born. I have seen idiots in high castes and I have seen geniuses in low castes. Numerically, when there's no difference between people's intelligence, there's no reason for us to pretend that there is.

Q: *What do you think about society now? Do you think anyone would do what you did today in India?*

I think so. We're in an increasingly progressive time in India. People don't look at caste anymore. Westernization has somewhat helped that, although it has ruined other things. So I'm happy the government instituted measures to help children in low castes attend better colleges and get better jobs. A lot of people complain about the quota system the government put in place, but if the government doesn't eliminate the advantage of the womb as much as it can, then we would be living in a kingdom and not a country.

Q: *Have you ever considered running for office and taking your ideals to a higher level?*

Absolutely not. Politics in India is nothing about politically helping people and all about gaining money. The civilian bureaucrats do most of the good work in the country. I don't want to run for any position. I have no desire to be known on a higher level. I want to live a life of service and subservience to good ideals. I want to die without having tainted my words with my own actions. If I can die not as a hypocrite, then I think I will have succeeded.

Q: *I see. So how do you see your role evolving in the future?*

I'm currently working for nonprofits helping children of lower castes attend school. I love doing the work I do and enjoy spending time with children. My role right now is to tend to those children I've committed myself to helping grow. You have loving parents who will take care of you and who are capable of taking care of you. You have a lot of comforts. A lot of children do not have those comforts. My job right now is to help children who need it and to enjoy myself with their beautiful souls.

PART III

A Richly Faceted Moral Courage

Ultimately, you had to decide whether you could sleep at night.
LORETTA LYNCH

10

When Nobody's Watching

> Judge a person not by what they do when people are watching but what they do when people aren't watching.
> SENATOR JOE[1]

> It all starts with values.
> HEATHER BOOTH

What does an empirical examination of moral courage reveal that we did not know before, both about the concept itself and about what causes it? These are the two questions that drove my empirical analyses of instances of moral courage as I began my work.

What Is Moral Courage?

The literature on moral courage assumes—as did I initially—that moral courage emanates from the actor's core values, and that the actor is aware of but disregards the risks and costs of acting. Indeed, the most commonly accepted scholarly characterization of moral courage defines moral courage as "acting on one's values in the face of potential or actual opposition and negative consequences."[2] My empirical examination confirmed this general conceptualization. "It all starts with values," as Heather Booth said (73). This view was illustrated by all our speakers. Consider Steve Zimmer, who explained his acts to protect undocumented students in the Los Angeles Unified School District (LAUSD) as driven by his desire to do the "right thing" and not worry about the consequences: "We're going to do what's right. We may pay a price for it, but that's fine" (45). While our narrative interviews confirmed the central, traditional conceptualization, fortunately, they also fleshed out further parts of moral courage as a concept, since the traditional definition remains somewhat vague.[3] So, what in particular did our empirical examination add to the existing knowledge concerning moral courage?

CHAPTER TEN

CORE VALUES AS THE DRIVER OF MORAL COURAGE

First, it was very clear that core values lie at the heart of moral courage. Moral courage is viewed as something that entails "doing the right thing." This somewhat general definition, however, was rejected by our interviewees. The people we interviewed were very clear that moral courage was not an abstraction to them. Moral courage was more than a general concept or an intellectual construct:

> The values we advocate don't stay as abstractions. It's not that we're for freedom, justice, and democracy. I'm for them, but you know that and a nickel won't get you much, since the nickel doesn't buy you much anymore. But I'm for a living wage. Is $15 an hour adequate? No. But it's better than starving. I'm for retiring student debt. I'm for long-term care for senior citizens. I'm for capping pollution. It's not everything we need, but it improves lives. We'll be able to breathe; we'll be able to walk safely in our communities. So I'm for improving lives as a standard. (Booth, 73)

Further, what constituted the "right thing" was something upon which our speakers were able to expand, and it always involved "issues that will improve people's lives" (Booth, 73).

While our speakers made clear that specific values might differ slightly, they noted several common values that were key and that featured prominently in most of the interviews analyzed. First among these was the valuing of a shared humanity to which all human beings were entitled. Working on "issues that ... improve people's lives" was a common theme (Booth, 73). Beyond this, virtually all our speakers demonstrated their belief that we should treat all people with decency, respect, and fairness because of their common humanity. Zimmer said he treated his workers as if they were family, as if it were *his* mother working in the school cafeteria or *his* father driving the school bus in the Los Angeles school district he headed. His decision to work so that no federal troops could come onto any Los Angeles public school property to search for undocumented students—the event that brought him to our attention—reflected not so much abstract principles of justice as it did the belief, deeply held, that America is a nation of immigrants and that we owe these new immigrants the same respect and support we would want for our own family members.

> Zimmer: I feel very, very strongly that we're a nation of immigrants ... The [undocumented] children and their families are trying to follow the same dreams my grandparents were trying to follow ... the dreams they had for my mom, my dad, my aunts and my uncles. I don't think the families I work with in Los Angeles deserve anything less than my family does.

Q: *So this is a pretty straightforward moral issue for you? It's not something predicated on the idea that the country will be better off if we have immigrants? It's more that this is just the right way to treat people?*

Zimmer: Yes. Look, I make decisions as a policy maker as if it were my own children in a classroom. If they were my son or my daughter who was affected by an instructional policy, an equity policy, or whatever it is. If my son or my daughter were at our most highly impacted school in this district and I were deciding about this school or our curriculum or whatever it is, I make the decision as if it were my own kid. When it relates to our employees, I also make decisions as if it were my mom or my dad working in the cafeteria or driving a school bus. So it is for issues around immigration: I treat these issues as if they were affecting my own family, for it *is* our family. It's not some community like, "those kids over there." This is our family. What would we want for our own family? What were the dreams my grandparents and my great-grandparents had? Well, it turns out it's the exact same dream a hundred years later. So I'm just doing what I would hope anyone would do if it were their own family, which is treating it as if the issue were affecting your own family. It may not be my mom or dad, but it's *someone's* mom or dad. When you dehumanize these issues, that's when you get policies like the executive orders of this president, President Trump. (44–45)

The concept of family is clearly evident in this statement. But other speakers—not just Zimmer—elaborated on this theme when they spoke of the need to move beyond thinking only of themselves and caring about a more all-encompassing community. Kay Monroe was especially eloquent in this regard as she spoke of quitting her job to care for her aging mother: "You have to forget about yourself and do what needs to be done. Look at life from a very large perspective . . . in a much broader way, from a view above the world, not from just a tiny little selfish 'me' town" (94). Vikram Tej also spoke of the value of community. Having had a successful career in the Indian government, he nonetheless puts this career into perspective, noting that professional success, while important, is not as important as family ties, community, and inner peace:

Career goals are great, but if your career is not based on the need to serve a purpose, then you don't know the value of community. . . . Community is everything. The worth of an action is measured in terms of contribution to the community, not the self. We live in a time, especially in your country [2017 in the United States], in which people like to fight against each other for resources, promotions, college, and everything you can do to elevate yourself. Selfishness is the death of one's soul. I tried, when I was very young, to do the best I could to join the best college, to get the most money, to get the highest promotions, and I got all of those. I thought I was very lucky. But I realized all I was doing was subscribing myself to an eternal form of torture. People don't realize that selfishness never ends. There is absolutely no end to wanting, but there is a stability to peace and inner strength. (130)

The specific values that drive this community, however, are also spelled out by our speakers. They contrast sharply with the values of the Nazis who threatened Nini (who as a young girl during the Holocaust rescued Jews), of the American South that discriminated against its African American citizens, or of any community that espouses an us-versus-them mentality and hate. Booth gives specificity to the values of the community she works for so diligently, in the Deep South of 1960s America and today as a social activist:

> What we need to do is to take the moral convictions we have and the interests we have, in addition to our moral values, and act on it. We believe we should have health care for everyone, that no one should be denied care when they are sick because of a previously existing condition or because they are not wealthy. That you should be able to walk on the streets and not be frightened you'll be picked up because of how you look. That you should have an education you can afford that helps gives you resources to make a decent life. (60)

Booth's community exhibits incredible faith in the common people and a strong commitment to equal laws, fairly enforced regardless of race, skin color, ethnicity, or economic position: "In 1965 I already had the experience of having been in the civil rights movement. Certainly that was transformative in my life and told me that if you have confidence in regular folks, they know what they need, and they can take action to change their lives. I also saw and learned the lesson that sometimes there are unjust laws that need to be confronted and need to be opposed, even if the risk is arrest" (61). Amal and Booth describe vastly different arenas of action—anti-Muslim bullying for Amal and advancing civil rights and the rights of women for Heather—yet each spoke of the desire for equal treatment of everyone based on this shared humanity. A college student at the time, who survived the 2004 tsunami in Thailand with literally only the bikini on her back, Amal describes how people helped each other regardless of nationality. She tells how fellow survivors shared in each other's joys and rejoiced when one of them—a total stranger until the tsunami—would find a living family member:

> Some of the most interesting emotional times requiring a lot of courage are really scary, something you wouldn't think you would know how to handle and get through until you are there and you *have* to get through it and survive it. What I learned from this experience was that all we had was each other,

and as much as it was important for each of us to survive on our own, we all really stuck together and functioned like a family. All the people with us, we saw humanity at its best. It didn't matter who you were, it didn't matter where you came from or what your background was. It was all of us being together, being safe, and making it out alive. (106)

Countries, time periods, and cultures apart, Vikram Tej in India and Nini in the Netherlands echoed the same desire for social justice that made up such a central part of identity for Booth as a 1960s American college girl and Janusz Reykowski as a middle-aged academic in Poland, risking his reputation and possibly imprisonment to try to bring together different political sides to protect a fledgling Polish democracy in the 1980s.[4] Booth shares that the most difficult night of her life was the evening she told her parents she was going to Mississippi and Alabama for the 1964 Freedom Summer. Her mother was crying so hard she could barely breathe out of fear Heather might be killed.[5] Booth nonetheless tells her parents it is the values *they* gave her that mean she *must* go:

Q: *Did your parents have any qualms about letting you go down there [to Mississippi]?*

Booth: On the one hand, I think they were very proud that I went. They realized I was living the values they had instilled in me. But they were desperately frightened. So frightened that the night before we were to leave for Mississippi, I had a rift with my folks over the strain it was causing. My mother, whom I love dearly, was crying so hard over the phone she basically couldn't breathe. She was so frightened. Even thinking about it almost makes me cry right now because I did love—I do love—my parents so dearly. To know how frightened they were is still painful for me. And yet, I did go down there. I was living the values they had instilled in me. I know they were glad about it. They did actively support the summer volunteers. My father, who was a physician, helped create the Medical Committee for Human Rights, MCHR, which was the medical arm of the civil rights movement. My mother went to lobby and support the summer project to get FBI assistance.

Q: *Let me go back a minute to the phone call. You're on the phone. You're talking to your parents. Your mother can hardly talk, you said, because she's so upset, she's crying so hard. What gave you the drive to go ahead and say to these two people you love dearly, "I'm sorry, I'm going do it anyway"?*

Booth: This was both—well, first, they raised me to try and do the right thing. Often, it's not that people want to do the wrong thing; it's that they feel confusion about "what can I do?" I often tell people that when I'm confused—and I'm often confused—I try to center myself with two thoughts. One, what is the right thing to do? Sometimes it's hard to know because it's just things competing for what's right. The second thing is to center yourself in love. And while I have deep love for my parents, I also knew the stories of what was happening to people in Mississippi. They were living with a level of terror, threat, and inequality worse than second-class status. They had absolutely no chance of breaking out. But if the northern students were there to support them, that could provide visibility, provide greater attention so people could hear their stories. So, with great sadness and [despite] the pain it caused my folks, I decided I would go. (62–63)

All of these quotes underscore the extent to which the core values driving moral courage center on caring for others, and for social justice, equal application of the law, and fairness. They provide specificity about the most widely held conceptualization of moral courage: "I would restrict the meaning of moral courage to people acting on genuinely moral values which serve moral ends."[6] It is clear that social justice and the law are critical core values, as is treating everyone with "decency, dignity, and respect": "I was born into an incredibly loving family that values social justice. I have had incredible luck and fortune to be raised believing we should not only try to live our values, but we should try to make this a world consistent with the values of treating everyone with decency, dignity, and respect" (54).

Zimmer linked the core value of equality and fairness directly to the Trump election and to his efforts to combat the division and hate that can emerge as a result of a lack of social justice, fairness, and economic equality:

> Q: Let me just ask you one last question. . . . How do you explain to yourself all the people who voted for Trump for these kinds of reasons? People who said they wanted to protect the country from foreigners, that they didn't like immigrants. How do you explain all the anti-immigrant feeling that is in the country?
>
> Zimmer: How do I explain it?
>
> Q: Yes. How do you explain it to yourself, and to the kids you teach? How do you change it?
>
> Zimmer: Hate is present. It's very hard to explain hate to people. I'm not sure it's important we understand hate, other than to know that it exists. To try and dissect what causes it, that's great work for sociologists, but it's not how I spend my time. I just think it is important to understand that working folks in this country struggle a lot. That's the reason Donald Trump and Bernie Sanders culminated at the same time. They both, in their own way, appealed to a core discontent in the fabric of our democracy, which is economic inequity, a system that benefits and is stacked precariously in favor of others. These core

> inequities and these core separations that infect our systems make it so there is a deep strain of discontent that throughout history we find repeatedly turns us upon the "other." The job we have is not necessarily to understand the hate or try to explain it, but rather to be working constantly to eradicate inequity and reduce the savage gaps between those who have and those who do not have in our economic system. . . . A lot of the rejection of the establishment that was part of the Trump vote was not actually this radically xenophobic, radically deregulatory kind of madness that's going on right now; it was a statement against the status quo. Some people within our electorate believe there is a ruling elite. Donald Trump is not part of that ruling elite; he's part of a different type of elite. But he was able to capture that antiestablishment feeling. I don't think every single person who voted for Donald Trump hates immigrants. I think it means that . . . look, when you're sick, you go to the doctor. If the sickness is serious, you want the doctor to give you medicine. Most of us are not deeply concerned with a multifaceted understanding of what caused us to be sick. We just want to be better. So when you feel like the economy doesn't work for you and you're told by a charismatic leader that all we have to do is build a wall and keep other people out and you're going to be okay, well, I don't blame people who want to feel better. It's our responsibility to have the courage to come up with real solutions for economic inequity and create an economy that truly works for the working class. (46–47)

Tej also helps move us beyond the traditional and accurate, if vague, understanding of moral courage. Like Zimmer, Tej suggests that a core value of moral courage is caring for others: "Moral courage to me just means doing the types of actions that can help other people without regard to how it will benefit me" (130).

Our interviews thus provide an answer to a question raised by most scholarly analysts: what are the moral values driving and defining moral courage? Concern for others is one critical value. This knowledge can help us distinguish between an act of moral courage and an act of ideological fanaticism. Concern for others can distinguish the terrorists who bombed the World Trade Center, thinking this would strike an important blow for their cause from someone who eschews such political acts in favor of protecting human life. I should not claim too much or oversimplify; differentiating my act of moral courage from your act of fanaticism or betrayal remains a tricky act of discernment. (What about an antiabortion demonstrator who kills someone to prevent future abortions? Is this morally courageous, especially if killing one person—the doctor performing abortions—saves other lives—all the unborn children?) The double-edged aspect of moral courage, the extent to which each act of moral courage also constitutes an act of betrayal, will be discussed in a later volume. But for now, as we think about moral courage as a concept, we need to ask: do I have to agree with someone's morals to find them morally courageous?[7] While each of our speakers touched upon this in some way, one important distinction was articulated most concisely by Reykowski, a distinguished social psychologist dealing with ethical concerns, who summed up his thoughts on moral courage at the end of several days of interviews:[8]

> Q: *So what would you say moral courage is as a concept? Is it an idea that is closely related to acting out of your values, or do the values themselves have to be values that are good in the sense that they further human life? Human flourishing?*
>
> Reykowski: Values are socially constructed within a particular society, and the well-being of this society may become the ultimate value. Therefore, the well-being of other people does not count. America First, or Germany or Poland First. What we think of as good values for one society can be bad values for others. We have to bear in mind that the values of one group can become anti-values for other groups. We face here not only problems of good versus bad values, but also the problems of universality versus locality of values. What is important about values is that they further human life, and the concept of human cannot be limited to an in-group.
>
> Q: *You're saying that courage can be driven by identity, by the feeling that there is nothing else you can do except that particular act, and that you feel compelled to act in a certain way because of who you are. But that to make courage moral courage, the values that make up the identity, and thus the values that drive the act, have to reflect values that are in accord with, in keeping with, or even the furthering of human well-being and human life?*
>
> Reykowski: Yes, I agree.[9]

This insight proves extremely useful in helping distinguish between courage and moral courage.

Finally, the eternal need for moral courage was also identified by our speakers:

> Under the current [2018] policies of President Trump, families will be separated. Voting and civil rights will be jeopardized. People will suffer. People may die because of these policies: the destruction of safeguards, guidelines for food, water, and health, on the environment, voting rights, and women's rights. It's an undermining of so many of the protections and caring, welcoming communities that we've created over the last fifty years. And it's not just at the federal level in Washington. In fact, over the last ten years there has been destruction of the same kinds of laws at the state and local levels. There has been a rise of forces in many states that are driven more by fear of each other rather than by caring and community. These policies are driven sometimes by

hate, race, and antidemocratic tendencies, limiting voting rights rather than expanding small-d democracy. So I think it's also a time of incredible peril. (Booth, 56)

Incredibly, the morally courageous are not daunted by the fact that the need for moral courage seems to remain constant. Consider Booth again: "Even in the times of greatest crisis, when you think everything seems hopeless and you just can't make a difference, it's often [then] when there is the greatest progress" (58).

IDENTITY AND VIRTUE ETHICS

Our conversations also fleshed out other areas of interest concerning moral courage. First, we can answer one series of questions posed in chapter 1 and left unanswered in prior analyses of moral courage. Is moral courage, in fact, best explained by an identity-based ethical approach, as virtue ethics would suggest? Can we think profitably about moral courage without putting ourselves into a virtue-ethics framework? Are character and identity the same—or simply different terms for the same phenomenon, utilized by different academic disciplines? (*Character* is the term preferred by philosophers, while psychologists speak more of *identity*.)

Our interviews clearly suggest that from a philosophical perspective, a discussion of moral courage is best embedded in a virtue approach to ethics. People spoke of knowing instinctively what to do; they seldom referred to rules. Even when they did refer to rule-like behavior, the conversation would be along the lines of "treating others as if they were you" and not in reference to following the Golden Rule. The heavy emphasis on being able to "look yourself in the mirror" (an idea expressed by several speakers) indicated the central place of character that dominates the virtue-ethics approach.

Empirically, we could find little difference between character and identity in the thought process described by our morally courageous exemplars. Regardless of whether we use the term *character* (as philosophers tend to do) or *identity* (as do psychologists), the importance of this concept was critical. Identity lies at the heart of the core values driving moral courage. Acting based on one's character, and protecting that character, was a central concern, reflected in the fact that many of our speakers alluded to the ability to live with oneself later or, as Tej said, the need to take an action because there was "nothing else I could do that would enable me to look in the mirror the next day" (128). So character is key. This primacy of identity helps explains how morally courageous acts can be spontaneous without being impulsive. As emphasized by virtue ethics, thinking about who one is and what kind of person one wants to be means that acts often must then follow naturally, flowing from the basic sense of self. Hence, if I want to be a kind person, certain cruel acts simply cannot exist on my cognitive menu. Doing something cruel is unthinkable. This was demonstrated most dramatically by Nini's suggestion that she could not walk away from Jews who needed help, even knowing that helping Jews would risk her life and the lives of her family as well. Acts can evolve instinctively, out of one's sense of who one is. But these acts are not impulsive, because they emanate from deep within a person's character.

Contra virtue ethics, however, we did not find that the people we interviewed fell into the somewhat rigid categories that virtue ethics seems to advocate. Our speakers' stories suggest human beings are more complicated, with person A having a proclivity toward moral courage that can be, but *need not always be*, called forth, depending on the situation. The framing of the situation seemed critical. For example, Kay notes that part of her kindness toward her mother was repayment for her mother's caring and generous treatment of her as a child: "I frequently went back in my memory to good experiences and things Mom had done for me when I was a child. Then I wanted to pay her back, I guess you would say, because she spoiled all of us. So she got her karma back, you know? Perhaps, if a person is dealing with a situation like that and the parent wasn't so good to them when they were young—I can't imagine what that would be like. I'm going to guess that the parent doesn't get so much back" (79). Reykowski also noted the importance of framing for evoking certain types of behavior. He referred to the impact of the environment—in his case, shifts in the rigidity of Poland's then communist political system—but suggests the impact was not so much on his acts themselves but rather on his perception of the actual danger and risk to him for pursuing morally courageous acts.

But what about the interesting question of whether person B might normally *not* demonstrate moral courage, yet might do so in some unusual circumstance? How critical is framing then? This is the type of situation illustrated in fiction by the character Sydney Carton in Charles Dickens's *A Tale of Two Cities*. We encounter a similar character in both fiction and reality in the form of Oskar Schindler, of *Schindler's List*.[10] Neither man was a model human being for most of his life, yet each nonetheless performed extraordinary acts of moral courage *at certain points in time*. Why? What triggered their morally exemplary behavior? We find little dispositive evidence to answer this question. So how do we keep in mind this possible variability and allow for a more complex human personality as we draw on general theories of ethics? This question cannot be answered by our data. I encourage further empirical studies to focus on this important question, and I will explore it in later volumes.

LITTLE AGONISTIC CHOICE

Much clearer is the fact that the need to maintain a certain type of character trumped choice. No one at all spoke of any kind of agonistic choice. While I had found this lack of agonistic choice in other work that touches on moral courage,[11] its absence was again surprising, given the extent of the potential sacrifice required by one's act of moral courage. Kay touched on this at the very end of her interview, summing up why she had dedicated thirteen years of her life to caring for her mother even though it cost her financially and in terms of health and friendships:

> Once I made the decision to care for my mother, I said, "I'm just gonna step up to this." You have only two choices: you do it or you don't do it. There aren't any other choices. You can't do something like that halfway. When you have a conflict in your life, when you have something that's difficult, you either step up or you don't. There's nothing else. Once you decide you're going to do it, you have to follow through. I never found myself saying, "Oh no, you shouldn't do this. This is too hard." I said, "I am going to do this. I am going to do this to the end!" And I did. (79–95)

Half a world away, and in a vastly different context, Nini expressed the same view when explaining, almost matter-of-factly, why she rescued Jews during the Holocaust: "A human being who is lying on the floor and is bleeding, you go and do something."[12] The simplicity and directness of this statement is striking. It captures the spontaneous but not impulsive aspect of moral courage—a courage that emanates directly from one's sense of self and makes any other option impossible. It is not that Nini ignored the costs and risks of her morally courageous acts; such obliviousness would have been foolhardy and dangerous for anyone in Nazi-occupied Europe. It was that Nini could not even contemplate turning her back on "a human being who is lying on the floor . . . bleeding" and remain the person she was.

RECOGNIZING BUT DISREGARDING
THE RISKS AND CONSEQUENCES OF ACTING

One important question in the literature asks how much risk must be involved for an act to be deemed courageous. To paraphrase Chemerinsky, if I criticize the president of my university for an action he took, and I am a tenured professor, am I doing anything courageous? Must there be a risk of physical harm for an act to be morally courageous, or is mere censure and criticism of people whose opinion I value enough to place my action in the morally courageous category? Further, what *type* of risk must be involved for an act to be *morally* courageous and not just *physically* courageous? This relates closely to the previous concern: how big must the risk of potential harm to me be to make my act one of courage?

In general, moral courage is held to differ from physical courage in that moral courage "involves facing other persons while upholding some morally motivated cause and enduring resistance or retaliation that may occur in response to one's actions."[13] So actions can be both morally and physically courageous, but moral courage usually involves other actors, not simply courage in the face of physical danger.[14]

It seemed clear in all of our interviews that the consequences of the act are not deemed relevant. Remarkably, the costs *are* noted, yes . The morally courageous are not unaware of the consequences of their actions. But these consequences do not enter into any calculus of action. They do not affect the decision to act or not to act. Booth, Zimmer, and Tej—among others—stated explicitly that they noted the costs but disregarded them. Others tended to minimize the courageous aspect of what they had done, as if it were nothing, something everyone would do if they had the opportunity, characterizing their acts as no big deal, as did Chemerinsky, Nini, Zimmer, and Reykowski. Chemerinsky tells the students his acts were not morally courageous, citing the fact that he was protected by his status as a tenured professor, even though he was working diligently, as dean of a new law school, to get jobs, contributions, and clerkships for his law students. He knew he risked offending establishment lawyers and wealthy donors by suing the sitting president: "I just want to insert one thing, and you can put it wherever it fits. You are very kind in calling these acts of moral courage. I'm a tenured law professor. I've been a tenured law professor since the spring of 1987. That means it would be very difficult to fire me. You can fire me as a dean; that's a whole different question. There's no tenure there. But I have a guaranteed job and a guaranteed salary. It's not moral courage to stand up for these things" (52). Similarly, Zimmer says the policy makers were not the ones deserving praise: "To be very clear, the heroes and heroines in this story are not myself or Jerry Brown or Eric Garcetti, or anybody else. The heroes and heroines are people whose names we'll never know, who have taken an extraordinary personal risk to bring their families here to escape oppression, to stand up to racism and xenophobia" (45).

AGENCY

Agency is frequently assumed to be a critical contributor to moral courage.[15] It makes sense that people who rank high on agency—people who believe they matter and can affect change in the world—will be more likely to engage in morally courageous activities than will someone who is low on agency, a passive person who does not believe he or she possesses the skills or power to change the world. As such, this traditional view of agency usually refers to the actor's sense of agency, of how important and strong they judge themselves to be. I found mixed evidence here. Clearly, some speakers—Chemerinsky, Booth, and Lynch—were powerhouses, dynamos with great abilities, people who know they are affecting things in the world. Yet others—Kay, Choo Tee Lim—describe themselves in quite different terms. Choo Tee is a Chinese woman sold into slavery as a child who then refused to sell any of her nine children after her husband died and left her destitute. She describes herself as a rather inconsequential person who merely obeyed the demands of duty to her family. Similarly, Kay begins her interview by describing herself as someone who feels somewhat inconsequential at this stage in her life.

> I'm not at a very good stage of my life right now.[16] I'm not as actively involved in things as I think I should be and as I used to be. I find myself obsessing about things from the past and having a lot of regrets. It's not good to do that. Not good at all. It's also pointless. It doesn't get you anywhere. But I think that happens to people whose lives have not turned out as they had hoped, and I would certainly put myself in that unappealing category. (76)

In terms of agency, then, our findings are mixed. Some of the morally courageous appear to have a high level of agency, while others do not.

What are we to make of this mixed finding? On the one hand, we want to empower people, assuming people who see themselves as strong will be happier and more comfortable trying to improve things in their lives. Yet, the very humanness of these speakers, the fact that they are not all wonder women or supermen, is ironically perhaps also a positive finding, at least insofar as it provides inspiration and perhaps hope for the rest of us. As Amal concludes, explaining why she would like to use her grandmother's name for the interview instead of her own: "Can we have my name as Amal? It's my grandmother's name. It means 'hope,' and it's what I wish my story to offer those who have been through hard times like mine" (chap. 7, n. 1).

ACCORDING ONE'S OPPONENTS AGENCY

Interestingly, the data lend insight into another important aspect of moral courage, one raised by Pianalto when he asks how we treat the person on the other side of the moral-courage equation.[17] One thing I investigated was the way in which the speakers acted toward their "opponents." What was striking was the extent to which the speakers did *not* belittle, malign, or disparage those they opposed. They rarely referred to those with whom they disagreed as objects or obstacles to overcome. All the people interviewed here fully recognized the humanity in their opponents. Doing so meant their moral courage could be conceptualized as asserting themselves as moral agents, taking responsibility for their actions, but treating others as moral subjects also. This meant justifying their actions to their adversaries—as Zimmer did, since he recognized the humanity and agency of those he was challenging. One's opponents were seldom denigrated, despised, or dismissed. There was little vilifying, and in fact, they were more interested in engaging in the kind of dialogue that might foster greater understanding and empathy on the part of those one confronts. As Zimmer said:

> Late 2016 is when I wrote this last policy [to protect undocumented students from ICE], but this was not new. I had been working on this issue for quite some time. . . . It was February 2016 when we passed what's basically a sanctuary schools bill; immediately after the [2016 presidential] election, we reiterated that policy. We just made very proactive direct statements to our kids and their families that all schools in Los Angeles would be safe. We would make absolutely sure we would not cooperate with ICE and would use our schools as resources.
>
> Q: *Was everyone on the board in agreement with this? I would imagine this was not a totally uncontroversial policy.*
>
> Zimmer: We have a pretty progressive board as it relates to immigrant rights. But yes, I definitely had to bring some people along. There's always a lot of outrage whenever you do something like that. That's part of it. (43–44)

Zimmer's respectful treatment of his opponents was reflected in the interviews with others as well. As a social activist, Booth describes herself as dedicated to convincing people through dialogue and direct contact. Reykowski worked hard to develop the Round Table Talks between the Polish communist government and the banned trade union Solidarność (Solidarity) and other opposition groups. Held from February to April in 1989 in Warsaw, the Round Table Talks emphasized mutual dialogue and are credited with aiding in the peaceful transition to Polish democracy. Although his actions cost him friends on both sides of a tense divide, Reykowski said it was worth it to ensure that no child was killed in what could have become a bloody conflict. Both Lynch and former California State Senator Joe ran afoul of the political establishment, but each told us they retain friendships with former colleagues with whom they disagreed. Perhaps most striking of all is Ceballos's discussion of the respect prosecutors must feel for those they prosecute, people who are literally courtroom opponents: "Prosecutors need to be reminded that we are different from other lawyers. Our obligation is not to any particular client, but rather to the entire criminal justice system. It's not just to the victims and witnesses, not just law enforcement, not just the defense attorneys and judges; rather, our obligation extends even to the defendants we prosecute. We need to ensure the defendants are being treated fairly. We represent the people, and while defendants are not our clients in the technical legal sense, they are still part of the people we do represent."

What Drives Moral Courage?

Let us now ask: what drives moral courage? We found many themes associated with moral courage among the people interviewed: empathy and a sense of being connected to all people; a sense that we all share a common humanity; commitment to an objective sense of fairness or justice; certain cultural influences or values provided by critical others, often family members; a sense of gratitude and wanting to give back to society; personal values that include modesty—little desire for glory or for the limelight; a desire to be able to look loved ones in the eyes without shame for not having "done the right thing"; and a feeling that one has to stand up and be counted and not be driven by one's fears. All of these factors figured into our respondents' acts of moral courage. We can divide these critical influences into (1) the personal characteristics of the people who demonstrated moral courage and (2) the forces that produced the values of the morally courageous. This distinction allows for the fact that there are people who possess the characteristics correlating with moral courage to such a degree that we can reasonably call them morally courageous. This distinction also recognizes, however, that many other people exist who may possess these same characteristics but to a lesser degree. This means we need to also focus on the forces that draw forth these morally courageous behaviors, as opposed to other traits.

In addition to the above-noted personal characteristics, moral courage also has been associated by prior analysts with the capacity or inclination to take decisions quickly and with being an action-oriented as opposed to a reflective or feeling person.[18] We found a more complicated decision-making process, with decisions emanating spontaneously out of one's sense of self—as discussed above—and no evidence whatsoever to support the idea that being an action-oriented rather than a reflective person relates to moral courage.

PERSONAL CHARACTERISTICS

Humility. Perhaps what strikes us first is the humility of the morally courageous. None of these people felt they had done anything remarkable. Choo Tee Lim, a Chinese mother sold into slavery as a child and later, after an arranged marriage, left a penniless widow with nine children to support, tells of refusing to give up any of her children, despite widespread pressure to do so. Her simple statement captures what all our speakers voiced, in one form or another: the complex drives behind moral courage and extreme humility about their actions.

> Q: Do you think this decision was morally courageous?
>
> Lim: No, of course not. This was my decision for my family. I have a duty to my family, and that was my responsibility.

As with Lim, any expression of praise for their actions was brushed away by those we interviewed, saying their acts were simply their duty, responsibility, nothing unusual, and not even remarkable. Zimmer told us, "I'm used to people yelling at me. I just try to do what I think is morally and ethically correct. I don't consider it courageous at all actually" (44). I have noted that Chemerinsky was the first dean of UCI's School of Law when he was interviewed by two of our mutual students. He interrupted the interview after the students asked about a few of his acts of moral courage. One of those acts involved his ongoing suit against Donald Trump for violation of the emoluments clause of the Constitution. Another entailed heading an independent investigation of a police scandal in Los Angeles that resulted in the dismissal, suspension, resignation, or retirement of many policemen and the election of a new mayor.[19] Despite the obvious potential significant fallout of these acts, Chemerinsky insisted that none of his acts was morally courageous: "I have a guaranteed job and a guaranteed salary. It's not moral courage to stand up for these things. Real acts of moral courage [come from] people who put their jobs or their liberty on the line. Being a tenured law professor provides wonderful security in life to be able to do these kinds of things. . . . So I'm not sure I agree that any of these things are acts of moral courage, in the scheme of moral courage. They *are* standing up for things I believe in, though" (52). I had to remind the students that Chemerinsky also was the first dean of a brand-new law school, which he was working very hard to make successful, and that most other deans would have felt they had to be careful and not offend potential donors or employers for UCI law school graduates.[20] So Chemerinsky, in my view anyway, was downplaying the potential costs of his acts.

This humility often was reflected in people's embarrassment at speaking about what they had done:

> To be honest, I don't like to think or talk a lot about what I've done. Obviously, I'm talking to you because you are my granddaughter, but I don't think that one should talk about what they've done. It sets the wrong tone for goodness. People who are good don't usually announce that they are good, because then they would be doing it to elevate themselves and not others. There's a fine distinction between being good for selfish reasons and being good for other people. It gives me no satisfaction to talk about things I have done because I don't think I have done any great things. One should act in a manner they would expect someone else to act toward them. (Tej, 130)

Perhaps the most striking remark, however, came from a teenage girl who risked her life to save Jews during World War II, an act that could have resulted in her death and that of her sister had she been caught. Nini did acknowledge she had "been fairly gutsy, always. That's true." But she hastened to add others had more guts. She cited her sister's bravery in telling off a general and her brother's giving his ID card to a Jewish friend who then used it to escape to Switzerland. This act of generosity meant her brother lacked identification and was forced to live underground for the rest of World War II. Said Nini: "There were people who had done so much more. What I did, that was just very little. . . . I thought that [what I did] was such a normal thing to do that I don't feel I want to be put on a pedestal. It's not that kind of thing. That's the way I feel." Nini actually refused the Yad Vashem medal, saying she should have done more and noting that the first people she tried to save were eventually caught by the Nazis, not when hidden by Nini but after they had gone elsewhere.[21] This extreme humility and modesty characterized all the people we interviewed.

Interestingly, a few people's refusals to accept praise seemed related to the image that might be painted of the people they had helped. Tej explains why he did not talk about his efforts to help lower-caste Indians, telling his granddaughter: "If I had told people about what I had done or what the Indian government had done because of my complaint, then people would think committing good acts gives you a right to boast. I didn't want people to think defending people of lower castes is a heroic act. It makes me seem like a hero and it makes them seem like poor victims, and they are not. They're just like anyone else, and they are human. So painting the story of moral elevation makes them subhuman, and I didn't want to do that" (131).

Restraint: moral courage or complicity? Amal, who was about Nini's age when she confronted Muslim bullying, offered another insight into moral courage, demonstrating the courage involved in simply doing nothing, of putting up with ill-treatment and not striking back. Restraint is not often discussed as part of moral courage, but surely refusing to retaliate or even the score in the face of bigotry, anger, and prejudice must take some strength and resolve, if not actual courage. Noted Amal: "We could have made a huge deal out of it [bullying, anti-Muslim treatment].... We could have been more vocal. But at the end of the day, that was where I went to school. Those were the people I was going to be around. Had I made it even more uncomfortable by creating more tension, it would have been worse. So we decided to just stay humble and stay a little quiet and peaceful about it, and it turned out for the best" (101). Being quiet is an interesting phenomenon, one whose effect may well depend on a critical distinction in intention. We can think of being quiet as a form of forbearance, refusing to engage in ugly or retaliatory behavior; or we can view not saying anything as an act of cowardice, in which case silence can be a form of complicity in wrongdoing. A Cambodian activist, Sophal Ear, captured this distinction this way: "Certain things don't always jive with the truth, with reality. So when you don't say anything about it, you're kind of taking part."[22] This strong sense that (1) failing to speak out is selling out yourself and that (2) shameful acts can damage your self-esteem ran like a leitmotif throughout the narratives of all our speakers. Consider Sophal Ear again, noting what we find and discuss later: the extent to which moral courage is more than just something done to help others, as important as that is—it is also *done to* the actor, to free the actor to be him or herself. Says Ear: "If I decided to not speak out anymore in order to be back on good terms with the authorities, then I'd be selling out and saying, 'Okay. I'll censor myself to the point where I no longer speak truth to power,' which is a responsibility we all have. I think the worst kind of prison is the prison of the mind where you have a metaphorical gun to your head and you're not able to think. Thoughts make you free. If you're too afraid to say what's right and wrong, or even think it, then you're too far gone."

Empathy and a sense of connectedness. The sense the morally courageous people we interviewed had of being rooted in one's own self was striking. Continuity of self played an important part of this desire to avoid shameful behavior. It was captured by Lim in a conversation with her great-granddaughter in which she explained why she refused to sell any of her nine children in China after her husband died : "You can never forget where you are from, even if it is dangerous." This sense of a self being rooted in one's own past acts is related to the fact that for our speakers, the sense of self was influenced by family and by a sense of empathy for others. Empathy meant more than simply the ability to understand how others might feel or view a situation. (Indeed, were empathy only this, the knowledge could be used to manipulate or exploit others.) Empathy also included a component of concern and care for others, a feeling of being connected to others through a shared humanity. We find a striking illustration of this in Zimmer's frequent references to the current immigrant community as being just like his grandparents and his insistence that every decision he makes about employees in the public schools—from students to staff—is made as if they were members of his own family. Empathy in this sense—as a sympathy-inducing identification with others—played a critical factor for all our speakers. Perhaps nowhere was this more remarkable than in the interview with Lim. As she told her granddaughter:

> Money was tight. Everyone around me was telling me to give up a kid. Because how could a single mom raise nine children by herself? People kept telling me I should give at least one up so I can feed the other eight. That's how hard it was.
>
> Q: *But you didn't. Why didn't you listen to the other people around you?*
>
> Lim: Because how could I? I knew what it was like to be sold. My children are my responsibility. I did not want my child to feel like they are not wanted.

Lim's ability to put herself in the mind of her child and want to protect that child from suffering by taking the hit herself was extraordinary, even though this is what parents frequently—and perhaps always should—do. She spoke of her distress at having to move to a different country, leaving Burma, where she was head of the household and knew everyone. She knew moving to the United States would be very lonely. But she did it anyway because she knew America held more opportunities for her children. Lim also spoke of riding the bus lines prior to her children's arrival, not knowing any English herself but memorizing landmarks near critical stops. She did this not because she herself needed to use the bus but because she believed her knowledge would enable her to take her children on the bus and show them the ropes, easing them into the transition she knew so well could be stressful:

> I didn't know any English, how to speak, read, or write it. I just memorized different things, like the houses near each stop.
>
> Q: *Why did you learn [this]?*
>
> Lim: I wanted to be prepared for when your aunts and uncles came to America. I wanted to make sure I could help them. I had to learn by mistake. If I got on the wrong one, I would have to find my way back. I didn't want my children to have to learn by mistake like me. So when they got here, I took them out on the bus lines and taught them.

If this behavior is perhaps touching but understandable in a good mother, who does not want her own child to suffer as she did, the empathy nonetheless runs deeper. Lim wanted to spare her children the feeling that "they are not wanted," as she herself once felt; she did not want them to undergo the difficulty of transitioning to a new society. Among our speakers, this empathic concern for others was not limited to their close relatives. We found it as well in Tej, who demonstrated that his empathy extended beyond his caste. Notably, he risked his job not because he himself was being discriminated against, but because lower-caste workers were. Empathy and its ability to link people with others figured high in the narratives of all the morally courageous. They consistently spoke of other people as if they could understand and feel the plight of others, repeatedly using the words "family" or "humanity" to describe the people for whom they demonstrated moral courage:

> I treat these issues [of immigration] as if they were affecting my own family, for it *is* our family. It's not some community like, "those kids over there." This is our family. What would we want for our own family? What were the dreams my grandparents and my great-grandparents had? Well, it turns out that it's the exact same dream a hundred years later. So I'm just doing what I would hope anyone would do if it were their own family, which is treating it as if the issue were affecting your own family. It may not be my mom or dad but it's *someone's* mom or dad. (Zimmer, 44–45)

Zimmer went on to note he felt his own experience with prejudice, bigotry, and hatred had given him the ability to know what it felt like. Instead of being bitter or trying to win acceptance, Zimmer used past hurts from anti-Semitism to bolster his empathic involvement and sympathy for others:

> Look, I understand white privilege. I understand the opportunities I've had because of that. I also dealt with anti-Semitism in my own life. . . . I actually think that I was lucky, in some odd way. I'm very grateful that I was exposed to hate. I feel like being exposed to hate as a child allowed me to both understand what that means on a personal level and to give me the opportunity to understand what my privilege means. I know what it means to not have to face systemic or institutional racism. When I have the opportunity to make decisions where I can use the undeserved privilege I have to take down instruments of institutional or systemic racism or to stand with a community that is facing oppression, a vulnerable group that is facing hate, well, that's a high honor. (46)

Halfway around the world, we find similar statements from people who showed moral courage in quite different circumstances. Nini, a Chicago-based psychoanalyst, described her work as a young woman saving Jews during the Nazi occupation of the Netherlands in World War II. Why did she do it? Empathy. She said, "There was emotion involved, certainly. I certainly wanted to thwart the Germans but I wanted to . . . I felt, 'God, if I were Jewish, this would be awful.' So . . . Yes, it was emotional. It was not a sense of duty so much, I don't think." Expanding on this, she added: "I didn't even think much about it [risking my life to help Jews]. . . . I was always for the underdog. And so if people came for help, that was what I felt." Nini continued, relating that her sister was a nurse and helped the wounded: Jews or others, it did not matter. Downplaying her own bravery, Nini dismissed it as "nothing uncommon in our family to do things like that."

Similarly, Tej explained his acts on behalf of lower-caste employees he felt were being discriminated against at the company where he worked in India: "I decided enough was enough. It was important to take this to higher officials because it not only violated my beliefs about how society should be, it also violated the Indian constitution, which I had pledged to protect. Indian democracy is beautiful, and it was designed so it works for all people, regardless of their caste, their color, or anything like that. It's designed to work for them" (129). When asked to elaborate on this idea, Tej revealed what drove his acts, and in doing so captured what lies at the core of empathy: "I didn't want people to think defending people of lower castes is a heroic act. It makes me seem like a hero and it makes them seem like poor victims, and they are not. They're just like anyone else, and they are human" (131).

The ability to recognize and appreciate the humanity in another, to find common ties and realize and feel how the other person was feeling and what it must be like to be them—the very essence of empathy—formed a central core of all our interviews. Perhaps Amal—a college student when a tsunami hit—captured this theme expressively, describing how "we just tried to support each other" (104): "What I learned from this experience was that all we had was each other, and as much as it was important for each of us to survive on our own, we all really stuck together and functioned like a family. All the people with us, we saw humanity at its best. It didn't matter who you were, it didn't matter where you came from or what your background was. It was all of us being together, being safe, and making it out alive" (106).

Gratitude and wanting to give back to society. Beyond being humble and empathetic, what kind of person risks censure, ridicule, or other losses in order to stand up for what they believe is right? Are they religious? Are they of any particular gender or belonging to any particular ethnic or professional group? Do genetic traits or socialization lead to moral courage? What other characteristics mark these people in terms of personality or character?

We found little evidence to suggest the religious were more inclined toward moral courage. Nor did we find gender a factor, or ethnicity. Our sample was not wide enough to make these findings dispositive, but it is noteworthy that we were not struck by the preponderance of any of these factors among the people we interviewed. Nor did genetic traits appear significant, although, again, this was not something we were able to test for conclusively.

We did find a high percentage of lawyers who showed a strong commitment to ideals of fairness and justice. One law professor—a former California state senator who ran several controversial governmental investigations into wrongdoing, even when that meant he had to break with former friends and political mentors—illustrated a common characteristic found among all our respondents: in minimizing their own courage in favor of those they were helping, all of these people revealed themselves as people for whom happiness consisted in giving back and making others happy. Said Senator Joe: "Frankly, we can die in poverty. But if you dedicate your life to just making life a little bit better for others that don't have a fair shot, that's gold."[23] One strongly held trait among the morally courageous was the view that life was more than just doing for yourself. Tej echoed this thought: "I'm currently working for nonprofits helping children of lower castes attend school. I love doing the work I do and enjoy spending time with children. My role right now is to tend to those children I've committed myself to helping grow" (132).

A slightly more complex variation on this theme came from Zimmer, who argued it was *he* who was lucky to be able to help people, not *they* who were fortunate to receive his help:

> I feel very lucky to have a chance to take a stand. Most people don't have that opportunity in their lifetime. But as it relates to standing up to the federal government or standing up to oppression, this is our Selma, in some ways. But there is no John Lewis. There's no Martin Luther King. These are just regular people going about their lives with very brave, ordinary acts of courage every day. The job of the high-profile people is to just stand at their side and make sure that they can continue to be the courageous people they are in their own lives and their own ways, to show that the American dream still means something. Those of us who have been the beneficiary of it from a previous generation have an obligation to stand up for it for a new generation. Those people who don't [recognize] this either don't understand history, don't understand their own family, or they have abdicated their obligation to pay back this country for the opportunities that their own families had. (46)

A DREAMer we interviewed, whom we are calling Raquel, echoed this thought: "So my mom kept telling me, 'You're so brave, you're courageous.' I came back and responded, 'No, no, no. *You two* [parents] are the brave ones. You risked it all.' "[24]

Another common characteristic was the sense of connection with others. This was often expressed through the language of family, as was the case for Amal, on vacation in Thailand when the 2004 tsunami hit. Amal was a Berkeley student, alone, literally possessing not even the shirt on her back, just the swimsuit she was wearing while scuba diving. When the tsunami hit, wiping out her hotel and everyone in it, Amal was safe but underwater.[25] The American government did little to help her, and she survived thanks, in large part, to the proverbial kindness of strangers. She described coming back into the harbor on a boat, where the captain made her and her friend go below to spare them the horror of viewing bodies in the water. Then came the nightmare of finding everyone at her hotel gone and seeing the desolation, not knowing where she would go or what she would do: "As difficult as it was, it was so beautiful seeing people help each other so much. The way the Thai government handled it, the way they created the crisis center out of thin air in twenty-four hours. They had clothes ready to give us, and they were offering us free tickets and giving us places to stay. It was all beautiful to see" (106). The experience marked Amal, changing her forever. Today she devotes her life to helping develop indigenous businesses in the Middle East.

> That's why I'm doing what I'm doing today. . . . I'm making an impact by helping these small businesses grow and be better and contribute to economies and create jobs. . . . Everything I do, I see it through that lens. I ask how it is contributing to a greater good, and if it's not , then I don't do it. That's the lens I see my life through, even in relationships. The reason I talk freely about my different experiences is that I sincerely believe that if I can change just one person's opinion or make that person feel . . . more connected to a good cause or make a difference, then that's what I want to do. Ideally one day I will be making very large-scale impacts, but for me, it starts with the individual. If you can do it in your own way on an individual basis, then eventually it starts to have a more exponential impact. (107)

Like Amal, other people also described their good deeds as part of cosmic karma, a paying back what one had been given, in Kay's case given directly to her by her mother: "I frequently went back in my memory to good experiences and things Mom had done for me when I was a child. Then I wanted to pay her back, I guess you would say, because she spoiled all of us. So she got her karma back, you know?" (79).

This sense of paying back was directed toward everyone, but especially one's family and children. Torres, a refugee from Central America, told us:

"The legacy I want to leave behind to my sons and to everyone else is that you should never give up. To do what needs to be done today and not put it off for tomorrow. If you are going to read, first read with your children so that they would learn too."[26] It is important to note that this sense of giving back extended beyond the immediate groups of family and friends. Yes, there was a desire to be good to one's family and friends, as the quote from Torres illustrates. But this desire to pay back (or pay it forward) also led people to act as a mentor, to try to use their own suffering, pain, and calamity as a way to help others, not just those who had been kind directly to them (as in Kay's case), or family (Torres), or strangers who had helped them (Amal). Amal's theme of giving back by paying it forward was strikingly evident in many interviews, as noted by the Cambodian activist Sophal Ear: "Of course, giving back also means trying to be a mentor to those who need help, who are younger, who are earlier in their careers. You try to be a beacon for other Cambodians who are coming up and don't see how they could possibly achieve the things that I've achieved. It's all trailblazing in that sense." No one articulated this sense of a kind of cosmic karma more eloquently than Tej, when asked by his granddaughter if it had been difficult to risk his job to protest the poor treatment of lower-caste Indians, especially since he had a family to support: "Parenting isn't always about giving your children money. Parenting is about leading your life in a way that you would want your kids to lead [theirs]. If my children encountered the same problem when they were working, I would expect them to do as I did, and [I would] chide them if they didn't do anything. I wanted my children to grow up strong, to understand that fighting for good will always enable you to live a happier life" (129). These are the most striking commonly held characteristics of the morally courageous. How were their characters shaped by the particular values the speakers held?

VALUES, ESPECIALLY CORE VALUES

Character was strongly informed by the values held by the morally courageous, values often imparted to them by family. Core values were key, constituting the essence of moral courage, as we learned in the first part of this chapter. One could compromise on certain issues, but not on the central values. Said Senator Joe: "There are certain issues [on which] I simply will not sacrifice my moral beliefs. If that means I lose the election, I'm okay with that. I get how you have to nuance a lot of votes and be careful, but there are certain ones that are so core, you just have to say, 'Look, my vote's yes.' [For example,] I believe marriage equality is the right thing to embrace, and if my constituents revolt and defeat me next time, it's okay. I'm fine. I'll go back to practicing law."

What are these core values? I noted the importance of core values in my discussion of moral courage as a concept. But let us now document more fully the specific values that constitute the core values of the morally courageous.

Fairness, justice, and respect for human well-being. First and foremost, the morally courageous demonstrated a strong sense of objective fairness, impartiality, and professional ethics. The idea that you "do the right thing" for and toward all people, even those you might not like, was a common theme in all our interviews. Noted Richard Ceballos, referring to his clients and his obligation to them, even the people he was prosecuting: "We also need to make sure the defendant is being treated fairly because, to a certain extent, the defendants are also our clients, even though we are trying to put them in jail or send them to prison. They are still our clients. They are still the people." An objective sense of fairness and justice constituted a large part of the identity of the morally courageous. It was part of their sense of who they were and what values they espoused. Ceballos continued, describing why he had endured the pain and financial costs involved in taking a case against his coworkers to the US Supreme Court:

> Justice [is] doing the right thing. It's abiding by the law and setting aside any personal animosity you have towards a person, whether it be a defendant, a defense attorney, or a judge. It's being impartial and not letting politics influence your decisions. You always strive to do the right thing, the ethical thing, and to abide by our ethics and abide by the law and the Constitution, regardless of who gets upset by that. If your friends, your co-workers, the people you work with on a daily basis get upset, well, that's just too bad. That's the way it's supposed to be. We're not here to make people happy. Doing justice sometimes means people are going to be unhappy. But that's okay. We just have to accept that. That's the price of doing justice—some people are not going to be happy.

This same professionalism and respect for the law, fairness, and justice surfaced in interviews with other lawyers, from Senator Joe to Erwin Chemerinsky and Loretta Lynch. In Lynch's discussion of her work as head of California's Public Utilities Commission, she related that on being nominated for the position she first read the law on the public utilities; it was the law that then guided her actions, not political commands or loyalties. In fact, Lynch notes she decided to go to law school because of her sense that things were not fair in the world and that lawyers might be given the tools to help correct this: "This was 1983, and I did not realize just how pervasive sexual harassment in a workplace was. So that prompted me to go to law school" (108). Once confirmed as Public Utilities Commissioner, Lynch realized she needed information in order to fulfill her professional duties to the California taxpayers she represented:

> With only a rudimentary understanding of the law, I realized we had subpoena power. I spent the month of September figuring out what to do because (1) my lawyers had never issued a subpoena and (2) many of the lawyers were too scared to do it. So I worked with a couple of legal advisors who were our political appointees, a band of four people, writing 127 subpoenas to all of the companies in the market for information, subpoenas which I then promptly issued at the end of September. No one at the PUC [Public Utilities Commission] would sign the subpoenas because they were too afraid the companies would come after them, so I signed them all. Technically it was supposed to be someone from the legal department, but I realized I had the authority as a California lawyer and president of the PUC to sign, and so I did. (113)

Lynch articulated the position of every lawyer we interviewed: professional respect for the law is critical. Following the law is indispensable for the people you represent:

> Ultimately, you had to decide whether you could sleep at night. I made sure I read a bunch of those letters; you know how Obama had penned letters given to him daily, or weekly? I forget. Well, I read a bunch of those letters all the time to remember who I was working for and why the law was written the way it was. It wasn't written—well, actually, sadly some of it is written for the companies, but a lot of the laws were written during the Progressive Era, the reform era, of the 1910s. Certainly during the Depression of the 1930s it was written for the consumers. Those consumers included businesses that were getting reamed by those prices. So from my perspective, I was following the law, and that helped a lot. The hard part was that people don't typically follow the law in my job. I guess I was a bit naïve to think that when you take the oath of office to uphold the constitution of the state of California, you follow those laws in your job setting. People just don't fulfill that oath on a routine basis. (119)

This respect and support for professional ethics were evident in each of the lawyers we interviewed. Witness Chemerinsky's statement that "no one, not even the president, is above the law" (53). Nonetheless, it is important to note that the professionalism and commitment to specialized ethics espoused by Lynch, Chemerinsky, and the other lawyers we interviewed were not restricted to lawyers. It was not just lawyers who had this sense of fairness and the idea that everyone is equal before the law. Tej made frequent references to his belief in the sanctity of the Indian constitution, revealing his own sense of strongly held professional ethics: "So why would anyone—why should anyone—praise me for defending a constitution I had pledged to defend?" (131).

At the core of all these statements was an often unspoken but nonetheless underlying respect for human well-being and human welfare. As highlighted in my discussion of the concept of moral courage itself, what often distinguished moral courage from other forms of courage was the desire to further the well-being of all. Janusz Reykowski made this distinction in his discussion of why he was a bridge builder in the 1980s. His acts of moral courage—speaking up for the need to compromise and work together—emanated not from a sense of honor, but from his fear that ideological courage could precipitate the harsh repression of Polish workers if the Solidarity unionists pushed too hard:

> Reykowski: There are extreme situations when people are facing the ultimate threat to their lives or the lives of their close ones or to their freedom, or they are facing an imminent existential threat to their nation and are unable to prevent such a course of action. The only thing they can do is to fight, being aware that they will be defeated and must die. This was the situation of the Warsaw Jewish Ghetto in the spring of 1943. But it was not the situation of Warsaw in August of 1944. This [1944 Warsaw] Uprising reflected the idea that the human cost doesn't count. This view, that what counts is showing to the whole world how brave we are and how important our honor is . . . this type of thinking is very dangerous. The 1944 Uprising was a deliberate political act that was supposed to prevent Soviet domination over Poland. It was a futile action that brought nothing except great catastrophe.
>
> Q: *So you rejected this view. You wanted slower change that would avoid political confrontation ending in the kind of catastrophe you saw in 1944. You're a bridge builder.*
>
> Reykowski: This was my intention.

As Reykowski explained his thought process during the time of the Round Table Talks, which pulled Poland back from the brink of civil war and/or Soviet repression, he argued that he was someone who believed in the value of human life. He did not want honor if it meant one more child was killed. Better to build a bridge, to find a compromise that would benefit all, and avoid the violence of war. Furthermore, this sense that he had the expertise necessary to help here was what drove Reykowski's feeling that if he did not act, he would no longer be the person he was. His values—which stressed the welfare of his fellow citizens—were so much a part of his identity that he had to act on them; otherwise he could not be true to himself. His actions were necessary to complete who he was, to not betray himself. This is an identity issue, but one tied to a sense that one's identity includes the value, indeed, is *based on* the value of human flourishing, human well-being. This key value of human well-being was intricately related to a sense of justice, fairness, and human integrity, a view echoed by others in our sample, who shared the view that moral courage is undertaken to improve lives, not just to following ideals: "Moral action is not the symbolic making of a statement. Those symbols *can* matter. They *can* electrify people. They *can* help us decide we should take action. But symbols that are only for our personal statement and acts of purification are a luxury that . . . it's not even a luxury; I think it's fooling ourselves" (Booth, 72).

Living one's values every day, which create a sense of self. These core values were principles to be lived by every day, not just when the limelight was on you. Said Senator Joe: "[The] admiration I really have is for those who show acts of moral courage when nobody's watching. It's that old saying that you can always judge a person not by what they do when people are watching but what they do when people aren't watching." Lynch reinforced this theme, noting that true character is shown in a crisis: "It is in crisis that you see the true character of people. It is in crisis that you have to choose" (122). Tej echoed this notion: "I thought everything was good as far as I was concerned, but I routinely saw people in the office get discriminated against because of their family's caste. That was wrong. The official—I don't want to name him continued to threaten to fire people. He called them derogatory names [and] told them they didn't deserve their position. So I decided to stand up [to him]. I nearly got fired, but there was nothing else I could do that would enable me to look in the mirror the next day" (128). The sense of self—captured by Tej's insistence that he needed to be able "to look in the mirror the next day"—was a critical part of these people's character. One had to live one's values or be a hypocrite. The concern for one's character, the feeling that one had to stand up and own this character, and the relation between character and self-respect were remarkably strong. Again, Tej articulated this view:

> Q: *Did your perception of yourself change after the incident [suing the government for caste bias]?*
>
> Tej: No, it did not. I didn't want my perception of myself to change; otherwise, if I felt any sense of elevation by doing what I did, then I would immediately feel guilty for having done something to elevate my image of myself. I did it and I never thought about it, or at least about how I would look to the rest of the world. It didn't matter to me what other people would think of what I had done, so I didn't share it with anyone besides my own family. (131)

I noticed another interesting phenomenon, suggesting how, in a circular fashion, self-respect, the expectations of others, and one's acts looped back and fed into each other. The power of self-respect freed people from the expectations of others and helped these people retain their sense of self-worth, which then fed back into their own sense of self-respect.[27] The importance of having one's actions reflect and in turn reinforce one's sense of self was captured beautifully by a young woman who was a social work student in Amsterdam during the Holocaust. Marion told of a time when she saw the Nazis throw Jewish children into a truck. She then watched as the Gestapo also arrested the Dutch women trying to protect the Jewish children. All the while she stood frozen, unable to comprehend or respond quickly enough to what she was witnessing. Marion said: "We all have memories of times when we should have done something and we didn't. And it gets in your way during the rest of your life."[28] This event, when she did nothing, led Marion to later help rescue Jewish children, in part because she was unhappy with what her failure to act did to her sense of self.

RELATIONSHIPS AND SUPPORT: FAMILY, RELIGION, AND LITERATURE

Being at peace with yourself is important. But it is also important to recognize that being morally courageous can feel lonely and isolated. How did these people find support in the tough times, times when they were under pressure to act differently or to say nothing? The answer is an unsurprising one: friends, family, loved ones. In addition to her boyfriend—now her husband—Lynch noted that she "also had longtime friends and allies who knew my character despite what people were telling them, saying I was a liar and disloyal, which are bad things politically" (119).

Amal echoed this thought in discussing her encounter with Muslim bigotry: "Sometimes it hurt my ego a bit and I felt uncomfortable, but at the end of the day what was really helpful was that I still had my close friends around me. They never let that be something that defined our friendship or that defined who I was" (100). Reykowski spoke of his situation in speaking out against both the Polish government and the union movement to which he belonged, as he tried to find common ground, all the while knowing he would probably end by pleasing no one:

> I was writing articles that people sometimes criticized, or I decided to work for an organization which for the most part was criticized. . . . Radical people from both sides were against those actions. For me, doing those actions was easier because the position of a professor at the Polish Academy of Science comes with a lot of authority and probably stopped the attacks a little, but of course not completely. Secondly, I have to admit that on both sides were people who realized that there were some advantages of those actions [that I

advocated]. They were my undercover supporters. I have to admit that sometimes I had open supporters as well, which in that situation was really important. But of course, there were times when I didn't have any supporters.

These critical others became ingrained in the mindset of the morally courageous, and not betraying their trust became an important factor for our speakers: "How could I face the people who were my friends and family if I made a deal? And a secret deal it would have to be.... Why go into government if you are not going to try to do the right thing?... When you are in a public office there is public trust, and to me that was a real thing" (Lynch, 125). While family and religion often provided critical support in tough times for the morally courageous, they were not the only structures on which people could rely. Kay spoke of her love for literature and how that provided strength and perspective in the darkest days of her mother's illness.

> I have read some of the great literature of the world, and most of the time people in great literature are suffering through something. That's just the way things are in great works. There's not a lot of comedy out there. That's one reason kids don't like to read great literature sometimes, because there's a lot of sadness and people are struggling. I thought back on some of those works and used them as a guidepost. I remembered Hester Prynne struggling, and after everybody rejected her, even as life went on for her, she began doing things for other people and growing and maturing as a person.[29] She struggled and struggled and did her best to stay on top in spite of how badly she had been treated by Dimmesdale and the townspeople. Tess, of *Tess of the d'Urbervilles*, did the same thing. She just survived each day and tried her hardest to do what was right and what was best for everyone. Maybe this sounds kind of goofy, but remember, I have a master's in English literature, so the guidance and inspiration from books I've read is very meaningful to me. It has been ever since I was a kid. All of that helped me. While religion might help some people, literature helped me. (95)

Family served not only as support; it was also what drove the morally courageous in the first place, often working through the love of family, family values, or a sense of duty and obligation, especially toward family. Lim notes she always did what was in the best interest of her family. At first this meant her birth family, even though they had sold her to another family because they did not have enough food for all of their children. Despite her tremendous sadness at leaving, Lim went without protest because she knew it was best for her family. Later, having been raised—fortunately for her—by a loving adoptive family, she was told she would be married, becoming the second wife of a man whose first wife could not have children. She again felt sorrow at having to leave her adoptive family but believed it was her duty to do as she was asked. Finally, when her husband's death left her with nine children and no way to support them, Lim made great sacrifices, often going hungry herself, to keep her children fed. Her own needs, even her own feelings, were secondary to those of the family, as witnessed in a conversation with her grandchild in which she expresses surprise—and a bit of exasperation?—that her feelings are the subject of so much interest:

Q: *How did that make you feel?*

Lim: You keep asking how I feel, but it was my job. I had to do what it takes to keep my family safe, even if that meant being by myself with my child. It wasn't easy. There were a lot of obstacles, but I made it. . . . It hasn't been easy, but when you have family, everything is worth it. Sometimes you have to take the difficult road for family, but in the end, everything will work out.

Family also drove Tej, who risked his job in the Indian government even though he had two small children to support. Asked why he did it, he referenced his views on parenting:

Q: *So you were never scared you would get fired? Fearful of what would happen to your children?*

Tej: Parenting isn't always about giving your children money. Parenting is about leading your life in a way you would want your kids to lead [theirs]. If my children encountered the same problem when they were working, I would expect them to do as I did, and [I would] chide them if they didn't do anything. I wanted my children to grow up strong, to understand that fighting for good will always enable you to live a happier life. (129)

VALUES THAT SHAPE CHARACTER

Self-sacrifice, costs, and what matters in life. If moral courage costs people, does this factor into their decision-making? No, surprisingly but resoundingly not. Said Lim, "My sacrifice helped someone, and that's all that matters. . . . I would rather have sacrificed myself so my children could eat just a little more. . . . That's what I did, you know. When we had just rice and salt, we were happy. I made the decision to keep my family together. Even though they all may have suffered more because I chose not to give one up, I took on that sacrifice."

But Lim's sacrifices were made for her children, something not unfamiliar to most of us. What about the costs of other sacrifices, often for people you do not know, or who know nothing of the risks you are taking on their behalf? Is the drive behind moral courage different in this type of situation?

Senator Joe captured a common theme: "Frankly, we can die in poverty but if you dedicate your life to just making life a little bit better for others who don't have a fair shot, that's gold."[30] Beyond this, being fair was a core value even when it cost the person acting: "Am I proud we went after those wrongdoers and we eventually proved their wrongdoing, legally as well as morally and factually? Yes, I am. . . . Did it cost me a lot of relationships and jobs and reputational slights? Yes, it did. Am I a stronger person for it? Yes, I am" (Lynch, 120). While Lynch notes that the costs of her acts were ones she recognized in advance, she also is very clear that these costs did not really enter into any rational cost/benefit analysis. Lynch was not the only person to speak of how painful it was to stand up against a powerful person, in her case Governor Gray Davis, a governor she had respected and who had, after all, appointed her to her position.[31] Nonetheless, for Lynch it was not possible to go along with the governor's request that she do something she found unethical. She accepted this fact, knowing that the cost to her career of following her conscience would be great. But not following her conscience was not an option: "I tried to do the right thing in spite of suffering the imminent political consequences" (118). Lynch even managed to retain her sense of humor in the face of intense and nasty organized political pressure. In concluding her discussion of the official hearings on which she was grilled for her acts as head of the California Public Utilities Commission during the Enron scandal, a scandal that ultimately vindicated Lynch but which was acutely unpleasant at the time, she noted:

> So I survived those hearings and I felt like I tried to do the right thing in spite of suffering the imminent political consequences.
>
> Q: *The consequences must have been significant; what were they?*
>
> Lynch: Well, I was cut off from the governor's office, called a traitor. The chief of staff told me I was the worst hire that Gray Davis or she had ever done. The deputy chief of staff told one of the legislators that when they passed me on the street in Sacramento, if she had a gun and nobody saw her, she would clip my head right off. Eventually, that same person was put on the PUC [Public Utilities Commission] after Gray Davis was recalled; he put her on the PUC for the express purpose of making my life so miserable I would quit. Oh, and Gray Davis offered me a judgeship if I were to quit. First it was a carrot and then it was sticks. I was not perceived as a "go-along, get-along girl," which, let us just say, was unusual at the PUC. I wouldn't play those games, take those trips, dinners, or gifts. I also wouldn't take private meetings. They all had to be noted, and I would give both sides the same amount of time. The companies hated me because I wouldn't go along. When I left PUC, the senior lobbyist,

the senior vice president for Pacific Gas and Electric, told me, "You know, Loretta, if you ever thought about running for dogcatcher, PGE would put in a million dollars in an independent expenditure against you, and we are not the only ones. Every single company will follow with pleasure."

I just told him, "Well, good thing I am not thinking about running for dogcatcher." (118)

In Poland, Reykowski also expressed the same feeling of needing to do something even though it was clear from the outset that action would exact a price. Reykowski explicated the complex idea so many other courageous people articulated only generally: (1) their acts did not really cost them that much, they insisted (thus downplaying their courage), and (2) you had to do it anyway, regardless of the cost. "I want to emphasize that from my perspective the cost of speaking the truth was not very high," Reykowski said, capturing a common theme. Like Lynch, however, as well as so many others we interviewed, Reykowski did pay a price: "One price that I paid was that I was nominated to receive the X Award of Ministry for my . . . scientific work, and I was denied this award."

Sophal Ear echoed the same need not only to speak truth to power but also to stand up and do the right thing even in the face of disapproval, antagonism, and potential physical harm to himself and to his family from powerful opponents in Cambodia. Still vocal despite death threats, this Cambodian activist articulates the importance of fighting for what is right, even if you run into opposition and criticism: "So the advice I can give you is to keep speaking truth to power, and obviously knowing what's right and wrong. You have to have your own moral compass; you know, true north. You should have enough now from your parents, adults, and your community to know what's right and wrong. Keep fighting for that." A generation and a continent away, Nini spoke of her acts in combating the Nazis during World War II, using similar language to describe how "you cannot help others unless you are in a position in which you are willing to take risks. I think life is full of risks, and we take risks whether we want to or not."

Perhaps the most heart-rending—if quiet—expression of this refusal to think about costs when doing something important, however, comes from Kay, the schoolteacher who gave up thirteen years of her life to care for an aging parent suffering from Lewy body dementia. Kay did this despite her own health issues and her siblings' concern, and even their advice to put her mother in a nursing home: "All that stress I'm sure was not good for me, but here's where I made a conscious decision. I was aware of all this, and I said, 'Okay, see what you can do. If you die, you die. But you can't just turn and walk away from this. Your mother needs your help.' This [doing nothing] did not really feel like an option" (84).

DUTY, FAMILY VALUES, AND "DOING THE RIGHT THING"

All our speakers expressed a strong sense of duty toward others—sometimes family, sometimes the country or even the world as a whole. Booth shares that the most difficult thing she ever did was to hurt her parents, causing them pain and fear for her safety when she defied their request and traveled to the American South to take part in the Freedom Summer of 1964. Hurting her parents, however, became an inevitable result of both honoring the values they had given her and helping others she felt were in greater need. Nini expands this circle a bit. She admits her values were those of her family; she even downplays her own contribution by drawing attention to the extent to which others in her family did more to help people. "People were always being helped in our family," Nini said, minimizing her acts in risking her life and those of her family members if caught rescuing Jews.

This view of family was not uncommon. Indeed, the sense of duty and obligation to do the right thing frequently could be traced directly to family or cultural influences. Zimmer credits working in a family business as having influenced his sense of duty and obligation. His family's immigrant background also gave him a sense of connection with other immigrant groups. In fact, immigrants are a group Zimmerman has tried to help throughout his adult life, in large part because of his close ties to his grandparents and his recognition that today's immigrants are just like his own grandparents; why not give them a chance, do something he would like to have been done for his own family members? This close link was articulated simply by Zimmer, connecting the personal to the national: "I feel very, very strongly that we're a nation of immigrants" (44). It is striking that Zimmer views his work on behalf of immigrants, and especially their children, as a gift, not a burden or something he is generously giving to the immigrant community: "I've been very blessed throughout my career to have been able to work directly with the immigrant rights community. My grandmothers were the first in their families to be born here in the United States. They both, along with my grandfathers, grew up in a monolingual Yiddish-speaking family. Then, because of labor unions and the opportunities of the public school systems, my parents' generation . . . were able to break out of the cycle of poverty" (43). Zimmer continued, downplaying his own acts of moral courage in favor of what the students he was trying to protect were going through: "My God, it's incredible what our kids go through. What we're doing around this issue is the least we can do. I don't think we're doing anything heroic. We're just doing what's right. The children and their families are trying to follow the same dreams my grandparents were trying to follow . . . the dreams they had for my mom, my dad, my aunts, and my uncles. I don't think the families I work with in Los Angeles deserve anything less than my family does" (44). The sense of family as both setting one on a particular course and serving as the mirror in which you must judge your own life ran throughout many interviews. Said Zimmer, "I just hope I make my elders proud every day" (48). And he was not alone in this view. Says Lim: "I listened to my elders because that was what was expected of me." Virtually all of our other speakers reflected the importance of family in our conversations. The family provided both the values from which our speakers acted and the support while doing the act. Reykowski remembered his mother during World War II and the Warsaw Uprising:

> [She] prepared food for soldiers. Not as an official . . . but for the people, for the soldiers who hung around. . . . She didn't get this from other people. . . . This was what we had and shared with them. At the same time, in May of 1939, when soldiers were coming from the unit that was destroyed by Germans, [they] just came to our house, escaping. So these who were fleeing, she was feeding them. . . . You just see it [Mother giving food] and remember. But it probably has some internal psychological impact that we feel.

Doing the right thing for one's family was a critical force for the morally courageous. As discussed earlier, Lim, the woman who had herself been sold into slavery in China because her family was so poor they could not afford to feed her, made many sacrifices to avoid having to do the same to any of her children: "I had to do what it takes to keep my family safe even if that meant being by myself [alone] with my child. It wasn't easy. There were a lot of obstacles but I made it." Lim went on to tell about how she nearly starved and *all* her children went hungry. She did what was necessary to avoid giving away a child, as she had been given away when young, sold into slavery to work for another family: "It hasn't been easy, but when you have family, everything is worth it. Sometimes you have to take the difficult road for family but in the end, everything will work out."

Parents and family played more direct and more traditional roles, too, influencing the morally courageous by providing specific values and a sense of where you came from and who you are. Senator Joe told of his father's influence on him: "I give that credit to my father. . . . [He] lived through the Depression, fought in World War II, came to life. He is Catholic. Raised Catholic. He was loyal to his Catholic church, loyal to his nation. . . . It was that intense loyalty that no matter what, those people and issues you believe in, you must remain loyal no matter what. No questions asked. If you want to predict what I'll do in the future: I'm Irish, Catholic, Midwestern, from the union." We have heard Lynch describe the support from her boyfriend, now her husband, during the darkest days of her ordeal; she also echoed the importance of other family members' support, in this case her uncle:

> Q: I would think, though, that at a certain point it would be very hurtful to feel that people don't like you that much. Who did you lean on [besides your boyfriend]?
>
> Lynch: . . . Longtime friends and allies who knew my character despite what people were telling them, saying I was a liar and disloyal, which are bad things politically, saying I had betrayed Gray Davis and whoever. They said my word was not good; things like that were very painful. The first person I worked for in the [John] Van de Kamp campaign, when I was the assistant campaign manager, the campaign manager—who was a wonderful woman and lawyer in Los Angeles—she told me my first week on the job, "If you are a woman in politics you have two choices: to be liked or respected. Choose now." I laughed and looked at her and told her I would rather be respected, and she said, "Great! Go fire this consultant." And I did. I understood that concept. My uncle was also a fifty-year member of the IBEW [International Brotherhood of Electrical Workers], which was for electricians. When I was on the PUC, he gave me his fifty-year pin and told me, "Remember working people." (119)

Lynch also echoed Reykowski's description of early socialization by parents, in which the parental values were transmitted via parental admonitions to her as a young girl: "My dad always used this expression, I must have heard it a million times growing up: 'Keep your nose clean.' I never really understood what that meant until I was very softly solicited for bribes. . . . I now have lived what it means to keep your nose clean" (127). And also: "My father . . . said, '[Bill Clinton] lied. I can't vote for a president I know has lied because character does matter in a president. The man also cheated on his wife. I can't vote for that either.' I really discounted that. In 1992 I was a true believer, but now I think my father was exactly right: keep your nose clean, and character matters in a leader" (127). And finally: "I survived those hearings and I felt like I tried to do the right thing in spite of suffering the imminent political consequences" (118).

SOME THINGS ARE MORE IMPORTANT THAN WINNING

Finally, I remind myself this book began in response to my students'—and my own—despair at the election of someone whose public persona oozed selfishness and a need to win whatever the cost. Part of the impetus for this book thus lay in our own need to spend time in a world filled with people who rejected this view of life. So let's return to the theme with which we began and ask: how do the people we interviewed contrast with those whose lives reflect the public morality of a Donald Trump? The people we interviewed could not be further from the worldview of a winning-at-all-costs kind of mentality. Said Ceballos: "A win-at-all-costs mentality sometimes overtakes the prosecutor's sense of doing the right thing, the ethical thing. When that happens, it does impact justice, and I think some prosecutors lose sight of that." Politicians are not known for their great morality. Senator Joe articulated critical distinctions here, however, distinctions that seem useful even for politicians who recognize that sometimes one does need to compromise in order to get elected and then do the good things: Joe argues, effectively, that there are some issues on which one should not compromise, even if one loses political office because of fidelity to these values or causes. Joe's view captures a core theme among the morally courageous. What matters in the end for them is not being reelected, not money, not material goods or even political power or fame. Instead, for the morally courageous, their goal in life is a particular form of happiness that comes from caring for others. Tej captured this well.

> Even if you don't have all the material wealth in the world, if you're a good person you'll always be one of the happiest people in the world for following your moral compass. I've known people who are a lot more successful than I am, but they always wanted more. They never paid attention to what they had. They never knew the value of family. They could never appreciate anything, because all they could think of was climbing another mountain and expecting praise for doing so. Career goals are great, but if your career is not based on the need to serve a purpose, then you don't know the value of community. (129)

This concept of personal happiness, the view of what matters in the end, the importance of a community in which all are treated well, and the notion of public service that then emanates from this view could not be further from that of Donald Trump.

Conclusion: The Moral Muscle

What is moral courage? Our analysis suggests that moral courage consists of acts emanating spontaneously—without regard for the opposition or cost to one's self—from core values of fairness, justice, and, above all, a concern for the well-being of others. Moral courage cannot be understood fully without reference to the actor's character or identity. It is rarely the result of agonistic choice and is usually taken in full recognition of, but a striking disregard for, the potential risks and consequences of acting. The people who engage in moral courage are not superhuman. Indeed, they are not even always people who would be judged high on agency. They are normal human beings, driven by their own need to do what they deem the right thing in order to help others and to be able to live with themselves later.

Further analysis of the people we found morally courageous reveals several striking traits held in common, in terms of both their basic personalities and their core values.

(1) All these people were surprisingly humble and modest about what they had done. They all denied they had done anything extraordinary. Their acts were simply those that—they insisted—anyone would do, even as many of them acknowledged their acts would not have been necessary if everyone had acted as they did.

(2) Each demonstrated extraordinary empathy, being able to put themselves into the place of the other and hence find the sympathy-inducing understanding that drove them to act to help others, even if only in some small way.

(3) This empathy gave them a feeling of connectedness to others, the sense that we are all part of a common humanity; their gratitude for this gift, and the recognition of the preciousness of what they had been given in life then led to a desire to give back to society and others in some way.

(4) The core values they acted upon often came from their families. Similarly, the support they needed during tough times also frequently emanated from families and friends.

(5) The values on which they acted—a sense of fairness, a desire for justice and equality, a feeling that all people have worth—were what made them the people they became. Living their values was important to them. "If I am someone who believes in justice and fairness, then I have to act on it or become a hypocrite" was the usual stance among our interviewees.

(6) All the above traits made them people for whom duty and conscience lay at the very core of their being. Not doing the right thing, pursuing winning at all costs, looking at the world from the perspective of "a tiny little selfish 'me' town" (in Kay's words)—these were not options for the morally courageous. They are willing to do the right thing regardless of the consequences, and are very clear that doing the right thing means working not for ideological causes but rather to further human well-being.

(7) I conclude with one of the most interesting aspect of our study of the morally courageous: what I call "moral muscle." A surprising number of the people we interviewed frequently engage in acts that require moral courage. Erwin Chemerinsky investigated the Ramparts scandal and took part

in other publicly controversial investigations long before he sued President Trump in 2017 for violation of the emoluments clause. After our interviews he moved to Berkeley and, as dean of the law school, tackled the thorny issue of freedom of speech as a cultural value and freedom of speech as a legal concept. Loretta Lynch went into law because of her concern for justice. Heather Booth has been a political activist since her college days. Stephen Zimmer has been working in the immigrant community most of his adult life, acting on his beliefs that we are all a family of immigrants in this country and that what newcomers want is the same thing our ancestors wanted. For Zimmer, newcomers are not threatening people sent here to rip off real Americans. They are people just like us, people in search of the same American dream that led our own forefathers to risk their lives in a new country.

We find a similar phenomenon among the rest of the people interviewed here. Slowly, through one small act at a time—even if the act was refusing to strike back when Amal was discriminated against or Kay's quiet determination not to walk away from her dying mother—these people developed their moral muscle. As Booth noted, "One struggle leads to another. The first physician I found to provide abortion services for the Jane movement was a doctor I found through the Medical Committee for Human Rights, which my father established [during the civil rights movement]. So it all comes around" (74).

This quiet aspect of character relates closely to how very commonplace they deem both their acts and themselves. Zimmer's comment, in explaining why he worked so hard to protect undocumented students against deportations he felt were immoral, is an apt one. It captures the extent to which all of our interviewees felt it was a privilege, not a burden, to be able to step up to the plate and protect others. Zimmer argues, in effect, that he is lucky to have the opportunity to be able to stand up and do the right thing. More important, he makes the connection between this belief and what makes the United States the special country it is, which in Zimmer's case is a country that still maintains the American dream of equal opportunity for all, immigrants included. No matter that protecting this vision might cost him in terms of public opprobrium or criticism, even hate mail and death threats. Zimmer—like all the individuals interviewed here—insists that this ability to stand up and be counted in a battle for human equality and dignity lies in us all. The opportunity to do something that is right, to join the ranks of what Zimmer calls "just regular people going about their lives with very brave, ordinary acts of courage every day," is remarkable on so many levels, not the least because it suggests that if other run-of-the-mill, ordinary people can find the courage to change history, so can we.

CONCLUSION

Learning from the Lives of Others

> When we are in the classroom and we talk ethics, it's very easy to give someone a hypothetical question and say, "What would you do in this situation if you were faced with it?" In a classroom setting the answers are easy because it's just a classroom setting. But in the real world, it's different.
>
> RICHARD CEBALLOS

So, what did we learn about moral courage? I described our substantive findings in the last chapter. But as we think about our empirical examination of moral courage with regard to real people in the actual world—not in laboratory experiments by social psychologists or armchair thought experiments by philosophers—we must ask: what does a narrative, empirical examination reveal that more traditional approaches do not? Our substantive insights into moral courage are important, yes; but their significance is heightened by what they reveal about how we study ethical questions in general and for pinpointing specific questions for future work on moral courage and ethics in the main.

Insights into Moral Courage: Future Work

MODIFY THE TRADITIONAL PHILOSOPHICAL APPROACH

We learned first that one of the most popular philosophical methods for analyzing moral courage is lacking in critical areas.[1] In particular, approaches emphasizing moral choice and rational decision-making need to be revised.[2] Our empirical examination of people most of us would agree exhibit moral courage suggests such courage emanates more from character and identity than from conscious calculation or internal debate. People seem not to engage in extensive deliberation before taking their morally courageous actions. There is less agonistic choice and more an awareness, akin to a slow realization, that they must do something they believe is right, even as they recognize their action may well be controversial, criticized, and/or condemned by others. Yet the morally courageous do not hesitate to act; they act because they feel compelled to do so, driven by something deep inside them that demands action because of who they are. Moral courage thus is moral action driven more by identity than by reasoning.

As we parse this further, our analysis reveals that, while there are many different ways to think about moral courage, most include three central components. (1) Moral courage appears to arise spontaneously based on the actor's identity, defined as the sense of self as determined by the actor's core values. (2) The actor is aware there are risks involved, but these risks are largely disregarded; they certainly do not play a dominant role in any conscious decision-making or consideration of whether or not to pursue the morally courageous action. The morally courageous recognize the act will necessitate a willingness for them to endure some unknown hardship, but this awareness does not factor critically into their decision; more surprisingly, it does not seem even to lead to agonistic deliberations or a struggle with choice.[3] (3) It thus is essential, when thinking of moral courage as a concept, to understand that the actor's values are key to the action precisely because moral courage usually reflects the actor's most strongly held core values. These values are so central to an actor's life that they come to constitute his or her very identity; they define and constitute the sense of who that person is as a human being, and thus demand action in harmony with these values.

The intimate relationship between moral courage and a person's core values is evident in Lynch's discussion of her political ordeal during the Enron scandal, when both Governor Gray Davis and the Clinton administration placed great political pressure on her. Lynch draws a clear link between moral courage and self-worth: "A person is only as good as their character and their word" (125). Lynch's comment illustrates how a morally courageous act arises from an actor's sense that they have no choice; to fail to act in a certain way would constitute a violation of their most basic core values, the beliefs and principles so fundamental and deeply held, and such an essential mainstay of a person's character, that they effectively make up the person's identity. Failure to act means they can no longer remain the same person they now are—or, perhaps even more important, the person they want to continue to be. From a philosophical perspective, this centrality of identity—the fact that core values are so fundamentally a part of one's basic self—embeds discussion of moral courage in a virtue approach to ethics.[4]

This relates closely to another, slightly different but nonetheless critical, aspect of moral courage. Moral courage emanates so directly from one's basic character or identity that it cannot be said to result from a conscious deliberation or agonistic choice. In this regard, moral courage again epitomizes the virtue-ethics approach, which emphasizes the development of a good character that then naturally leads one to good actions.[5] Our reading of the stories of moral courage in this book underlines the extent to which moral courage is, in fact, best explained by character, by an identity-based ethical approach. Whether we can distinguish between character and identity—and we did not find that distinction useful—we cannot think profitably about moral courage without putting ourselves into an approach in which character trumps agonistic, deliberate, conscious choice.

EXAMINE CRITICAL CORE VALUES

Here we find three related topics of great importance. If moral courage flows naturally from identity, which is based on core values, can we determine what these values are? It is correct—but incomplete—to be content with the solution of prior analysts, who found that moral courage exists when people feel compelled to "do the right thing."

Traditional explanations of moral courage as "doing the right thing" are too vague. Our analysis was able to identify seven correlates of moral courage that give specificity to the general and accurate yet imprecise traditional definition of moral courage.

1. Moral courage requires empathy, putting ourselves in the place of others in order to view the world as they do and thereby finding the sympathy-inducing understanding that drives us to help others, even if only in some small way. This empathy creates a sense of connectedness to others, the feeling that we are all part of a common humanity.
2. Moral courage involves gratitude for what we have been given in life; this then leads us to want to pay society back in some way. Indeed, many of those interviewed described themselves as lucky for having the opportunity to stick up for others.
3. Core values usually come from the family.
4. These specific core values are (a) respect for human well-being, (b) the belief that all are equal, especially under the law, and (c) a commitment to justice and fairness. These values, especially (d) the refusal to denigrate or deny dignity to their opponents, differentiated acts of moral courage from fanaticism.
5. The values impelling them—a sense of fairness, a desire for justice and equality, and a feeling that all people, not just those in their immediate group, have worth—combine to make the morally courageous the people they become. Living one's values is paramount. "If I am someone who believes in justice and fairness, then I have to act on it or become a hypocrite" was a common explanation given for their actions.
6. All these traits make the morally courageous people for whom duty and conscience lie at the very core of their being. Not doing the right thing,

pursuing winning at all costs, and looking at the world from the perspective of "a tiny little selfish 'me' town" (Kay, 94)—these are not options for the morally courageous. They did the right thing regardless of the consequences. Significantly, they were adamant that doing the right thing means working not for ideological causes but rather to further the well-being of all people, not just members of their own group.
7. Moral courage also provides remarkable restraint, a willingness to be silent, ignore abuse and not strike back, even when justified.
8. All those interviewed possessed what I call "moral muscle." One small act begat others. Surprising numbers of those interviewed had engaged in multiple acts of moral courage.
9. The quiet aspect of character relates closely to how very commonplace the morally courageous deem both their acts and themselves. They do not view themselves as heroic. Each of these individuals insists that the ability to stand up and be counted in a battle for human equality and dignity lies in us all.

Future work: is moral courage a universal ethical phenomenon, or is it morally relative? Prior analysts have tended to presuppose we all agree on what exactly constitutes the "right thing." What is designated as moral courage is perhaps by definition highly dependent on the values of the observer. What constitutes my act of moral courage may be viewed by others as an act of fanaticism or betrayal. The viewpoint from which we assess moral courage—or betrayal—thus relates closely to the values held by the observer. Determining what constitutes the "right thing" lacks an objective metric, making moral courage especially susceptible to moral relativism. A closely related problem, therefore, is to ask about acts of moral courage by people whose basic values we reject or share only partially; can't they, too, demonstrate moral courage within their different ethical frameworks? This question is, surprisingly, overlooked in the literature. Accordingly, we need empirical work that includes a wider range of moral courage, searching for acts of courage we can recognize even when they reflect values we ourselves do not share or may even abhor. I consider this in a second volume, in which I focus on Thomas More in Tudor England and Martin Luther in Reformation Europe as illustrations of moral courage by people whose values we might not totally share. In this second volume I also analyze acts purported to be morally courageous by Franz Stangl, Albert Speer, and Wilhelm Stuckart—all high-ranking Nazis who claimed they had behaved courageously to slow down and temper the Third Reich, yet who operated comfortably within a moral system most of us would find morally abhorrent. Ethicists frequently speak of the value of loyalty or community, but what if the loyalty is to Hitler and the community

Nazi ? Surely most of us would be aghast at labeling as "morally courageous" behavior that encourages loyalty to the Nazi Party. This simple exercise shows us how we immediately confront a host of questions that cluster around one theme: do we have to agree with someone's morals to find them—the actions and the person taking them—morally courageous?[6] Is a terrorist who risks his life to blow up the World Trade Center morally courageous or just ideologically fanatical? What about an antiabortion demonstrator who kills someone to prevent future abortions? Is this morally courageous? There are many variations one could discuss here, but the central question remains: how does an act of moral courage differ from an act of ideological fanaticism? Can we distinguish critical differences between moral courage in the liberal, democratic, humanistic world in which most of us—and certainly most contemporary scholars—live, and the moral courage of someone in the Third Reich, Tudor England, or Reformation Europe? Our narrative interviews in this second book provide only partial answers but do suggest that the key to distinguishing between fanatics and the morally courageous may reside in the different treatment of human life and in recognizing what part of moral courage is universal and what responds to the moral context.

More important for our discussion here, this distinction raises further questions. Would the morally courageous do everything possible to avoid harming others and preserving life? Can an act be morally courageous if it kills one—or a smaller number—of people in order to save more human lives? (Were those involved in the July 20 plot to kill Hitler morally courageous? Or were they traitors, as many Germans believed at the time? What about John Wilkes Booth, whose assassination of Lincoln was widely cheered by southerners who believed Lincoln had killed both their country and their way of life?) Can we distinguish between moral courage and fanaticism, then, by reference to the preservation of human life? Would fanatics be less concerned with protecting human life and more driven to protect their causes?

I suspect this last statement is correct. But we lack direct evidence for it, and empirical insight must await further interviews that highlight the distinctions people actually make when they think of moral courage. This will be considered in a forthcoming book.

Awareness but disregard for risk: perception or reality? Another important area on which our work suggests the need for future research concerns risk, and the distinction between the perception versus the reality of risk. It seemed clear from our interviews that the morally courageous are aware that they risked harm because of their actions but simply disregarded those considerations when acting. Yet as we analyze their acts, we find ourselves asking: must there be some potential harm for an act to be morally courageous, and if so, how much risk must be involved for an act to qualify as morally courageous?[7] Is the actual risk what is critical, or is the critical factor the risk perceived by the person acting? If there is no real danger, but the actor believes danger does exist, does that lessen his or her moral courage? Conversely, if an actor engages in a dangerous act while totally unaware of the danger, should this act be considered morally courageous? Further, how can we as outside observers ever actually *know* what the person acting is in fact thinking as we view her or his action? Here the empirical answers are intriguing.

Many people we interviewed insisted they had done nothing unusual, claiming that anyone would have done the same thing and that their actions did not require moral courage. In many instances, however, it seems abundantly evident this is *not* the case. Nini's rescuing of Jews during the Holocaust is perhaps the most dramatic illustration of this. But even in cases such as Chemerinsky's—who insisted his tenure protected him from retaliation—we need to factor in the modesty factor. If they themselves do not view their acts as morally courageous, should we? How can we distinguish between modesty and a genuine lack of moral courage? If I don't feel fear—either because I am stupid, uninformed of the risks, or extremely brave—does that lessen my act of moral courage? If someone takes an action that looks morally courageous—such as a kamikaze pilot—but takes that action only because it is a direct and punishable order given during war, is that a morally courageous act? Is the same act morally different when it is motivated not by fear of punishment if one disobeys an order but rather by a desire to further a cause in which one truly believes? Again, empirical answers to these questions should be pursued in future work.

Such questions are difficult to answer with a limited number of interviews. Nonetheless, we can provide some insight into a few of these issues. Consider Chemerinsky's actions in suing President Trump. Chemerinsky insisted this act was not morally courageous because he had tenure and there was little the university could do to punish him. In discussing this with the students who interviewed Chemerinsky, I noted that in making his protestation of humility, he ignored his other acts of moral courage, such as his role in investigating the highly charged Ramparts scandal.[8] Further, Chemerinsky's assessment of his own actions was important in raising several interesting definitional issues concerning moral courage. Must there be risk of physical harm for an act to be morally courageous? Is mere censure and criticism of people whose opinion one values enough to define action as *morally* courageous? Must risks be actual? Or is it the *perception* of risk that is critical? If Chemerinsky felt his position was secure, does that lessen the admirable and noteworthy aspect of his act, as he seems to imply it should? In this case, I personally felt it did not, since I knew Chemerinsky was the dean of a brand-new law school and that he was expending massive amounts of energy and time to secure jobs, clerkships, fellowships, and the like for his law students. Suing Trump could jeopardize those goals. At the very least, securing clerkships and jobs could be made much more difficult by his outspoken criticism of Trump. Certainly, rich donors, employers, or judges—all groups that frequently skew politically conservative—might find it unpatriotic to sue a sitting president and hence not want to help the law school Chemerinsky headed. But Chemerinsky did sue Trump anyway. All of this raised the question: in designating an act morally courageous, what is critical, perception or reality? The analyst's assessment or the assessment of the actor himself or herself? How do we, in speaking with the actor after the fact, assess their perception of the risk when there may be a modesty factor to function into the analysis?

These questions are not restricted to Chemerinsky. A Pole who helped make the transition to democracy peaceful in the 1980s, Reykowski also minimized his bravery by noting that his actions to help foster democracy in Poland would have been riskier at an earlier time, when communist control was more complete and opposition and criticism of the communist government hence more dangerous. Similarly, Booth minimized the danger to herself from her participation in the Mississippi Freedom Summer of 1964. (We know now that people indeed *were* killed as part of this social and political movement, including the grandson, son, and one of the women with whom Booth stayed.) Former California Senator Joe laughingly told about the Capitol Hill Police coming to protect him during his controversial Senate hearings. Joe too downplayed the actual threat to himself, chuckling about how he teased the ladies at the senior citizen center where he had been calling a Bingo game when the police entered. Like the other morally courageous, Joe minimized the actual risks his actions presented to his own safety and well-being:

> The first time [the death threats] were with Enron. Enron brought the first death threats. I remember when the first one came I was calling Bingo at a senior citizen center in Buena Park. Out of the blue in come the CHP [Capitol Hill Police], the group that protects the state legislators. They grab my chief of staff, who happened to be with me.
>
> It created quite a shuffle, getting me out with all those police. It created a lot of excitement for the seniors. When I finally returned, I told the older women, I said, "You loved it! All those young CHP officers in uniform" [*laughs*]. We had a good time about it.

Do our interviews answer our question about the direct relevance of whether risk must be involved to be morally courageous? Partly. I would argue that they suggest the critical factor is not actual risk so much as the perception of risk that must be involved in order for an act to be deemed courageous. Certainly, most of these people noted they were well aware of some of the risks they ran but discounted them. Even when they made light of the risk, however, most of the speakers acknowledged that they were aware there was at least some vague possibility that harm would come to them because of their actions. They all recognized that it would have been far easier to do nothing. So we can tentatively conclude, based on the limited empirical evidence we have here, that moral courage *does* seem to involve some risk, or at least the perception of risk on the part of the actor that there may well be unfavorable consequences of their actions. Nevertheless, it was abundantly clear, in all our interviews, that the risk seemed overshadowed by the compassion the morally courageous had for others, for their belief that their acts are necessary, and that the risks thus must be run. To walk away and do nothing because of the risk was not an option.

But if we are to conclude that *some* risk must be involved for an act to be morally courageous, what about the *type* of risk that must be involved for an act to be *morally* courageous and not just *physically* courageous?[9] How big must the risk of potential harm to me be to make my act one of *moral* courage? Our analysis here was not able to address this question with any reliable empirical data. I encourage others, perhaps using experimental or survey data, to explore this aspect of moral courage further.

Moral courage: people or acts? The question of varying degrees of bravery—or ignorance—raises another question: what distinction do we draw between a morally courageous act and a morally courageous person? Can weak, infallible, even morally repugnant human beings nonetheless perform morally courageous acts? Such a selflessly atypical act is what Dickens creates for Sydney Carton at the end of *A Tale of Two Cities*, when Carton substitutes himself for the husband of the woman he loves, taking the husband's place in the cart to be guillotined. His words while en route to die—"It is a far, far better thing that I do, than I have ever done; it is a far, far better rest that I go to than I have ever known"—seem to imply that this one act ennobles a life otherwise spent in dissipation, self-loathing, and despair. Similarly but in actual reality, Oskar Schindler performed morally courageous acts during World War II, yet was by all accounts a less than admirable human being otherwise.[10]

These two illustrations raise a host of further questions. What is the role of the scenario in leading to a morally courageous act? How key is the framing of a situation? What is the difference between values that can be held abstractly but never be acted upon and actual acts? Is a morally courageous character key? If so, how do we explain individuals who usually are morally courageous but fail at a critical moment?[11] Or individuals like Carton or Schindler who surprise us with a rare but morally courageous action? Indeed, is action key? What about moral courage through non-action, as expressed via principled silence, such as that demonstrated by Amal when she refused to strike back at the Muslim prejudice she encountered? Does forbearance count as moral courage, or must moral courage be an action to promote values toward a greater good in some way? Is it enough simply to help another person, or must a larger principle be at stake?

Spontaneous but not impulsive. Can morally courageous acts be impulsive? Must I have thought through all of the implications of my act for it to be courageous morally? Or does a spontaneous act—which may appear impulsive but which emanates from deep within my character—qualify? Here the evidence seems much clearer. To speak of an act as impulsive misses the point for the morally courageous. The term *impulsive* implies that an act is rash, reckless, and above all hasty, not well thought out and hence somewhat irresponsible and offhand. *Spontaneous* carries a totally different connotation and is the word that more aptly captures the actions of the morally courageous we interviewed. The main distinction here is that the spontaneous aspect of their acts emanates from deeply held convictions and values, values that create the very being of the morally courageous individual. It is the *values* that have been thought about in a deeply philosophical way. The values then lead inevitably to the act. Because the actors' actions emanate from their identity, which in turn originates in some part of the nonconscious calculus of reason, the acts may appear impulsive, but they are not, at least in the usual sense of that word as acting without forethought. We thus find nothing impetuous, hasty, or irresponsible about the acts of the morally courageous. Indeed, they reflect thoughtful and deep consideration of what is important to the actor; they thus are the very opposite of actions taken without forethought. Spontaneous, yes; impulsive, no.

MORAL COURAGE AND ALTRUISM

Is there a difference between moral courage and prosocial behavior or altruism? It was not originally my intention to parse this distinction. But since I am known as a scholar who has studied altruism, it is perhaps natural for such a question to arise.[12] I find a certain overlap in the origins of the two phenomena. Both moral courage and altruism seem to emanate from identity and function through spontaneous acts that reflect this basic identity. Again, as with altruism, the morally courageous are quite clear that acting in certain ways is simply not on their cognitive menu. With moral courage, however, the process seems to be more one of a negative nature. Not to act would constitute a betrayal of my own character. Altruism is more of a cognitive factor. Altruists simply do not see that there is a different option. Certain choices are not on the altruist's cognitive menu. For the morally courageous, there seems to be an awareness that other options exist, hence their awareness of the risk to themselves in taking certain actions. But they also know that not acting would be to turn away from their most deeply held values. This suggests that altruism and moral courage are closely related, and that the two groups—the morally courageous and the altruistic—may constitute intersecting sets. But the most relevant distinction seems to center on the perception of different alternatives and the knowledge that there is the option of doing nothing.

VIRTUES AND AGENCY

I have already discussed how our findings relate to the excellent literature, mostly in philosophy, on moral courage. But there remain additional, if smaller, questions that relevant to some of the issues that concerned us, and many of these relate directly to the subjective aspect of determining whether an act is morally courageous or fanaticism or betrayal.

For example, Philippa Foot's general discussion of virtues (not just moral courage) is relevant to thinking about how to distinguish moral courage from fanaticism. Foot asks whether virtues such as courage are always virtues.[13] Can a virtue operate uncharacteristically? Consider a poison—arsenic, for example. Foot suggests that there are at least *some* occasions—glass-making, for example—upon which we might say, "The arsenic does not act as a poison here." It may be poison in a necessary way, unable to ever escape its lethal nature. But insofar as it is being used to form glass, it does not *act* as a poison. Likewise, courage might be a virtue in a necessary way, never losing its power as such. But insofar as it is being used by a terrorist, then courage is not acting according to its characteristic operation. Foot suggests that "not every man who has a virtue has something that is a virtue in him."[14] This perspective may allow us to consider an act morally courageous even if we disagree with the particular values involved; we can say that the courage of the terrorist is virtuous while it is not acting as a virtue in him. Yet empirically, when we describe an act as morally courageous, how often are we describing an act of value with which we disagree? In our use of the term *moral courage*, then, how often do we distinguish between a virtue operating characteristically and a virtue failing to act as a virtue? Initial analysis—without systematic consideration of contrasting empirical data on moral courage in societies whose values we reject—suggests that moral courage is a term used to describe only those acts that hold a positive connotation for the analyst.[15]

More recently, Matthew Pianalto explores moral courage as a matter of agency.[16] As moral agents, Pianalto argues we must face our opponent as a subject, or a moral agent himself or herself, rather than as an object or obstacle to overcome. It is only with this recognition of humanity in our opponent that we can face our "fear of having the contingency and contestability of our own convictions exposed."[17] Here, moral courage is seen as asserting oneself as a moral agent, taking responsibility for one's actions *and* treating others as moral subjects themselves. This may entail justifying our actions to our opponents, since we recognize their humanity and agency, and also conceding that they too have justifications for their actions.

This distinction was very much one we found justified empirically in our speakers' conversation about their acts. Neither Senator Joe nor Loretta Lynch, for example, demonized the governor who gave them such grief and tried to ruin their careers. They still consider him "a friend" (Joe's words). Similarly, Booth wants to engage her opponents in positive dialogue, and Amal tells of reconciling with the young woman who was given the class presidency after Amal was denied it because she was Muslim. Finally, and movingly, Ceballos notes that the people he prosecutes are his constituency: "Prosecutors need to be reminded that we are different from other lawyers. Our obligation is not to any particular client, but rather to the entire criminal justice system. It's not just to the victims and witnesses, not just law enforcement, not just the defense attorneys and judges; rather, our obligation extends even to the defendants we prosecute. We need to ensure the defendants are being treated fairly. We represent the people, and while defendants are not our clients in the technical legal sense, they are still part of the people we do represent." So, how one treats those one opposes is a relevant factor to consider in future discussions of moral courage.

ENCOURAGING AGENCY IN OTHERS

Do the morally courageous judge themselves high on agency? Evidence was mixed here but generally weakly supportive of this claim. Clearly, their acts emanate from their need not to deny their own values. But the morally courageous vary on the extent to which they think of themselves as powerful movers and shakers. Booth falls at one extreme point on the continuum. Her entire life as an organizer is dedicated to the principle that "if you organize, you can change the world" (56). Booth's strong sense of agency—the feeling that she matters and can affect the lives of others—is evident in her discussion of her work as a college student. We note especially Booth's discussion of her participation in the 1964 Freedom Summer, where she helped work to improve the civil rights of African Americans in the South, and in her establishment of the Jane organization at the University of Chicago, where she helped find doctors who would perform safe but then illegal abortions. It continues in her work today, as evidenced in her activities organizing with Move On, the Affordable Care Act, and the establishment of the Midwest Academy, designed to train other organizers:

> At one point (when I was not trying to organize) I was fired for standing with others for fair treatment of clerical workers on the job. I won a back-pay suit, and with that funding I started a training center called Midwest Academy, which still exists and does terrific training for organizers.[18] It trains organizers at all sorts of levels and kinds of groups, from NAACP and Planned Parenthood to little groups you may not have heard of.[19] It addresses all kinds of issues. From there I helped to create new models of organizations. We helped to build statewide organizations at a time when there were only community groups and national groups. We formed multi-issue organizations at a time when there were mostly single-constituency groups. You were either an environmentalist or a senior, for example, a labor person or someone working for women's rights. But if you were both, where did you go? To address this issue, we helped create multi-issue organizations. (55)

Booth may be one of the most imaginative, and certainly one of the most vocal, in revealing her belief that we can change the world. But she is not the only one. Most of our speakers shared this view to some extent. We heard it from young girls in high school, such as the teenage Amal's fight with bigotry against Muslims in contemporary America or the young Nini's fight against anti-Semitism under the Nazis. We also found it among older people concerned with the notion of legacy, wanting to leave behind an example for others. Note that Tej risked his job and his children's security and financial well-being to fight against caste discrimination in modern India because he believed that being a parent involves more than simply putting food on the table. For Tej, showing children how to live in a manner that expresses your values is also important. Even when the speakers do not rank themselves high on agency—as Lim and Kay would not—they seem to want to instill a strong sense of agency in others. Tej wants his children to realize they too can effect change. They too need to be people whose values should make them leaders. Booth wants to establish more leaders, and the Midwest Academy is designed to provide training skills so others can go out and change the world. Amal chose as her pseudonym her grandmother's name. Her reason for doing so stemmed from her awareness that we all can affect and influence others through our acts, even an act as insignificant as the choice of name in an scholarly book on moral courage that few may read (see chap. 7, n. 1).

RETHINKING MORAL COURAGE

All of this suggests the need to revise the kind of abstract pictures of moral courage presented to us by philosophers. As a general principle, it is extremely useful to construct the kind of philosophical theoretical framework from which to speak ideally about what we think *should* be considered morally courageous. But that theoretical framework needs testing and revision by the examination of empirical reality. Consequently, the kind of analysis presented in this book complements the philosophical approach and can offer valuable insight into how the basic philosophical understanding of moral acts needs to be modified to allow for the complex and often shifting reality of actual life. Some of these ways were suggested earlier in this conclusion and in chapter 10. But these various revisions also reveal the highly complementary aspect of our work. Theoretical philosophical discussions are invaluable in pointing to critical distinctions. But the distinctions worked out carefully by a philosopher can—and must—be tested and revised by actual empirical understanding of moral courage in action in the real world, not just the classroom. In this sense, we hope our work can serve as a valuable supplement that tests philosophical discussions of moral courage.

Fortunately, recent years have seen an increase in this kind of empirical examination of philosophical concepts. George Lakoff and Mark Johnson's work on the embodied mind is one of the more theoretically sophisticated works calling on scholars to ask how actual people really do think about moral issues.[20] I now find the behavioral economics movement encouraging a similar movement in philosophy, the experimental philosophy movement, which uses tools of survey research or experiments to address questions philosophers traditionally consider, such as the ones I posed above, to ask whether people actually do think about ethical questions this way.[21] One limitation of the experimental approach, however, arises from its reliance on surveys and/or experiments. Experiments are conducted in a laboratory, a controlled but artificial setting. This permits precise delineation of different situations but also limits examination to a conscious act, and as we have just found, much of moral action emanates spontaneously, outside the domain of consciousness or reason in preference to one's sense of self or identity.[22] Survey research is limited by the same situational factors and requires the respondent to locate the answers in only a few critical boxes: yes, no, a little, a lot, on a scale of one to ten, and so on. Surveys further ask only the questions posed by the researcher. A narrative allows a more nuanced and complex way for the speaker to select the "right answers." A narrative accordingly is less a reflection of the researchers' preconceived vision of reality and more a drawing forth of the speakers' own worldview, opinions, and so on. Advancing knowledge of how the mind thinks about ethical issues requires the tools of all types of research, including variations on the ones discussed above.

VIRTUE ETHICS AND AGONISTIC CHOICE

Finally, I return to my original point about philosophical analyses. Beyond the call for a more broad-based methodological approach, our interviews also speak to other philosophical debates. In particular, our analyses of the narratives confirm the virtue-ethics account of moral courage. It suggests that identity is key. Reasoning and cognition enter the moral realm more through reflection on values and the kind of person one wants to be rather than through any conscious decision-making at the time of action. This includes the much-touted agonistic choice favored in Western philosophy and literature. Many of our most important ethical acts reflect character, not agonistic choice. This is true for a wide range of morally courageous acts. It holds for the somewhat consciously recognized act of boldness we know will threaten our own well-being, as exemplified by Nini when she saved Jews from the Nazis. We find it in a series of acts of quiet, everyday courage, such as Kay's care for her mother despite the risk to her own health. And we find it in morally courageous acts of restraint, such as Amal's refusal to strike back against those who had treated her unfairly because of her religion. Some acts are instant and spontaneous, requiring that the actor effectively forsake a cost-benefit analysis. Other acts are chosen in spite of rationality; that is, people know the risks but disregard them anyway. This power of personal identity to override cost-benefit calculus reflects the fact that the actor is incapable of doing otherwise. This phenomenon is captured over again by our speakers. We find it in Kay's refusal to walk away from her mother and Amal's rejection of striking back. It is reflected in Zimmer's and Booth's willingness to risk physical harm. And it exists in Lynch's and Tej's risking their careers. The morally courageous can "do no other."

These are some of the more substantive insights our examination provided into moral courage and the questions these answers in turn raised for future work that can move us toward a better understanding of moral courage and related ethical concerns. These are crucial questions for scholars in the area. Beyond this, however, what did the work teach the students—and the professor—involved in this study?

Learning from the Lives of Others

This book evolved from a class project with three goals: (1) to help students better understand moral courage as a substantive phenomenon; (2) to determine whether the more personal experience of interviewing someone about their moral life brings insight and understanding of ethical issues that more traditional teaching of ethics does not; and (3) to assist the students—and the professor—as they addressed their deeply personal confusion and despair over the political victory of someone they found unqualified for the presidency in terms of character and experience and to ask what that meant for their own responses to the changing political system. I have addressed the first two questions above. But as we consider the third, we must also ponder its broader implications. In particular, I wondered if this one exercise could carry more far-reaching significance for young people, who would surely encounter other periods of confusion and despair in their lives. Had our project taught the students anything of deeper, more lasting significance about the moral life? I hoped so. But I remain an empiricist, so I needed to ask directly: what did the students themselves say they learned? Here is where things got interesting.

Any professor who assigns a final paper that asks, in part, what the student learned from the assignment must expect to find a certain amount of flattery. Wouldn't most students who submit a final paper have thoughts of their grade in mind? Would it not then be natural for them to find something positive to say about the course? I expected this, and I did find a certain amount of it. I also was struck, however, by the students' honesty. Many confessed they had taken the course only because they needed to fulfill an upper-division writing requirement and my course fit their time slot. (So much for sycophancy.) One student related this to Martha Nussbaum's book *The Fragility of Goodness* and its discussion of moral luck.[23] This student—I'll call her Alison—analyzed the interview with Amal and was struck by Amal's discussion of the tsunami and how this natural disaster still affects her. Alison noted that Amal asks why, out of the 35,000 people who died that day, she had survived. Alison was struck by Amal's answer: God had another plan for her; God intended Amal to live. Alison then proceeded to describe how Amal's whole life revealed the slow development of Amal's moral muscle. This was evident, Alison said, in three separate instances: (1) Amal's refusal to condemn Christians at her high school who tried to convert her using quite heavy-handed techniques, such as telling her she would burn in hell if she did not convert; (2) her remarkable forbearance in refusing to strike back in the face of Muslim discrimination that took away her rightfully won high school class presidency; and finally, (3) her takeaway from her tsunami experience, which emphasized the importance of kindness and treating others like family. All of these, Alison noted, led Amal to dedicate herself to pursuing her passion in a way that would help others. But for Alison, the lesson was slightly different:

> Being an atheist, I do not necessarily believe that actions are the result of a god's will. Nussbaum's thoughts on luck strike me as a more correct answer to the "Why me?" question [which Amal poses, asking why she survived when 35,000 others perished]. Just happening to be in the perfect place [underwater in the ocean] in the event of an emergency doesn't mean you survived because you have some greater purpose or that you survived because you deserved it more. It means you were lucky. The question should not be: "Why did I survive?" Instead, people should say, "I survived. What am I going to do because I survived to benefit the people and world around me?" ... Ultimately, though she used religion to get there, Amal arrived at the same conclusion as I did. (Alison, paper, 4–5)

Alison continued, arguing that moral courage is "not some distant thing. It does not require a highly unattainable level of morality or intelligence or altruism. You do not have to do something incredible, like saving Jews from the Holocaust. Moral courage can be exhibited in small, personally meaningful ways. Anyone can choose to show moral courage" (Alison, paper, 7).

Alison then captured the response of most of the other students on so many points. It is that moral courage "is not defined by large, astonishing acts. People can be morally courageous in day-to-day life, in small personal ways. These personal victories may not seem to have a large immediate effect. However, the ripples of the small act can open the door for other people to make morally courageous choices and show compassion. Moral courage begins with consciously understanding your morality and defining what you believe in. Moral courage is then fostered through having the inner strength to follow the moral compass you feel best defines you" (Alison, paper, 1).

THE DELAYED IMPACT OF MORAL COURAGE

Students commented on several other factors that struck them. First, they noted the development of moral muscle through small acts, such as the progress Alison charts for Amal. Second, they noted how other people can be influenced by seeing other acts of moral courage, as highlighted by Amal's choice of her grandmother's name—meaning "hope"—for this pseudonymous interview. The idea that struck students here is the importance of understanding and knowing what your own values are. Like leitmotifs, found in the papers of virtually every student, I noticed a strong link between these core values and one's very essence as a person, and the conclusion that one was lost if one did not follow "the moral compass you feel best defines you."

The interviews presented in this book were only some of the oral histories my students analyzed. Several students reached their conclusions about moral courage through the analysis of interviews with undocumented students. (Our concern with protecting the identity of these students means that I quote none of them here.) Other students spoke with El Salvadoran refugees, a few with Syrian refugees. One student drew on the experience of someone who resisted the Taliban. I am always astonished by the resourcefulness of students in finding fascinating people to interview. For all the students, however, analyzing oral histories—listening as people they know tell stories about their lives—seemed to provide an alternative and valuable way to think about ethical issues and moral choices, one they said offered a context and specificity that allowed them to take the lessons of others and find relevance to their own lives.

DRAWING ON EMOTIONAL INTELLIGENCE

I tried to draw upon the students' emotional intelligence by asking them to write about people they knew, people for whom they would feel affection, in the hope that this affection would facilitate and provide them with the empathy that might help them recognize how complex the moral life could be in reality. One student interviewed a friend who was at risk of having to drop out of school in order to care for his younger siblings. The young man's father was absent from his life, and his mother was in jail on a drug conviction. The young man did not want his sisters to have to grow up on their own, as he had done. Conducting an interview with him led my student—I'll call him Don—to conclude: "Through my interviewee's story we can see why morality is infinitely complex. We can see what experiences led to a decision and how his character was developed throughout his lifetime. We can see the guilt but also the mercy in making decisions that may be considered good for one person (his sister) but bad for another (his mother)" (Don, paper, 8)

Like the other students, Don was inspired by the person he interviewed. Time and again, I found such statements as: "This story very much reinforces my ideas about how I want to live my life. . . . I am inspired by the level of maturity Amal had at my age, and aspire to be able to have a positive attitude toward life like she does. I also hope one day to be able to let go and live without anger or resentment like she has been able to do" (Alison, paper, 8).

The ability to inspire comes from more than just a rousing or motivating story. So many of the interviewees were young when they performed acts of moral courage (Nini, Amal, the college-age Heather Booth), and so many of them were people my students knew personally (Chemerinsky, Ceballos) or family members (Lim, Tej). This personal tie made a critical difference. These were people *like them*. Hearing about acts of moral courage performed by normal people, often described with an honesty that revealed the speakers' confusion and uncertainty as they sometimes bumbled from one step to the next, lurching toward wherever their acts of moral courage took them—this helped the students relate the speakers' acts to their own lives.

I noticed this immediately, the first year I taught this course, before the focus was on moral courage; at that time it was simply a course that asked how we all use stories to understand ethical issues. One student wrote on her final exam that she was graduating and didn't care about her grade since her path after college was already set. But, she confessed, she had been a big party girl so far in school and had thought the course, with its emphasis on literature and films, looked easy. Like so many other students, the course fulfilled an onerous requirement—of an upper-division writing course—and she chose my course because it fit into her schedule.[24] But then, she continued, we showed a video clip from *The Courage to Care*, an Academy Award–nominated documentary about people who rescued Jews during the Holocaust. One of the speakers was the grown-up Marion Prichard, who had moved to the United States and lived in New England, where she worked as a psychotherapist. Marion described how as a young student in the Netherlands—roughly the same age as my students—she came out of her class in social work in Amsterdam to find herself viewing Nazis rounding up Jewish orphans and throwing them into the back of a truck in preparation for transport to a concentration camp. Marion watched, horrified yet unable to move, as a few Dutch women protested and fought to save the children; the women themselves then were thrown into the truck for arrest by the Gestapo. Marion said she did nothing but resolved then that if she later *could* do something, she would. Marion concluded the description of this event by commenting, "We all have memories of times when we could have done something and we didn't. And it gets in the way during the rest of your life."

I did indeed remember this film and Prichard's moving statement. But I did not recall what followed, as my student continued: "You then said, 'It is never too late.' And when you said those words, I felt a huge door open in my life and I realized I did not have to continue being someone who just spent my life partying and getting drunk. I quit partying and got serious and read all the books for this course."

At some level I am always surprised to hear from a student that some little thing I did affected them, changing them in some way. But this recognition also always makes me a bit nervous, anxious I am pushing students too hard. What if I am being too judgmental? Who am I to tell them to think about their moral lives? Isn't that offensively presumptuous of me? Shouldn't I be more responsive, less insistent that they think about who they are and what choices they make, and how those choices will feed back and bite or warm them later in life?

I therefore wondered how the students responded to my unorthodox approach to teaching ethics. Most felt the course pushed them gently to examine their own morality and life experiences. "The course forced me to talk about sore spots and things I often repress," one student noted. But, as many students continued, the writing and sharing of personal stories eventually came to feel cathartic. Said my student Pauline:

> Listening to other people's stories helped me realize that I am not the only one with issues. I was not the only person in the room with a messed-up family, with overly critical parents. I am not alone. I feel as though for the first time in my college career I truly learned something. This class forced me to examine my morality, to examine the construct of morality as a whole... These stories and prompts helped me redefine and establish my own personal moral code. This class opened up dialogue about my family between my parents and me. I am so thankful for this class because it has given me so much more than a check box on a list of mandatory courses.

STORIES AND UNDERSTANDING THE ETHICAL LIFE

Most students noted the ability of stories to locate us in their context and reveal critical values. Not only did thinking about ethics via stories teach the students that context is important for understanding acts such as moral courage; the pedagogical approach also suggests that gently forcing students to locate themselves in the middle of their analysis of ethics can be transformative for them. Stories not only help us understand the speakers' context; they also help *us* view *our* own selves more clearly. They help us reveal many of the complexities surrounding our own moral choices and concretize our own moral life in a way abstract philosophical discussions do not. As noted by many students, sharing stories with those we trust helps lessen the existential loneliness of life. It can build community and increase our own moral imagination as we think about how to conceptualize our own way out of ethical dilemmas. When we read the narratives of others, whether they be stories of moral courage, as in this book, or stories of moral failure and despair, we find reflected and concretized, and thus made more intelligible, many of the ethical questions we ourselves will encounter in life. This helps us ask what is

LEARNING FROM THE LIVES OF OTHERS 193

really happening and why. We can gain new insight into how bad things can be, whether natural disasters, such as Amal's tsunami, or manmade tragedies, such as Sophal Ear's Khmer Rouge. Even these bad times can help build our character, preparing us for later challenges, much as Amal's early teenage experience with religious discrimination helped prepare her for later, greater challenges in life. As we think about how the stories play out, we can ask how we can help shape and construct counternarratives, perhaps ones with happier endings.

Stories of moral courage—indeed, all stories—are about the speakers' lives. But such stories also highlight the values of community—however that community gets defined—and thus can be national stories. When we find Chemerinsky (chap. 3) suing Trump for violating the emoluments clause of the Constitution, what kind of statement is he making about our country? Our president? Our past? When Kay tells us (chap. 6) how people treated her mother in a nursing home, what does that reveal about our own time? About how we value and treat elders in twentieth- and twenty-first-century America? The time and culture surrounding the story can be critical. As Kay's story illustrates, the current model for caring for elderly family members has shifted dramatically from the norm of a hundred years ago, when most parents who were widowed and infirm lived with their children until they died. Juxtapose that context with the one of present-day America, when nursing homes are becoming the accepted way to deal with the elderly.

Lynch's discussion makes a direct link between past instances of public moral courage with the present-day situation with Trump. Her comments support the conclusion, highlighted above in conversations with both Kay and Chemerinsky, suggesting how the individual links to the national in critical ways:

Q: So it wasn't a choice for you; it was something you had to do, given that you had taken an oath and what that oath meant to you.

Lynch: Yes, but also, politically, I thought a person is only as good as their character and their word. How could I face the people who were my friends and family if I made a deal? And a secret deal it would have to be. Ugh. Why go into government if you are not going to try to do the right thing? I do not see the government as pigs at the trough. I don't believe you should eat the spoils, as the Trump administration clearly does. Even after what I have seen, government can be a force for good. It can also be a force for immense cynicism, and [things can] devolve into a banana republic. But I was never going to go down that path. Shoot, I could make more money in a law firm; why not just go back there? From that perspective, when you are in a public office there is public trust, and to me that was a real thing. Gray Davis was the fourth Democratic governor in the twentieth century. The other three were Culbert Olson, Jerry Brown, and Pat Brown, so I understood this was a special opportunity and responsibility to be able to be in government. It would be a violation of the public trust to not do all I could to stop the wrongdoing.

Q: *That was important to you?*

Lynch: Absolutely.

Q: *You mentioned the Trump administration. What are your reactions, what are your thoughts as someone who does seem to take very seriously oaths of office and the idea that being a public servant is a noble profession? How does it make someone like you feel when you look at the Trump administration today?*

Lynch: Well, it was a travesty. We knew it was going to happen, right? This man was going to become a tin-pot banana-republic dictator if he possibly could. He was going to unleash his people to be pigs at the trough. I don't think he made any bones about that. . . . From that perspective, it is not surprising what Trump is doing. But does it tear the fundamental contract we all made as citizens of this great United States of America? Yes, it does. We are at a fundamental point of taking a stand because it is so clear that the Trump administration is destroying that public trust. So are we going to protest? Are we going to fight them? The Republicans essentially did a good thing with Nixon, and when you look at that situation versus this, Nixon is a schoolboy compared to Trump, which is something scary to say. (126)

As these stories reveal, a great deal about the complex relationship between micro and macro stories is often critical, as when both Lynch and Chemerinsky effectively argue that it is Trump who has broken trust with the people, indeed, with the history of America. (They argue it is they who are loyal and Trump who has betrayed American values.) The structural transformations of the private sphere into the public domain are evident in Kay's conversations about nursing homes in contemporary America, and in Tej's comments (chap. 9) on how he sued the Indian government for caste discrimination as an act of conscience. He took this act in his role as an officer working for the Indian government, because caste discrimination violates the spirit of freedom in the Indian constitution he venerates.

As we read these stories of moral courage, then, we are reminded of the need to think about how the construction of political narratives speaks to ethics and politics. (Remember, almost all narratives that address how we deal with others should be defined as "political.") How does the strategic use of narrative construction serve to move people from a traumatic past into a future that is richer and more peaceful instead of one that is more destructive and violent? How does the construction of one particular narrative rather than another lead the speaker—or the listeners—to a happier outcome, in which their trauma seems to have served a purpose, to have ennobled a person? This ennoblement occurred for Booth, who notes her awareness of all the troubles of the world but insists on Gramsci's pessimism of the intellect yet optimism of the spirit? Such a critical difference in interpretation is what Booth offers us. Kay's story, too, is remarkable in its open discussion of how her kindness to her mother was spurred by her mother's kindness to her as a child. Her mother's kindness thus shaped the entire rest of Kay's life. But Kay's returning this care to her mother also ennobled Kay, making her a better person. Rarely are people so honest and revealing.

THE CALL OF STORIES AND THE MORAL IMAGINATION

Joan Didion, a master storyteller, reminds us that "we tell ourselves stories in order to live"—to figure out life and our place in it. As my student essays reminded me, however, we also tell ourselves stories in order to bridge a gap between ourselves and others. When this happens, stories become communicating and bonding experiences.[25] Stories also construct bridges between the personal and the public. Zimmer's experience as head of the LAUSD, where he worked to protect undocumented students, makes clear how his acts as a public official were informed and shaped by his more personal experience—being close to grandparents who were, themselves, immigrants. Both Tej and Kay also link their personal narratives to that of the broader community and thus also illustrate the bridging effect of stories.

Finally, storytelling can recreate history as opportunity. Stories can trigger the moral imagination, suggesting new possibilities, as they did for Reykowski, whose sponsoring of the Round Table Talks in Poland helped establish a new democracy without bloodshed but meant Reykowski had to serve on the Politburo in order to oversee this peaceful transition. At ninety-four, he is still working, trying to establish a liberal think tank in Poland to protect Polish democracy, which is again under attack as it was when he initially helped put it back on track in the 1980s. I find this detail—part of the minutiae of daily life—immensely touching and helpful in bringing into tangible form more general theoretical concepts academics like to toss around for our students' and our own edification.[26]

Unspoken tales told to a loved one. The importance of listening to stories of moral courage cannot be overestimated, especially when we consider the role stories play in showing alternative routes to action. A story of moral courage can inspire by example but also by helping the reader imagine specific alternative narratives to the one the listener might otherwise fall into or accept as the norm. As a result, narrative imagination creates a sense of the possible. It extends the idea of what could exist and helps us visualize and conceptualize this new way of living. As a consequence, it reveals new potentialities, letting us reach beyond our own limits to search for different scenarios, different options, different actions, and different outcomes. I hope some of the spirit and bravery of these speakers will inspire readers, as they did the students who participated in this project.

In listening to stories, however, we need also remember to ask: how is the story told? When is the story told? Under what circumstances? To whom? Several speakers gave their stories to students in their classes (Chemerinsky). Others told their stories to members of their families (Lim, Tej, my cousin Kay). Reykowski is a friend of many years, someone whose oral history I had always wanted to capture. He never wanted to publicize his past, always insisting he had done nothing of importance. However, when he asked if his grandniece could stay with me, in order to improve her English and give her a different life experience, I unhesitatingly said yes but laughingly told him the payment would be to tell his life story to Zosia. He did so, I believe because he loved her, just as Tej told his granddaughter his personal story but might not have told others. (Tej's request for a pseudonym is perhaps emblematic of this fact.)

The context of Reykowski's story also is relevant in another vein. He told me the fuller story when I visited him in Warsaw in the spring of 2018. I did not want to push my friend to do anything with which he was not totally comfortable; I wanted to be sure he had no reservations about having his story printed and distributed in a book. He asked why I thought his story was important, why it deserved to be published. I told him that just hearing one story of moral courage from a normal person might inspire others to think they too might find the strength to do one brave thing. I reminded him that Polish democracy had benefited from his actions and that this democracy was now again under threat in Poland as in many other parts of the world as well. I believe it was these comments, plus our twenty-some-year friendship, that established the element of trust necessary for a modest and private man to share his story so publicly. Personal stories told to a dear friend or family member involve trust but also a desire to set the record straight for someone you love and who you believe should know the truth, especially in times of political crisis, when similar acts of moral courage may again become morally salient.[27]

THE LIVES OF OTHERS, THE UNSPOKEN STORY, AND HOPE

One final note: how we decode and find meaning in the narrative of a particular story involves interpreting what is not said. What is not commented upon is often taken for granted. In this sense, the unspoken may reflect many things, and one of them may be the speaker's implicit understanding of the world at such a deep level that it is assumed, and thus presumed that others also understand and share that belief as well. (Ancient people believed the gods caused events and thus demanded human sacrifice, or they believed their kings had a divine right to take land and fight wars without consulting the people they ruled.)[28] In *A Darkling Plain* I asked how people kept—or regained—their humanity during wars.[29] I was surprised that none of the people I interviewed talked about the war they had lived through in dramatic terms evoking honor or glory. Such an omission I found significant, even remarkable. In speaking of their wartime experience, there was no burst of patriotic passion, no rush of glory, no justifying their suffering and loss through reference to a greater good. Instead, everyone spoke of the war as the most horrible thing they had ever known; after such trauma, they all desperately wanted to return to the life of the everyday.

Determining whether there is an unspoken message in stories is extremely difficult, of course, and must be done with great caution. How do we establish whether something not mentioned is there as an underlying assumption—the way the divine right of kings was once accepted as a given, widely accepted by people and not commented upon because that was the normal course of life—or is something that simply is irrelevant to the speaker? Perhaps it is something that interests the researcher but is genuinely not germane for the speaker? (One of the people I interviewed about their rescue activities during World War II told me, half in amusement, half in exasperation, that one researcher wanted to know details about his sex life. "What does my first sexual experience have to do with my rescuing Jews?" he asked, perplexed. I guessed that the psychologist doing the interviewing was using a fairly crude Freudian framework, a paradigm I found somewhat inappropriate in this instance. Otto never told me about his first sexual experience, and I never asked. Neither of us thought it relevant to his rescue activities.)

As I read the student papers and the interviews for this book, I wondered if there were something unspoken but of importance in our interviews. After reading the stories many times, I realized that the thing that had gone unspoken in the interviews in this book seemed to center on hope. Its significance for moral courage was considerable albeit complex, as I trust the following discussion will make clear.

I have spoken about the importance of stories for building a bridge between people.[30] The heart of ethics—or at least, something very close to the core of ethics as a discipline—concerns how we interact with others. People are social beings, and our lives are inextricably intertwined with the lives of others. We interact and influence them, just as they influence us, every day, defining who we are and shaping who we become. We learn from others, and the quality of our interactions shape and mold how we feel about ourselves in deeply profound ways.

I was reminded of this as I wrote the penultimate draft of this concluding chapter. By chance, a book that began in response to the presidential election of 2016 ended the week of the 2018 midterm elections. Again as fate would have it, I was spared the roller coaster of election-night returns by having an evening seminar, this one for a class entitled "Morality during War," which focused on asking about how people keep their humanity during wars. Again by coincidence, the syllabus topic on November 7, 2018 asked how people found ways to keep their integrity while living in a politically repressive regime. We read John Steinbeck's novel *The Moon Is Down*, about a fictionalized town—possibly in Norway—during the Nazi occupation, and Vercors's *Silence of the Sea*, about a man and his niece forced to house a German major in their home in Nazi-occupied France. Both books were published initially by Éditions de Minuit, a clandestine press that published in occupied countries of Nazi Europe; it reflected the agonizing of intellectuals—in this case, writers—trying to find an appropriate venue in which to produce their work without selling out to the Nazis, people whose politics the writers found morally reprehensible. The class supplemented these readings by viewing *Das Leben der Anderen* (*The Lives of Others*). This Academy Award–winning film about a playwright and a Stasi agent is set in the former German Democratic Republic, the authoritarian communist state operating in East Germany from the end of World War II until the fall of the Berlin Wall in 1989 and German reunification in 1990.

The movie begins with a Stasi agent being asked to run surveillance on a well-known East German playwright, Georg Dreyman.[31] Dreyman is a man of integrity who loves his country even though he finds the political regime repressive. Somehow Dreyman manages to write serious, high-quality plays, even within the constraints of the autocratic state. Dreyman is in love with a beautiful actress, Christa-Maria, who has the bad luck to have attracted the attention of a top cabinet minister named Kempf. Kempf wants to find something on Dreyman so Kempf can send Dreyman to prison, leaving Kempf free to make romantic inroads with Christa-Maria. Thus, lust results in the tapping of a Stasi agent, Gerd Wiesler, for the surveillance job. Wiesler begins spying on Dreyman twenty-four hours a day; but in doing so, Wiesler suddenly finds himself an unknown observer in a world he never knew existed, a world of art, great literature, beautiful music, and friendship groups unknown to him.

A critical scene involves Kempf picking up Christa-Maria and forcing her into his limousine, where he then rapes her. The acting is brilliant and the scene incredibly disturbing, as Christa-Maria alternates between refusal and the hopeless compliance of someone who knows she is trapped and has no other option. Kempf paws her breasts, and the scene ends in a particularly ugly manner as Kempf pulls down his trousers and climbs onto Christa-Maria, tugging at his old-fashioned white underwear to reveal his rather large bottom.

The next scene shows Wiesler, the Stasi agent, noticing that Christa-Maria is being dropped off from the minister's limousine. Wiesler smiles to himself and says, "Time for some bitter truths." He then connects two wires that ring the doorbell to the flat where Dreyman is quietly working at his desk, writing. After a few moments of minor annoyance, Dreyman gets up to go downstairs and let into the building whoever is buzzing. As he opens the door, Dreyman sees Christa-Maria exit the limousine, still pulling her clothes together as she crosses the street. Dreyman cannot know about the rape but in an instant realizes that Christa-Maria has been with Kempf. His face expresses a myriad of emotions as he steps quickly behind the door so Christa-Maria can enter the apartment building without seeing him. She charges right past him and goes to the apartment, where she immediately takes a shower, trying figuratively to wash away the foulness of what has just happened to her. She then curls up on the bed in her bathrobe, in a fetal position. Dreyman enters the bedroom, and when she hears him come in, Christa-Maria asks him to "just hold me."

The face of the Stasi agent shifts from the anticipated glee at what he had expected to be a scene of confrontation and anger from a betrayed lover to one of confusion and bewilderment as he realizes Dreyman says nothing to Christa-Maria. Dreyman utters not one word of accusation, expresses no hurt, no anger of his own, just sorrow and compassion for Christa-Maria. He simply—silently and tenderly—lies down on the bed and holds her. This scene signals the beginning of the Stasi agent's realization that there is an alternative way of living, a different way of interacting with people. It is one of several small moments of truth when he shifts in his character and is transformed by the life of another.

I thought about this scene as I mulled over the striking manner in which even small acts of moral courage can beget similar acts, stimulating not just the moral imagination and strengthening the moral muscle of the actor but also rousing others, including the students who worked on this project. That the project took on a life of its own, one in which both I and my students learned a lot about moral courage as a topic, was not a surprise. This intellectual phenomenon I understood; this is what I did. Like other scholars, I have been trained to be objective, to stand back and analyze data dispassionately, and I have certainly tried to do that here.

But I also had asked my students to do something more: to open themselves up to a deeper kind of analysis, one that partook of emotional intelligence as well as the analytical ability or learning facts. I challenged them to engage in the kind of work that would shake up, even disturb their current thinking and question their most basic assumptions about life. Don't I then owe them the same honesty?

Of course, although writing this section is difficult and goes against my years of training to be objective and impartial. It is so much safer to leave myself out of the analysis. I ultimately felt obligated to my students, however, to acknowledge how deeply personal teaching is to those of us on the other side of the desk—to admit how this kind of project also led *me* to reexamine some of my own deeply held beliefs about the world.

So, what did I learn, not just about moral courage but about myself and how I think about the world? Did the project force *me* to reexamine my own inherent views about life? To encounter a new way of looking at things, as Wiesler did through his contact with Dreyman? The answer here is incomplete and unsatisfactory, far darker than I initially wanted to recognize or admit, leaving me less confident and more resigned than I ever thought I would be, less sanguine about a world of progress and hope.

The project made me acutely aware that I had grown up believing the world was a good place. Not good, exactly—perhaps more a place filled with dangers but one in which my parents were on top of things, protecting my brother and me from harm. The deeply ingrained belief that the people in charge were both loving and competent took its first hit when I began graduate school. Moving to the South Side of Chicago after the 1968 Democratic National Convention left me with a visceral and profoundly troubling sense that the people running the country were *not* doing a good job of it. The ugliness of the convention—in the city that was to become my new home, where police beat peaceful demonstrators—left such a bad taste in my mouth that I still can view Chicago as a city only through that filter. Further, the Vietnam War left me in despair, intensely conscious that my government—*my own government*—was engaged in what felt like immoral behavior toward both the Vietnamese and America's own citizens, especially its young men being shipped off to die for a cause I found unjust.

Alienation is the word to describe what I felt, but it does not fully capture the essential feeling of foreboding and dread this memory even now evokes in me. I can liken the sensation itself only to another period in my life—the beautiful summer days in June 1973, after my father had been killed in a sudden and unnecessary car accident.[32] I had just submitted the first draft of my thesis and was spending a few weeks in England with my then-boyfriend. I immediately flew back to St. Louis for Daddy's funeral and to stay with my mother to help her. (This was what I told myself then. In reality, staying with Mother probably was more to help me cope with my own pain and loss, as well as the sheer disorientation I felt in a world suddenly turned upside down.)

For the first few days after I returned home, I would wake each morning in my childhood bedroom on Pine Lake. All my things were there, just as they always had been. The white curtains with violets on them would lift lightly in the summer breeze. The sun streamed through them, and the birds provided a familiar and soothing background, mixed with the usual comforting noises from the other part of the house as I could hear breakfast being prepared. All was peaceful and serene, just as I always remembered it. Yet there was this cold chill around my heart, a panic so intense it frightened me to my very bone, and each morning when I awoke I felt my mind stumbling wildly, racing to escape, to find somewhere to hide. But from what? I would lie there a few moments, deeply disoriented. Everything had seemed normal, safe, and secure in what had always been a pleasant, happy, and very protected little world; yet now there was a sense of pure terror at some unknown horror.[33] I would lie there like this for a few minutes, feeling unanchored, and then, suddenly, everything would click into place, my subconscious and my conscious worlds aligning. My father had been killed. Daddy was dead. He was no longer there to protect me, to take care of business, to make sure the world functioned as it should, and the day suddenly went dark, a bleak filter descending and coloring life in a way I had never known before.

The consequence of my alienation over Vietnam meant I did not go to law school, as I had always planned. As much as I admired my father, as much as I still feel at home with lawyers and their passionate talk of constitutional issues, I realized I could not accept the tenets of the legal system, the core assumption that the system works and hence lawyers have to do everything they can to fight to protect their clients. No matter that some people had advantages others did not. No matter that the rich could afford better lawyers, that the deck was stacked against the have-nots. The system worked, and that was what signified. Once that belief was gone I could not become a lawyer, and my new love called to me. Social science provided a freedom and an integrity the law no longer held for me.

Like any other thoughtful person, regardless of political conviction, I have many times been critical and unhappy with the political and legal system since then. But the visceral sense of betrayal and estrangement has returned only twice since the time of the Vietnam War. During the 2000 presidential election, when I felt the system had been corrupted, was the first time. Surely the courts would intervene in the correct way and order a recount, my judge's-daughter memory told me. Surely. The day the Supreme Court handed down its decision in *Bush v. Gore*, the feelings of duplicity and disaffection came flooding back. The second time this happened was when Trump was elected. I was first in denial and then in despair that the antiquated American Electoral College was giving us someone so unqualified in terms of experience and character to lead the country. Worse, I realized Trump was a manifestation, not the cause, of incredible divisiveness and hate. This book reflects my attempt to deal with that, as I said in the introduction.

But what sense does this all make in terms of my own participation in these interviews? Did my own deep-seated views on life change as a result of this project? Did I learn anything new? Did I find greater insight into life and my own way of dealing with it when the world around me descended into confusion and despair? Did my experience differ significantly from those of the students involved in this project?

The answer to the last question is easy: yes. The students found hope in the interviews. Most shared Booth's optimism, her faith and confidence, both infectious and striking: "We often keep thinking about how far we have to go—and it's important to keep thinking of how far we have to go—but we shouldn't lose sight of where we've come from" (59). The students identified—correctly—with the hope inherent in this statement. They quite accurately concluded that moral courage was driven in part by the hope that one could make things better.

I was not so sure. I found the question of hope deeply disquieting to me, triggering a thought process I can explain only by reviewing the troubling reflections that analyzing these interviews generated for me.

I still believe the world is a cruel place, but I no longer believe the big folks out there safeguarding us are on the job. My father is gone, and there is no one to replace him. Most political leaders today disappoint me. I know intellectually that I have to be my own parent. I have to—and can—learn to be the one to take care of myself. Part of growing up is abandoning the childlike desire to be protected. Becoming an adult means many things, of course, but one of them is clearly learning to care for one's self, forming bonds with others who have your back and whom you love, cherish, and look after in return.

But I was born with the nurturer gene, and the recognition that I can do so little to shield and safeguard those I love from all the ugly things in life hits hard. I share Booth's pessimism of the intellect but lack her optimism of the spirit. In good moments, I can tell you that even though life is futile and hope too often a cruel illusion, the struggle alone to create something good is enough to fill your soul. Camus's *Myth of Sisyphus* got that one right.

That's on the good days. On others, I feel overwhelmed. I have too little to give the students who come to me and ask what they can do in a world of such anger and hate and us-versus-them. We live in a political climate in which, unfortunately, this ugly reality extends far beyond Donald Trump. How, then, does a decent human being respond? Create one's own world? Live one's life in cameo, doing as much good as one can and letting go of the frustration and upset when the outside world and all its nasty viciousness caves in on one? Was Albert Hirschman right in saying that we must cling to hope in order to live in a world we know is often so foul? Is that enough to sustain us? Do we have any other alternative?

The last question is perhaps the critical one. Is there any option other than taking the heartache we feel in a world filled with so much misery, desolation, and sadness, and turning it into something good, some little thing—a child we can make laugh, wonderful books we can introduce to students? I have tried here to create a small volume documenting the moral courage of some unusual yet normal, average people we meet in our everyday lives, wishing that this book might inspire others, making clear that moral muscle develops slowly and among us all, if only we can find the strength to begin exercising it. Is finding moments of opportunity born of tragedy and despair enough, enough to do for others, enough to sustain us?

I don't know. I accept that being human means experiencing pain, and I realize adversity often helps build character. Without challenges, life can leave us insipid, vacuous people with little depth. Perhaps things like moral courage are drawn forth only in hard times.

But how then does hope figure into all of this? As I reviewed the project and what the morally courageous said to the students, it seemed that hope plays a vital part in moral courage. People usually act in the hope that their actions will make things better. Indeed, analyzing the interviews suggests an argument could be made that the unspoken aspect of moral courage—that essential thing which is so central to the character of the morally courageous that they take it for granted and thus need not even articulate it because they assume everyone else understands it, too—is hope. Hope is both a facilitator and an initiator of moral courage, making hope's relation to morality key.[34] It clearly was for my students.

It was not for me. As I read these interviews and assessed their impact on me—as a person, not as a scholarly analyst—hope indeed did count; but for me, the bottom line often located moral courage outside the boundaries of hope. What struck me as central was that one can engage in acts of moral courage without having any hope at all, without even thinking of the consequences of one's actions. Why do we engage in acts of moral courage? Because we must. We must stand up and be counted, staying true to the values that make us who we are, because that is what it means to remain human.

Morality, then, is more basic than hope. Moral courage emanates—at least in some instances—from something more fundamental than the hope that our actions will improve the world in some way. Hope can facilitate, initiate, and drive moral courage, but hope is not necessary for moral courage to exist. We can have integrity, honesty, and moral courage even in the face of hopelessness.

For most of us, when we live in a world without hope, the world becomes a scary place, one filled with confusion and despair. My students certainly picked up on that. But immersing myself in this project took me to a different place. It shifted my sense of the possibilities and taught me something new about searching for alternative scenarios.

Even when the world around us seems to be falling apart, when everything seems lacking in decency, we can still find integrity in ourselves. Individually, there is always something we can do. Even in times of bewilderment and despondency, personal or political, moral courage can emerge from the least of us, and it can do so without any hope that our actions will have any impact at all. We can operate ethically without hope. We can behave morally simply because that is who we are. Because that is what we must do in order to remain human. Morality, then, involves acting as an end in itself, without hope, without praise, without any concern for the consequences of our acts. Understanding this helped me find a purity in ethics that I had not found before.

We can never control the outside world, never make it perfectly good and right for those we love, any more than we can expect others to provide a safe, decent world for us. But we can become our own protectors. This is true not just for the morally courageous, not just in times of world turmoil. Any one of us, anytime we find ourselves disoriented, lost, uncertain of our bearings, can dig deep within ourselves to imagine new scenarios, new ways of viewing the world. We can be the ones to stand firm and assert moral values in the face of oppression, cruelty, and hatred, and take strength from our own most basic humane values anytime we need to rediscover our own moral compass.

Acknowledgments

This book grew out of a 2017 project for a class called "The Moral of the Story" (Political Science 138AW). Research continued over the next few years, including two iterations of the class and two summer internship programs in which I mentored students at the UCI Ethics Center. I am deeply grateful for the students in my classes at UCI and for the summer interns, especially those in the 2021 summer program. Too numerous to list individually here, all of these students are acknowledged in a working paper on the UCI Ethics Center website. Special thanks go to the students who worked particularly hard on the project: Ali Ansari, Risha Bat, Kali Bate, Anne Chen, Kendrick Choi, Kaytlin Cui, Hannah and Isabelle Dastgheib, Daniel Delpassand, Alex Fu, Victoria Gutierrez, David Han, Adam Hernandez, Joelle Hwang, Aniket Kamat, Nate Kang, Alexis Kim, Michelle Kim, Thivinya Kobbekaduwa, Connor Lee, Eunice Lee, Michelle Lee, Brock Lichthardt, Bella Liu, Steven Ma, Arya Marwaha, Lauren O'Neill, Antonia Park, Max Razmjoo, Luca Shakoori, Grant Sheft, Samuel Shih, Bridget Swineford, Sophia Sun, June Shin, Andrew Tsang, Anna Ulrey, Ria Varmi, Abigail Wang, Anqi Wang, and Daniel Yoon.

Next, of course, are the many individuals who agreed to be interviewed for this project. I thank them for both their trust and their moral courage. I have selected only a few of the interviews to present in full here, and all of the speakers have approved the publication of their interviews. Some of those interviewed were comfortable having their names used. Others requested anonymity or pseudonyms; for these people, I can give only general thanks here. In a very few of these published stories, then, I have modified noncritical identifying details—such as the speaker's name or city of origin—while keeping the substance of the interview itself. In these cases, I also omit the name of the person who conducted the interview, to fully protect the interviewee's anonymity. Although I did work closely with all these speakers and their interviewers, all the final editing and analysis of the interviews was done by me, and I alone am responsible for any errors. In this vein, I must thank Barbara Norton for her kindness; her careful copy editing caught many infelicitous phrases, and her attention to detail corrected many errors.

Beyond this, I have the usual cast of suspects to thank: colleagues and friends whose regular conversations instruct and inspire me. My cousin Kay Monroe generously allowed me to use an interview with her in this book. Lily Gardner Feldman and Jennifer Hochschild gave especially insightful comments, as they so often do. Andrada Costoiu, Barbara Dosher, Jim Glass, Rose McDermott, Janusz Reykowski, Etel Solingen, Kay Schlozman, Lawrence Sporty, and Ervin Staub all provided their always generous support. Beyond this, I remain especially indebted to three of my graduate students, Monica De Roche, Jessica Gonzalez, and Ben Hoyt, who worked with me on the project during the summer internship program. It is a joy to have such students and a gift to watch them become wonderful colleagues and friends. My daughter, Chloe Wilmot Lampros-Monroe, assisted in the editing of transcripts, and my son, Nicholas Monroe Lampros, commented generously on both their substance and their presentation. I benefited from comments on this work presented at meetings of the International Society of Political Psychology, the American Political Science Association, Harvard University, and the UCI Ethics Center. A mini-conference at UCI brought me into contact with other participants who provided especially useful comments, chief among them Jim Glass, Artemis Jankowski, Barbara Heisler, Martin Heisler, and Peter Suedfeld. As always, I am grateful to Chuck Myers, my editor, for the integrity and thoughtfulness he brings to his job. Chuck's dedication to his work was especially evident in this instance, since he continued to work on my project even after he retired.

Finally, I gratefully acknowledge the generous financial support of the Institute for Humane Studies. It is rare to find an organization funding basic ideas that underpin our liberal, democratic society. As we find both liberalism and democracy under attack, at home and abroad, we all owe a great debt to such organizations.

This book is dedicated to my father and my maternal grandfather. It also honors my dear, departed friend Cheryl Nichol Hawkins, too modest to ever want any attention drawn to her but whose love and affection enriched the lives of all she knew. None of them lived to read this book, but then none of them needed to learn anything about moral courage, for their lives embodied it.

Notes

Preface

1. I was fortunate to know Albert Otto Hirschman at the Institute for Advanced Study at Princeton. Hirschman was an influential economist and the author of several books on economic development, political economy, and political ideology. *Exit, Voice, and Loyalty* (1970) posited three different responses to the kind of political repression Hirschman encountered as a young Jew living in Berlin when Hitler came to power. The book argued that people can leave (as Hirschman did, moving to France only later to have to flee Europe entirely), remain and protest, or be loyal. Until it became too dangerous for him, Hirschman worked with Varian Fry to help smuggle to safety people in jeopardy from the Third Reich. His actions, and his life and intellectual contributions, are discussed more fully in Jeremy Adelman's superb biography of Hirschman (Adelman, *The Essential Hirschman*; Adelman, *Worldly Philosopher*). The story I describe was told to me by Hirschman at lunch at the Institute in the early 1990s. The conversation was not taped.

2. Varian Fry was a journalist who was crucial to the establishment of the Emergency Rescue Committee (ERC), a private American relief organization designed to help rescue writers and artists targeted by the Nazis. Hirschman was a member of Fry's staff. Some of the two thousand people saved by this group included Alma Mahler Werfel and her husband, Franz; Thomas Mann's family members; Marc Chagall; Wanda Landowska; and Lion Feuchtwanger.

3. *Go Set a Watchman* was published in 2015 by HarperCollins.

4. Richard Ceballos's interview was analyzed but is not included here for reasons of space.

5. This later volume addresses the question of historical context and moral relativism by examining the moral courage of individuals (such as Thomas More and Martin Luther) who demonstrated moral courage in the past, although they were driven by societal values most of us today would reject. We also analyze the values of Franz Stangl, Albert Speer, and Wilhelm Stuckart, three Nazis who presented their acts as morally courageous. These acts were, to varying degrees, endorsed by postwar courts; and yet, most of us would consider the core values of these individuals to be morally repugnant.

6. The full name of the Center is the UCI Interdisciplinary Center for the Scientific Study of Ethics and Morality. See www.ethicscenter.uci.edu for details on the free online summer program, open to anyone above the age of fourteen.

7. The names of these students who participated in the internship are found in the acknowledgments. The acknowledgments can only begin to note my gratitude to these students for allowing me to work with them and watch them grow intellectually.

8. Heather Booth's story (chap. 5) illustrates this well.

9. No interviews are included in the analysis without the explicit oral permission of the speaker. I did the editing of all interviews. Therefore, any errors are mine alone, and not the responsibility of the student who may have done the initial interview. Most of the interviews were done jointly or by me and transcribed by students, with my edits being the final ones. Although I have not identified particular individuals who conducted the interviews—in part to protect the identity of the speakers—I am most grateful to all the students and interns who worked with me on these interviews.

10. What our values are and how we define what moral courage means in action is another, extremely large topic—one I address in chapter 1. Chapter 10 identifies the particular values most closely associated with moral courage among our interviewees.

11. This project helps clarify the nature of that choice, however, and links it closely to identity or character, not to agonistic choice.

Introduction

1. Closely related questions are addressed in two later volumes. If values determine what we find morally courageous, can we find moral courage in societies that do not share our values? How does moral courage look in such societies? And does moral courage look different in liberal, humanistic democracies than it does in societies whose values we do not share or perhaps even find morally repugnant? These are big questions and will be answered in the two later volumes of the trilogy on moral courage of which the present volume is the first.

2. Was Daniel Ellsberg a traitor or a patriot? Were the Republicans who voted against Trump's impeachment disloyal Republicans or the stalwart guardians of true Republican values?

3. I am grateful to Jessica Gonzalez, Kyle Stanford, and Peter Ditto for this insight.

4. I should note that Kay is my cousin.

5. Officially known as the Abortion Counseling Service of Women's Liberation, the Jane Collective, or simply Jane, operated as an underground service in Chicago from 1969 to 1973, when abortion was illegal in most of the United States. Booth laid the foundations for the organization when she helped find a doctor to provide a safe abortion for the sister of a friend in 1965. Since the Supreme Court overruled *Roe v. Wade* in 2022 in its *Dobbs v. Jackson Women's Health Organization* decision, abortion has now again become illegal or highly restricted in many American states. As a result, commentators note the likely rise of underground abortion organizations such as Jane.

6. The nature of this choice is complicated, as we discover in part 3.

7. Interviews are ongoing, so the eventual number of cases will exceed fifty.

8. We interviewed a wide range of people who exhibited moral courage, including some whose moral courage might be judged marginal by some readers. For example, we interviewed Choo Tee Lim, sold into slavery in China as a child, who resisted poverty and cultural pressure to give up her own children. Was this moral courage or simply parental love? To avoid any confusion, I focused my analysis on cases in which moral courage seems unambiguous.

9. The literature review in chapter 1 makes clear the extent to which scholars focus on

classical Greece. Perhaps a more important role in limiting existing works on moral courage, then, is the fact that most contemporary scholarship comes from *analysts* who hold liberal, democratic, humanistic values.

But can't we find moral courage in societies that do not emphasize or even share these values? What about societies most of us find morally repugnant, such as the Third Reich? Or societies whose values seem quite alien, if not morally objectionable, such as a Europe that honored the divine right of kings and thought it normal to burn people at the stake because they worshipped differently? What about these societies? Can we find moral courage in all societies regardless of their specific values and beliefs? Does moral courage look the same in different ethical polities? Moral courage in these societies is analyzed in the two forthcoming volumes of this trilogy. Volume 2 presents portraits of moral courage in societies whose values we may relate to in part but do not totally share; hence, we examine the moral courage of Thomas More in Tudor England and Martin Luther in fifteenth-century Germany. We also consider the touted moral courage of Franz Stangl, Albert Speer, and Wilhelm Stuckart, all Nazis whose claims of moral courage in "opposing" the Third Reich were given some legal credence after World War II but whose values were set firmly in a society whose moral values most people find morally repugnant: the Third Reich. Volume 3 analyzes moral courage in situations where the boundary between moral action and betrayal quite evidently tends to shift and blur. In this volume, we examine whistleblowers such as Richard Ceballos, Geoffrey Wiggin, and Linda Tripp, all commended by some and vilified by others. We also consider patriots—or spies—such as Daniel Ellsberg and Edward Snowden. Finally, we consider moral courage in the age of Trump by focusing on "rogue" Republicans such as Mitt Romney, John McCain, Liz Cheney, and Rick Wilson, a prominent member of the Lincoln Project, to examine partisan political moral courage.

Chapter One

1. This chapter was written with Benjamin Hoyt, who headed a group of talented interns at the UCI Interdisciplinary Center for the Scientific Study of Ethics and Morality during the summers of 2020 and 2021. Under Ben's direction, the students helped research the literature on moral courage. I am deeply grateful to them and especially to Ben for their assistance in putting together this review of the literature. Monica De Roche assisted with updating the literature from social psychology, and Jessica Gonzalez provided valuable insight into the literature from cognitive psychology and philosophy.

2. James, *The Moral Equivalent of War*; Kateb, "Courage as a Virtue"; Rorty, "The Two Faces of Courage"; Scorza, "The Ambivalence of Political Courage."

3. The predominant view is that liberalism doesn't need courage. James, *What Pragmatism Means*; Kateb, "Courage as a Virtue"; and Scorza, "The Ambivalence of Political Courage" all think courage is (to a varying degree) antiliberal. Sparta is the quintessential example of a society hooked on courage. The idea is that if we (as a society) value courage too greatly, then we risk becoming a collection of boorish, nationalist bootlickers. In addition, most people agree that (for example) the 9/11 hijackers exhibited a great deal of courage in the service of their values. That highlights the problem: how do we distinguish between acts of moral courage and acts of fanaticism and betrayal? These questions are discussed as part of our empirical examination and are examined empirically in the two later volumes on moral courage.

4. Rate, Clarke, Lindsay, and Sternberg, "Implicit Theories of Courage."

5. MacIntyre, *After Virtue*; Avramenko, *Courage: The Politics of Life and Limb*.
6. See the psychologists O'Byrne, Koetting, Lopez, and Petersen, "Building a Theory of Courage"; and Lopez and Snyder, *Positive Psychology*. For philosophers, see Rorty, "The Two Faces of Courage," and Avramenko, *Courage: The Politics of Life and Limb*.
7. Rebecca Tan, "A Black Officer Faced Down a Mostly White Mob at the Capitol: Meet Eugene Goodman," *New York Times*, January 14, 2021.
8. Avramenko, *Courage: The Politics of Life and Limb*.
9. Avramenko, *Courage: The Politics of Life and Limb*.
10. Gable and Haidt, "What (and Why) Is Positive Psychology?"
11. Kennedy, *Profiles in Courage*; Kennedy, *Profiles in Courage for Our Time*; McCain and Salter, *Worth the Fighting For*.
12. Lopez and Snyder, *Positive Psychology*.
13. Rate, Clarke, Lindsay, and Sternberg, "Implicit Theories of Courage."
14. Houser, "The Virtue of Courage"; Aquinas, *The Cardinal Virtues*.
15. Hobbes, *Leviathan*.
16. Aristotle, *Nicomachean Ethics*.
17. MacIntyre, *After Virtue*, 192.
18. Avramenko, *Courage: The Politics of Life and Limb*.
19. Cicero, *On Obligations*.
20. Miller, *The Mystery of Courage*, 14.
21. Balot, "The Dark Side of Democratic Courage."
22. Dent, "The Value of Courage."
23. Proposed by O'Byrne, Koetting, Lopez, and Petersen, "Building a Theory of Courage"; and by Lopez and Snyder, *Positive Psychology*.
24. Cox, Hallam, O'Connor, and Rachman, "An Experimental Analysis of Fearlessness and Courage"; Rachman, "Fear and Courage"; O'Connor, Hallam, and Rachman, "Fearlessness and Courage."
25. Sanford, "Are You Man Enough?"
26. Aristotle, *Nicomachean Ethics*.
27. Miller, *The Mystery of Courage*; Avramenko, *Courage: The Politics of Life and Limb*.
28. Avramenko, *Courage: The Politics of Life and Limb*, 77.
29. Rorty, "The Two Faces of Courage," 153.
30. Balot, *Courage in the Democratic Polis: Ideology and Critique*; Kateb, "Courage as a Virtue."
31. Shklar, "The Liberalism of Fear"; Scorza, "The Ambivalence of Political Courage"; see also Gay, "Courage and Thumos," for a contrasting view on "traditional" courage in Aristotle.
32. Dent, "The Value of Courage."
33. Shelp, "Courage: A Neglected Virtue."
34. Shelp, "Courage: A Neglected Virtue," 357.
35. Shades of that old joke: What's the difference between God and a doctor? God knows he's not a doctor. Shelp, "Courage: A Neglected Virtue," 358–359.
36. Lindh, Barbosa da Silva, Berg, and Severinsson, "Courage and Nursing Practice"; Hawkins and Morse, "The Praxis of Courage as a Foundation for Care."
37. Finfgeld, "Becoming and Being Courageous in the Chronically Ill Elderly."
38. Finfgeld, "Becoming and Being Courageous in the Chronically Ill Elderly."

NOTES TO CHAPTER ONE

39. Putman, "Psychological Courage."
40. O'Byrne, Koetting, Lopez, and Petersen, "Building a Theory of Courage"; Williams, *Truth and Truthfulness*.
41. Rousseau, *Rousseau: The Basic Political Writings*; Avramenko, *Courage: The Politics of Life and Limb*.
42. Rousseau, *Emile, or The Education*.
43. Tillich, *The Courage to Be*.
44. Plato, *Plato: Laches; Protagoras; Meno; Enthydemus*.
45. Yearly, *Mencius and Aquinas*.
46. Thoreau, "Civil Disobedience."
47. Sekerka and Bagozzi, "Moral Courage in the Workplace"; Sekerka, Bagozzi, and Charnigo, "Facing Ethical Challenges in the Workplace"; Chapa and Stringer, "The Path of Measuring Moral Courage in the Workplace."
48. Avramenko, *Courage: The Politics of Life and Limb*.
49. Frankfurt, *The Reasons of Love*. The relationship between authenticity and liberalism is fraught with conceptual tension. As some have noted (Waldron, "Superseding Historic Injustice"; Williams, *Truth and Truthfulness*), the kind of identity appropriate to the citizenry of contemporary liberal societies is ill-suited to a moral psychology defined by unalterable commitments to unchanging values. Citizens of liberal democracies should be allowed to change their affiliations and commitments, while authenticity has typically been associated with communitarian alternatives to liberalism. While space does not permit me to explore fully the architecture of authenticity, I presuppose here that some citizens of liberal societies feel morally bound to stand up for the principles of justice, fairness, and the rule of law, and that their commitment to these values tracks the schema of moral courage and authenticity described in this book.
50. Williams, "Practical Necessity."
51. Taylor, *Pride, Shame, and Guilt*; Williams, *Shame and Necessity*.
52. Williams, *Shame and Necessity*.
53. Rawls, *Political Liberalism*.
54. Plato, *The Trial and Death of Socrates*; Balot, *Courage in the Democratic Polis: Ideology and Critique*.
55. Aristotle, *Nicomachean Ethics*, 44.
56. Ward, "Nobility and Necessity"; Pangle, *The Moral Foundations of Aristotelian Political Philosophy*.
57. Balot, "The Dark Side of Democratic Courage."
58. Balot, *Courage in the Democratic Polis: Ideology and Critique*.
59. Balot, *Courage in the Democratic Polis: Ideology and Critique*, 41.
60. Balot, "Courage in the Democratic Polis."
61. Balot, "Courage in the Democratic Polis."
62. Plato, *The Trial and Death of Socrates*.
63. Tessitore, "Courage and Comedy in Plato's *Laches*"; Devereux, "The Unity of the Virtues in Plato's *Protagoras* and *Laches*"; Penner, "What *Laches* and *Nicias* Miss."
64. Dobbs, "For Lack of Wisdom."
65. Dobbs, "For Lack of Wisdom," 849.
66. Plato, *The Republic of Plato*.
67. Hobbs, *Plato and the Hero*.

68. This lovely phrase is Ben Hoyt's. I am grateful to Ben for his assistance in writing this chapter as part of our Ethics Center 2021 summer internship program.

69. See Locke, *Second Treatise of Government*; Rawls, *Justice as Fairness*; Mill, *On Liberty and Other Writings*.

70. Shklar, *The Faces of Injustice*; Shklar, "The Liberalism of Fear"; Williams, *Truth and Truthfulness*; Williams, *In the Beginning Was the Deed*.

71. Williams, *Truth and Truthfulness*.

72. Williams, *Truth and Truthfulness*.

73. Williams, *Truth and Truthfulness*.

74. Shklar, "The Liberalism of Fear," 33.

75. Shklar, *The Faces of Injustice*.

76. Shklar, *The Faces of Injustice*, 108.

77. Jennifer Schuessler and Elizabeth Harris, "Artists and Writers Warn of an 'Intolerant Climate': Reaction Is Swift," *New York Times*, July 7, 2020.

78. Williams, *Truth and Truthfulness*. The Q-Anon movement might be such an example.

79. Elizabeth Anscombe is frequently mentioned as the founder of contemporary virtue ethics (*Intention*; "On Brute Facts"; *Metaphysics and the Philosophy of Mind*). Martha Nussbaum (*The Fragility of Goodness*; *From Disgust to Humanity*; "The Future of Feminist Liberalism") is one of the most important virtue ethicists, along with Bernard Williams (*Ethics and the Limits of Philosophy*; *Morality*), Philippa Foot (*Moral Dilemmas and Other Topics in Moral Philosophy*; *Natural Goodness*; *Virtues and Vices and Other Essays* [1978 and 2002]; and her introduction to Quinn, *Morality and Action*), and Amélie Rorty (*The Many Faces of Philosophy*; *Mind in Action*; Rorty and Flanagan, *Identity, Character, and Morality*).

80. A major critique of virtue ethics concerns its failure to provide guidance on how we should act, since it stipulates no clear principles for guiding action, no ultimate value—truth, duty, etc.—to be fostered. It specifies only that one should act as a virtuous person would in a given situation. Beyond the somewhat vague admonition to develop "human flourishing," the particular values and the individual's ability to cultivate the right virtues will be determined by factors beyond a person's control, such as the time and culture in which one is born.

81. Balot, *Courage in the Democratic Polis: Ideology and Critique*.

82. Dobbs, "For Lack of Wisdom."

83. Pangle, *The Moral Foundations of Aristotelian Political Philosophy*.

84. James, *What Pragmatism Means*; Scorza, "The Ambivalence of Political Courage"; Kateb, "Courage as a Virtue."

85. Avramenko, *Courage: The Politics of Life and Limb*.

86. Avramenko, *Courage: The Politics of Life and Limb*; Gilligan, "Hearing the Difference"; Simola, "Understanding Moral Courage through a Feminist and Developmental Ethic of Care."

87. Care ethics focuses on relationships and dependencies. It contextualizes and promotes the well-being of care receivers and caregivers in a network of social relations, asking what motivates some people to care for the vulnerable and the dependent; further, it assumes that memories of being cared for oneself influence this care. In *On Caring*, Milton Mayeroff provided a precursor to care ethics, but it was the psychologist Carol Gilligan and the philosopher Nel Noddings who really shaped the field of care ethics by charging traditional moral approaches with male bias. They claimed the "voice of care" offered a legitimate alternative to the "justice perspective" of liberal human-rights theory. Other feminist theorists who advocate for a

broader conceptualization of the political include Virginia Held, Eva Feder Kittay, Sara Ruddick, and Joan Tronto, some of the most influential among many subsequent contributors to care ethics.

Typically contrasted with deontological/Kantian and consequentialist/utilitarian ethics, care ethics has affinities with moral perspectives such as African ethics, Confucian ethics, and others. Critics fault care ethics with a slave morality, essentialism, parochialism, and ambiguity. While not synonymous with feminist ethics, much has been written about care ethics as a feminine and feminist ethic, in relation to motherhood, international relations, and political theory. Care ethics has been widely applied to a number of moral issues and ethical fields, extending to the care of animals, the environment, bioethics, and, more recently, public policy. Originally confined to the private and intimate spheres of life, care ethics recently has branched out into political theory and social movements designed to foster a broader understanding of, and public support for, caregiving activities in full scope.

88. Avramenko, *Courage: The Politics of Life and Limb*.

89. Avramenko, *Courage: The Politics of Life and Limb*; Sekerka and Bagozzi, "Moral Courage in the Workplace"; Corlett, "Virtue Lost"; Lindh, Barbosa da Silva, Berg, and Severinsson, "Courage and Nursing Practice."

90. Madison, *Federalist* No. 51.

91. Arendt, *The Human Condition*.

92. Shklar, *Ordinary Vices*.

93. Tocqueville, *Democracy in America*.

94. Scorza, *Strong Liberalism*.

95. It is important to note that Staub's major work focuses on heroic actions; it is based on research on rescuers, on the development of caring and helping, and recent discussions about heroism, not on moral courage as a separate phenomenon, except in part. But part of Staub's larger enterprise asks: how do socialization and life experiences develop personal characteristics that join with people's immediate surroundings and their broader circumstances—what is happening in their group, culture, society, and world—in giving rise to or inhibiting "active bystandership"? (Staub, *Positive Social Behavior and Morality*). Staub's work, like much of the literature that draws from social psychology, focuses on the socialization of children and the experiences of children and adults that lead them to become caring and helpful (or not). Another focus is on the socialization and experiences required for moral courage in the face of opposition and at the risk of potential or actual negative consequences. Because Staub finds that socialization and life experiences are fundamental to this development, he holds that by changing these factors, one can individually (and collectively) create a world in which people are caring and then use that caring to help others and promote well-being. In other words, things such as moral courage can be taught. Interestingly, however, Staub's 1970 study suggests that children do *not* become more helpful as they age, with more time to learn to care about others and with more competence to help (Staub, "A Child in Distress"). But some social psychologists find that children were much less likely to help as they got older. Further analyses revealed that, as children learn rules of appropriate everyday behavior, these rules may, in certain circumstances and under certain conditions, inhibit helping (Eisenberg, Spinrad, and Eggum, "Emotion-Related Self-Regulation and Its Relation to Children's Maladjustment").

96. Staub, "The Roots and Prevention of Genocide," 1.

97. Staub, "The Roots and Prevention of Genocide," 1.

98. Staub, "The Roots and Prevention of Genocide," 2.

99. The specifics of the risk and the potential cost to the actor need not be known, but the evidence suggests some awareness of risk and cost is central to moral courage.

100. See Locke, *Second Treatise of Government*; Rawls, *Justice as Fairness*; Mill, *On Liberty and Other Writings*.

Chapter Two

1. I do not give page numbers for quotes from these individuals since their transcripts are not printed in full here. Full transcripts are available on request and will be available in print in later volumes.

2. Monroe, *The Heart of Altruism*.

3. An excellent introduction to narrative analysis is Andrews, Squire, and Tamboukou, *Doing Narrative Research*, which discusses narrative methodology in a multidisciplinary manner. The different chapters by some of the key players in the development of narrative analysis highlight the theoretical underpinnings of narrative analysis. Opening with a discussion of how one makes the initial decisions about what kind of form of narrative to employ, the book considers more intricate issues of interpretation, research context, and issues of reflexivity. Andrews's own book *Narrative Imagination in Everyday Life* analyzes the link between narrative and imagination and speculates on why stories lead us to ponder what it means to be human. Andrews argues that stories and imagination influence our thoughts about what we see and do as well as our ability to contemplate what is possible and what our limitations are. See also Andrews, *Shaping History*, which draws on extraordinary personal accounts to provide a unique lens through which we can view some of the major political changes of our time.

4. See the appendix in Monroe, *The Hand of Compassion*.

5. The *perestroika* movement in political science was all about increasing methodological pluralism (Monroe, *Perestroika! The Raucous Revolution in Political Science*). Thankfully, today most researchers advocate a multimethod approach in which one examines the same phenomenon from different vantage points.

6. See the works of Barthes listed in the bibliography: *A Barthes Reader*; *Critical Essays*; *Criticism and Truth*; *How to Live Together*; *New Critical Essays*; *The Responsibility of Forms*; and *The Semiotic Challenge*.

7. Andrews, *Shaping History*; Monroe, *The Hand of Compassion*; Tilly, *Stories, Identities, and Political Change*.

8. See Hanisch, "The Personal Is Political." This association flows from good reasoning. An American feminist, Hanisch argues that many personal experiences originate in a person's—especially a woman's—place in a system of power relationships. (If Jane is being abused by John, society's oppression plays an important part in explaining this abuse.)

9. Twenty-first-century feminist activists define the personal as political, as when it argues that beauty and thinness in particular are associated with a woman's success. Beyond Carol Hanisch and Betty Friedan, see interesting related work by Simone de Beauvoir (*The Second Sex*) and Catharine MacKinnon (*Feminism Unmodified*; *Pornography as Defamation and Discrimination*; *Sexual Harassment of Working Women*), who was among the first to argue that pornography is a civil rights violation and that sexual harassment in education and employment constitutes sex discrimination; and activists such as Waris Dirie, who argue against that most personal political problem: female genital mutilation.

10. This approach also draws on care ethics, which itself owes a debt to a broader conceptualization of the political. Care ethics originated in the feminist philosophical perspective that emphasizes the importance of a relational and context-bound approach toward morality and ethical decision-making. It contrasts starkly with ethical theories—such as Kantian deontology or utilitarianism—that rely on principles to highlight moral actions; it is not intended to be absolute and incontrovertible. See Noddings, *Caring: A Relational Approach*, and "Stories and Affect in Teacher Education," in which the author stresses relationships between people and finds the impulse to care a universal one.

11. Didion, *We Tell Ourselves Stories in Order to Live*.

12. See again Noddings, *Caring: A Relational Approach*; Noddings, "Stories and Affect in Teacher Education."

13. It is not just my students who were deeply affected by the interviews they did. The transcribers of the interviews with both Loretta Lynch and Heather Booth wrote telling me how impressed they were by these two individuals, and that they hoped they could meet them one day.

14. At ninety-four years of age, Janusz just published his latest book (Reykowski, *Disenchantment with Democracy*).

15. Brockmeier, "Pathways of Narrative Meaning Construction."

16. See the interesting work of Francesca Polleta on the drawbacks of narrative. For example, readers may be so absorbed by a story that they do not offer a counterargument. Polleta notes that the traditional view of stories holds that they create the empathy necessary to make us want to aid someone because we can put ourselves in another's place. But simply knowing about someone may not necessarily make one more sympathetic to that person's plight, nor do stories necessarily empower or persuade people (Conversation in seminar at the UCI Ethics Center, April 2019.-.

Chapter Four

1. The Rampart scandal in 1990s Los Angeles, so called because it revealed extensive police corruption in the antigang unit of the Los Angeles Police Department's Rampart division (full name: Community Resources Against Street Hoodlums [CRASH]), was the largest documented instance of police corruption in American history, with offenses ranging from unprovoked shootings and beatings to bank robberies and the planting of false evidence. Also included were dealing narcotics, theft, and, of course, the resultant perjury and cover-up of evidence of these activities. Eventually, over seventy police officers associated with the Rampart CRASH unit were found to have committed some kind of misconduct. Seventy officers were accused, but only fifty-eight were charged; charges against the other twelve were dismissed for insufficient evidence. The internal administrative board found only twenty-four of these officers guilty of wrongdoing. Twelve were suspended, seven resigned or retired, and five were terminated. Because of findings that the police falsified evidence and perjured themselves, 106 prior criminal convictions eventually were overturned and more than 140 civil lawsuits were filed against Los Angeles, costing roughly $125 million in settlements. The political fallout from the scandal was enormous. Mayor James K. Hahn refused to rehire police chief Bernard Parks in 2002, and this decision, coupled with the scandal, probably led to Hahn's defeat by Antonio Villaraigosa in 2005.

2. Vandenberg is actually a space force base. It is located nine miles northwest of Lompoc, California.

3. During a protest commemorating the seventieth anniversary of the bombing of Hiroshima, Dennis Apel, a longtime political activist and founder of the Catholic Worker community in Guadalupe, California, was arrested; he served four months in federal prison for crossing what is called the "green line." Apel and his wife were protesting US military expenditures while, the Apels argued, the government ignored the poor and failed to provide adequate housing, health care, education, food, and transportation for the working poor. The case turned on whether or not Apel had been on military property and, since technically, at least, the Pacific Coast highway runs through the military base, the Court found against Apel, 9-0.

Chapter Five

1. The murders to which Heather refers are known as the Mississippi Burning murders, the Freedom Summer murders, or the Mississippi civil rights workers' murders. The activists Andrew Goodman, Michael Schwerner, and James Chaney were abducted and murdered in June 1964 in Neshoba County, Mississippi. Like Heather, the three men were attempting to register African-Americans in Mississippi so they could vote, thereby overturning the seventy-year policy of disenfranchisement of Black voters, by-laws, and practices that began immediately after the Civil War. Sadly, since 2021 we have again been seeing serious state attempts to limit the ability to vote.

2. Transcribed by Sunny Sun.

3. According to various sources, out of roughly 73,199,999 million votes cast, Nixon received between 31,710,470 and 31,783,783 votes and Humphrey between 30,898,055 and 31,271,839 votes, with 9,901,118 going to George Wallace and 47,118 to Dick Gregory.

4. Interestingly, an example of this is Jerome Tobis, Heather's father, who was a physician at the medical school at UCI. Among the many things that he did after he retired was to set up a free health clinic with other retired doctors. Because they didn't charge anything, they didn't have to go through all the forms with insurance. When Tobis was in his nineties, he was diagnosed with stomach cancer, which is very painful. The drugs he took for the pain made him groggy, so he had only a few good hours each day when he was awake. The last thing he did on the day he died was spend his precious four waking hours with patients at the free clinic he'd established: he went to see patients. Jerry Tobis's death, that's the kind of death you want to have. That's the kind of life that you want to have, where he did something concrete to help others. He had a skill. It wasn't a political skill in the way that some of Heather's skills are political. It was political in the sense that it helped other people, and so that's a very good example of how everyone can do something that matters. Heather's story also related how one of the things her father did when he realized Heather was determined to go down south was to organize a network of physicians so that if people working on the civil rights movement got sick or were harmed physically, they could find medical personnel who would treat them, because not every doctor was going to treat a civil rights worker or a Black person.

Chapter Seven

1. While finalizing the editing of these transcripts, I wrote each speaker for their approval, asking if they wished to use a pseudonym, to protect their privacy. The woman interviewed for this chapter wrote back: "Can we have my name as Amal? It's my grandmother's name. It means 'hope,' and it's what I wish my story to offer those who have been through hard times like mine." The interview was done via phone.

2. A coastal city in southwest Cameroon, Doula dates from the German colonial period.

3. Also called the Festival of Breaking the Fast, Eid al-Fitr is a major Muslim religious holiday. It marks the end of Ramadan—the Muslim holy month of fasting—and is the first and only day in the month of Shawwal when Muslims are not allowed to fast.

4. An island group in Thailand, the Phi Phi Islands are found between the large island of Phuket and the Straits of Malacca coast of Thailand.

Chapter Eight

1. As of this writing, Judge Dorothy Wright Nelson is a senior United States circuit judge of the United States Court of Appeals for the Ninth Circuit.

2. FERC refers to the Federal Energy Regulatory Commission, the US federal agency that regulates the transmission and wholesale sale of electricity and natural gas in interstate commerce. FERC also regulates the transport of oil by pipeline in interstate commerce.

3. John Van de Kamp was a top Los Angeles county prosecutor before running for governor. He was accused of being too robotic and dull to be governor, criticisms that stuck during the 1990 Democratic primary, when he ran against Dianne Feinstein. Van de Kamp never again sought high political office and died in 2017 at the age of eighty-one.

4. A college professor, Delaine Eastin is the only woman elected California State Superintendent of Public Instruction (1995–2003) under Governors Pete Wilson and Gray Davis. Eastin was a Democrat who represented parts of Alameda County and Santa Clara County in the California State Assembly between 1986 and 1994.

5. Hyatt is an entrepreneur, lecturer, philanthropist, former attorney, and Democratic politician who raises funds and has served as a foreign policy advisor. He founded Hyatt Legal Services and Current TV.

6. Metzenbaum was a millionaire and Democratic senator from Ohio (1974, 1976–1995).

7. Lay is now remembered best for his involvement in what is commonly known as the Enron scandal. Lay founded and was CEO and chairman of the Enron Corporation for most of its existence. At its peak, Enron was valued at $63 billion, but it was shown, as the crisis Loretta describes was unraveling, to have used misleading and illegal practices to hide and embezzle funds and to mislead its auditor, Arthur Andersen, the fifth-largest accounting company in the world. The deception was discovered in 2000, making the Enron scandal the largest bankruptcy in the world, and one that destroyed Arthur Andersen because it had failed to discover the fraud. Lay was tried and found guilty of ten counts of securities fraud. Three months before his October 23 sentencing, Lay died at sixty-four, while on vacation, probably from a heart attack caused by coronary artery disease. Because his case was under appeal at the time of his death, his conviction was vacated.

8. Rubin served as Secretary of the Treasury under President Bill Clinton. Before this he had spent twenty-six years at Goldman Sachs, where he was a board member and co-chairman (1990–1992). While in office, Rubin was critical in loosening regulations for the financial industry, especially for weakening regulations that had been in place since the 1930s and were designed to protect investors. After leaving the Department of the Treasury, Rubin returned as director and senior counselor of Citigroup, which benefited immensely from the reforms he had instituted. When Rubin resigned as chairman of Citigroup on January 9, 2009, he was given over $126 million in cash and stock for his service to the company, through and including Citigroup's bailout by the US Treasury. Rubin has been strongly criticized for his policies, especially his

opposition to any regulation of collateralized debt obligations, credit default swaps, and other so-called derivative financial instruments, which, it is widely accepted now, created havoc for companies and disastrous consequences for the economy but were nonetheless the chief engine of profitability for Wall Street, including Rubin's former employer, Goldman Sachs.

9. In terms of Loretta's story, Rubin generated controversy in 2001 by contacting an acquaintance at the US Treasury to influence it to convince bond-rating agencies not to downgrade Enron's corporate debt. Enron at that time was a debtor of Citigroup. The Treasury official refused Rubin's request, but Rubin was subsequently investigated by Congress, which cleared him of having done anything illegal.

10. Kuehl is a politician, former child actor, and most recently a member of the Los Angeles County Board of Supervisors for the Third District. In 1994 she became California's first openly gay legislator.

11. Joe X was also interviewed for this project. We quote from him occasionally but were not able to include his full interview here. We thank Joe for his cooperation.

12. Once a popular governor and possible presidential candidate, Davis's career came to a halt largely because of the electricity crisis Loretta describes. Davis also had a damaging budget crisis caused by the bursting of the dot-com bubble and a car tax. Davis's fundraising efforts and negative campaigning were key additional causes behind a recall election on October 7, 2003. Davis was succeeded in office on November 17, 2003, by a Republican, the actor Arnold Schwarzenegger. As this book manuscript goes for review (May 2019), Davis is a lecturer at the UCLA School of Public Affairs and an attorney at Loeb & Loeb, as Loretta describes.

13. In 2021 Gavin Newsom also survived a recall vote.

Chapter Nine

1. Vikram Tej is a pseudonym for a man who was seventy-two years old when interviewed.
2. Tej is speaking to his granddaughter.

Chapter Ten

1. California State Senator Joe was included in the analysis and gave tentative approval of his interview but never responded to our many requests for formal approval, so his interview was unable to be included. We thank Senator Joe for his participation in the project, along with so many others whose conversations we recorded and analyzed but could not present in this book for reasons of space. Our quotes from the interviews in this chapter are often shortened (that is, some material is omitted from the full quote) to keep the analysis focused and brief. Full citations are noted in parentheses after each quote so the reader can find them in the transcripts printed as chapters 3–9 and be assured that the omissions were made simply for brevity and clarity. None of the deletions change the basic substance of the quotes.

2. Staub, "The Roots and Prevention of Genocide," 1.

3. What values? How much opposition, and of what sort? And what does "doing the right thing" mean in more concrete terms? These are some of the questions into which we needed to gain more insight.

4. Interviews with Janusz and Nini were analyzed but are not printed in full here, for reasons of space. Their full interviews will be included in a forthcoming volume. Other interviews

quoted and analyzed but not published here in full are those of Senator Joe, Choo-Tee Lim, Richard Ceballos, and anonymous undocumented immigrants (DREAMers).

5. The danger Heather's parents feared was real. Indeed, the woman Heather stayed with was killed by the local sheriff, who fired a gun directly into her face. This grew out of a class-action lawsuit over the equal distribution of municipal infrastructure and services. *Hawkins v. Town of Shaw*, 437 F.2d 1286 (5th Cir. 1971). The case came to the United States Court of Appeals for the Fifth Circuit. The plaintiffs were all Black citizens of Shaw, including the Hawkins family, with whom Heather stayed. As Heather describes in her interview (chap. 5), the tax monies for municipal services were disproportionately spent in the white neighborhoods, which had paved streets, storm drains, street lights, good water pressure, etc. The Black community had few if any of these facilities. The Court of Appeals overruled the United States District Court for the Northern District of Mississippi, finding in favor of the Black plaintiffs, and ordered Shaw to draw up a plan to equalize its services. During this time the Hawkins family had its house set on fire twice; the second fire killed the Shaws' son Andrew and two of their granddaughters. In 1972 Mary Lou Hawkins was shot and killed by a Black Shaw police officer, who was eventually tried for manslaughter but was acquitted.

6. Staub, "The Roots and Prevention of Genocide," 1.

7. See Foot, *Moral Dilemmas and Other Topics in Moral Philosophy*; Foot, *Natural Goodness*; Foot, *Virtues and Vices and Other Essays* (1978 and 2002); Pianalto, "Moral Conviction."

8. Reykowski has written extensively on questions concerning ethics through his academic work on democracy, justice, prosocial behavior, altruism, and social identity, as is revealed in a list of his major books and articles over a long and distinguished career. See Staub, Bar-Tal, Karylowski, and Reykowski, *Development and Maintenance of Prosocial Behavior*; Eisenberg, Reykowski, and Staub, *Social and Moral Values*; Reykowski, "Patriotism and the Collective System of Meanings"; Reykowski, "The Justice Motive and Altruistic Helping."

9. Janus Reykowski's interview was analyzed but has not been included here for reasons of space.

10. Keneally, *Schindler's Ark*.

11. Monroe, *The Heart of Altruism*; Monroe, *The Hand of Compassion*.

12. Nini's interview was analyzed but is not included here for reasons of space.

13. Pianalto, "Moral Courage and Facing Others," 165–166.

14. "Moral courage requires facing others as moral subjects/agents." Pianalto, "Moral Courage and Facing Others," 166.

15. Pianalto, "Moral Courage and Facing Others"; Staub, "The Roots and Prevention of Genocide."

16. As Kay notes in the coda to her interview, her life has changed dramatically since our conversations took place.

17. Pianalto, "Moral Conviction"; Pianalto, "Moral Courage and Facing Others." The latter was the winning entry for the Robert Papazian Annual Essay Prize on Themes from Ethics and Political Philosophy,

18. Staub also includes "the ability to take others' role or perspective: walking in their shoes" ("The Roots and Prevention of Genocide," 4), but he does not clarify how this differs from empathy. We do not find a clear distinction between what Staub calls "personal characteristics" and what he identifies as the contributing factors (such as agency), so we put them all in the category of personal characteristics.

19. "Since Donald Trump took office one year ago, perhaps no American has called into question the legal and ethical behavior of the president with more persistence and authority than Erwin Chemerinsky. One of the country's preeminent constitutional scholars, and the [new] dean of the University of California, Berkeley's law school, Chemerinsky has sounded the alarm from day one of Trump's administration—most strenuously over the president's alleged daily violation of the emoluments clause of the Constitution. Those provisions bar the president from receiving any form of payment from a foreign government, and also from receiving any payments beyond the salary of the chief executive. Last month, a federal court dismissed a lawsuit that Chemerinsky and other leading legal authorities had helped prepare seeking to stop the president from accepting any further payments—that decision is currently being appealed." Danny Feingold, "Erwin Chemerinsky and the Case against Trump," *Capital & Main*, January 9, 2019, 1, accessed October 6, 2020, https:capitalandmain.com. In the end, Chemerinsky's suit came to naught. The Supreme Court vacated opinions from the 2nd US Circuit Court of Appeals and the 4th US Circuit Court of Appeals and returned cases brought by the attorneys general of Maryland, the District of Columbia, and a government watchdog group, holding them moot since Trump was no longer in office.

20. By all accounts, Chemerinsky did a wonderful job as dean of a new law school. Since I interviewed him, Chemerinsky has become dean of Berkeley's law school.

21. Instituted in 1963 to recognize and honor those who helped save Jews during World War II, the Yad Vashem medal is given by the state of Israel to people—or their next of kin—who rescued Jews during the Holocaust. The award is given only after a rigorous process of certification. The Yad Vashem Law authorizes Yad Vashem "to confer honorary citizenship of the State of Israel upon the Righteous Among the Nations, and commemorative citizenship if they have passed away, in recognition of their actions." The medal and the designation of Righteous Among the Nations is given only to individuals, not to groups. The phrase comes from the Talmud and translates roughly to "whosoever saves one life, saves the entire world." As of 2019, there are over 26,973 Yad Vashem medal recipients, but, as Nini's story illustrates, many more people did risk their lives to save Jews.

22. Sophal Ear's interview was analyzed but is not included here for reasons of space.

23. Senator Joe's interview was analyzed but is not included here for reasons of space.

24. We did not include any interviews with DREAMers, although we interviewed several. In part, this was for reasons of space. But we also did not want to risk—however inadvertently—revealing the identity of anyone in a vulnerable position.

25. On December 26, 2004, a magnitude 9.1 earthquake struck beneath the Indian Ocean near Indonesia, generating a massive tsunami that claimed over 230,000 lives in fourteen different countries. The tsunami Amal survived was one of the deadliest natural disasters ever recorded.

26. Torres's interview was analyzed but is not included here for reasons of space.

27. This process reminded me of a Joan Didion quote: "We are well-advised to keep on nodding terms with the people we used to be, whether we find them attractive company or not. Otherwise they turn up unannounced and surprise us, come hammering on the mind's door at 4 a.m. of a bad night and demand to know who deserted them, who betrayed them, who is going to make amends. We forget all too soon the things we thought we could never forget. We forget the loves and the betrayals alike, forget what we whispered and what we screamed, forget who we were." Didion, *Slouching towards Bethlehem*.

28. Marion Pritchard, in Gardner, *The Courage to Care*.

29. Hester is the heroine of Nathaniel Hawthorne's *The Scarlet Letter* (1850). Set in Puritan Massachusetts in 1642–1649, Hester Prynne has an affair that results in an out-of-wedlock child and, as a result, is forced to wear the scarlet letter "A," for adultery, on her dress. The book dwells on topics of sin, guilt, redemption, and dignity, and Hester struggles to forge an honorable life for herself and her daughter, Pearl; in the end, she succeeds. It is considered a classic of American literature.

30. Interview analyzed but not included for reasons of space.

31. The thirty-seventh governor of California, from January 4, 1999, to November 17, 2003, Davis was known for having a pay-to-play administration and was recalled in November 2003.

Conclusion

I am indebted to Monica De Roche, Jessica Gonzalez, and Ben Hoyt, extraordinary UCI graduate students who worked at the UCI Ethics Center during the summers of 2019, 2020, and 2021, for their work on both the literature review and the data analysis for this book. Each of them worked closely with me to lead a team of high school and college students, mentoring them to show them how to do research by working on this project. Additional thanks go to Barbara Dosher, Chloe Lampros-Monroe, and Lawrence Sporty for helping me understand my own thoughts about moral courage and ethics. Finally, I was greatly assisted in the analysis of findings presented here by the students in the UCI Ethics Center Summer Internship program, 2019–2021, mentioned by name in the acknowledgments and on the UCI Ethics Center website. Special thanks go to Hannah and Isabelle Dastgheib, Aniket Kamat, Alexis Kim, Steven Ma, Maximilian Razmjoo, and Samuel Shih.

1. I think of the dominant philosophical approach in the United States as the Anglo-American tradition, growing out of the social-contract theory and utilitarian and Kantian philosophy, with a heavy emphasis on moral reasoning and moral choice. But virtue ethics, as noted in chapter 10, also has limitations, according to my analysis.

2. Without going into an elaborate discussion of the various schools of philosophy, and recognizing that these schools may not be separated along hard and fast lines, we can juxtapose what is often thought of as analytical philosophy with continental philosophy and virtue ethics, among others. By analytical philosophy, an approach that perhaps dominates the philosophical tradition in the Anglo-American world, we refer to works characterized by an emphasis on language, rigor, and clarity in arguments, and an emphasis on formal logic and math. This approach might be juxtaposed to continental philosophy, especially Hegelianism, existentialism, and phenomenology, or to virtue ethics.

3. See Kidder, *Moral Courage*.

4. The virtue approach, which grew out of Aristotelian ethics, was picked up by Anglo-American philosophers in the early 1950s. It focuses on character rather than action dictated by moral principles or rules, such as the Ten Commandments in Christianity, the Quran in Islam, or the Talmud in Judaism.

5. Moral courage thus falls into the virtue ethics camp in the philosophical gap between virtue ethics and approaches such as the two major approaches in the Anglo-American world, Kantian ethics and utilitarian ethics, which place greater emphasis on conscious, deliberative ethics and agonistic choice. In her excellent article "Virtue Ethics: A Misleading Category?," Martha Nussbaum argues that the distinction between these approaches is weaker than traditionally assumed, with both Kantianism and utilitarianism containing treatments of virtue.

Nussbaum finds one group of virtue ethicists antiutilitarian because (1) of their concern with the plurality of value and (2) what they find is the susceptibility of passions to social cultivation. This group of virtue theorists argues for enlarging the place of reason in ethics, suggesting that reason can both modify the passions and deliberate about ends as well as means. Nussbaum contrasts these theorists with virtue ethicists who are primarily anti-Kantians, believing that reason plays too dominant a role in philosophical accounts of ethics. This group of theorists want to increase the role attributed to sentiments and passions. Nussbaum investigates these differences and concludes by finding it less helpful to speak of virtue ethics as a separate field than to characterize the substantive views of each thinker, at which point we should conclude what we ourselves wish to say.

6. See Foot, *Moral Dilemmas*; Foot, *Natural Goodness*; Foot, *Virtues and Vices and Other Essays* (1978 and 2002); Foot, "Introduction," in Quinn, *Morality and Action*; Pianalto, "Moral Courage and Facing Others."

7. See Miller, *The Mystery of Courage*.

8. Chemerinsky was intimately involved in investigating the Ramparts scandal. As of 2018, the full extent of the Rampart corruption is not known, with several rape, murder, and robbery investigations involving Rampart officers still unsolved.

9. Pianalto, "Moral Courage and Facing Others."

10. See Keneally, *Schindler's Ark*.

11. The role of Pope Pius XII during World War II presents a complicated illustration of this phenomenon. Pius XII has been accused of helping the Nazis or at least remaining silent during the Holocaust. The Israeli consul Pinchas Lapide, in *Three Popes and the Jews*, examines the pope's acts during the Holocaust and concludes that he helped save 860,000 Jews from Nazi death camps (214). But should the pope have done more, especially by speaking out to the Roman Catholics in Poland? The argument traditionally advanced in Pius's defense is that this might have made things worse. Defenders of the pope quote Albert Einstein: "Being a lover of freedom, when the revolution came in Germany, I looked to the universities to defend it, knowing that they had always boasted of their devotion to the cause of truth; but, no, the universities immediately were silenced. Then I looked to the great editors of the newspapers whose flaming editorials in days gone by had proclaimed their love of freedom; but they, like the universities, were silenced in a few short weeks. . . . Only the Church stood squarely across the path of Hitler's campaign for suppressing truth. I never had any special interest in the Church before, but now I feel a great affection and admiration because the Church alone has had the courage and persistence to stand for intellectual truth and moral freedom. I am forced thus to confess that what I once despised I now praise unreservedly" (*Time*, December 23, 1940, 38). I make no assessment of this extensive debate, noting only that the negative assessment of Pope Pius XII seems to date to 1963 with Rolf Hochhuth's play *The Deputy*. Hochhuth saw the pope's silence as cold indifference. He finds unacceptable the idea that Pius XII was powerless against the fascists, viewing the pope as a diplomat whose first charge was to preserve Vatican neutrality so that Vatican City could be a refuge for victims of the war. The best recent work on this question is Zuccotti, *Under His Very Windows*.

12. See Monroe, *Ethics in an Age of Terror and Genocide*; Monroe, *The Hand of Compassion*; Monroe, *The Heart of Altruism*.

13. Foot, *Virtues and Vices and Other Essays*.

14. Foot, *Virtues and Vices and Other Essays*, 17.

15. The review of the literature on moral courage reveals the surprising extent to which most analysts conceptualize moral courage as acts they find morally admirable. But people can hold

NOTES TO CONCLUSION 223

dramatically different moral values and still demonstrate moral courage, can't they? Human beings are complex. How do we parse acts of courage among people whose values we reject? How do we distinguish moral courage from fanaticism? What about brief acts of morality by an otherwise immoral individual within an evil moral system, such as the Third Reich? Do we judge certain acts as admirable simply because they reflect our own moral values? Can a close examination of those who demonstrate moral courage based on *different* standards of morality from those one holds oneself help answer these questions? Can we find a kernel of ethical action that is universal and timeless, or is all morality relative? The second volume will address these questions by contrasting the kind of moral courage in this book—which reflects the liberal, democratic, humanistic values to which most scholars today pay at least lip service—and contrasts this with the moral courage of Thomas More and Martin Luther and the moral courage of Franz Stangl, Albert Speer (Hitler's architect), and Wilhelm Stuckart (co-author of the Nuremberg laws and participant in the Wannsee Conference, at which the Final Solution was that developed).

16. Pianalto, "Moral Courage and Facing Others."
17. Pianalto, "Moral Courage and Facing Others," 170.
18. According to its website (http://www.midwestacademy.com), "The Midwest Academy is a national training institute committed to advancing the struggle for social, economic, and racial justice. From local neighborhood groups to statewide and national organizations, the Midwest Academy has trained over twenty-five thousand grassroots activists from hundreds of organizations and coalitions. Midwest Academy teaches an organizing philosophy, methods and skills that enable ordinary people to actively participate in the democratic process. Courses and consulting services are designed for progressive organizations and coalitions that utilize civic engagement activities to build citizen power at all levels of our democracy. Over the years, the Academy has been instrumental in helping to build statewide coalitions in many states. Today, the Academy continues to provide training to these multi-issue, statewide organizations, as well as to numerous other groups, ranging from students to senior citizens and from neighborhood to national organizations."
19. A civil rights organization, the National Association for the Advancement of Colored People (NAACP) was formed in 1909 to advance justice for African Americans. Leading founders included W. E. B. Du Bois, Mary White Covington, and Moorefield Story. Its goal was "to ensure the political, educational, social, and economic equality of rights of all persons and to eliminate race-based discrimination." The NAACP does political lobbying, publicity, and litigation, expanding on the original twentieth-century mission to address concerns about economic development and inequality, police misconduct, and the status of Black foreign refugees. The organization has retained its original name—thus retaining the once-common term *colored people*—to refer to those Americans with some African ancestry.
20. Lakoff and Johnson, *Metaphors We Live By*; Lakoff and Johnson, *Philosophy in the Flesh*.
21. See Knobe, "What Is Experimental Philosophy?," and Knobe and Nichols, "An Experimental Philosophy Manifesto," as illustrations of work in experimental philosophy.
22. Monroe, *Ethics in an Age of Terror and Genocide*; Monroe, *The Hand of Compassion*; Monroe, *The Heart of Altruism*.
23. I had assigned Nussbaum's *Fragility of Goodness*, one of my favorite books but not easy reading for most undergraduates. I told the students it was a more difficult book to tackle than the rest of the reading and suggested they give it extra time, and that they would be rewarded by being in the presence of a first-rate intellect thinking seriously about ethics and how stories

could teach ethics. Many students commented on how excellent and insightful they found the book, noting it was indeed tough but well worth the effort.

24. I was pleased to hear such comments, feeling these were not students who were particularly drawn to a course on ethics, but merely students who chose the course to fulfill a graduation requirement. If an ethics course could affect these students, I figured, all the better.

25. It is not just my students who were deeply affected by the interviews they did. As I conducted follow-up interviews to supplement those done by the students, I needed to find people to transcribe the recorded conversations. The transcribers for the interviews with both Loretta Lynch and Heather Booth wrote to tell me how amazed they were by these two individuals and express their hope that perhaps they could someday actually meet these two remarkable women.

26. Reykowski's most recent book, *Disenchantment with Democracy*, published when he was eighty-nine, contains his thoughts on democracies.

27. Readers interested in more specifics about the deeper lessons my students learned from this project may write asking to view essays from students about their interviews, such as the one written by the granddaughter of Choo Tee Lim.

28. Not sharing this belief, I remember being struck the first time I saw an enactment of the execution of Henry VIII's wives. Both women paused before being killed to praise their wonderful king and husband for his compassion, generosity, and wisdom. What was wrong with these women, I wondered? The guy is cutting off your head because he wants to marry someone else, and you're thanking him for being so wonderful? Of course, later reflection made it clear that this was standard operating procedure for those executed in Tudor times (and probably others); it was an attempt to keep the king from taking vengeance on the victim's remaining family members. This was especially important for Anne Boleyn, whose brother Henry had already been killed, and who wanted to ensure the survival of her child, Elizabeth—a child who grew up to be a greater monarch than Henry ever thought of being.

29. Monroe, *A Darkling Plain*.

30. Monroe, *A Darkling Plain*.

31. The Stasi was the Ministry for State Security (Ministerium für Staatssicherheit) for the GDR. It was one of the most repressive and effective state police ever to operate. Based in East Berlin, the Stasi motto was "Schild und Schwert der Partei" (Shield and Sword of the Party), which referred to the Stasi's dedication to protecting the ruling Socialist Unity Party of Germany (Sozialistische Einheitspartei Deutschlands). Resembling the Soviet KGB, the Stasi was headed by Erich Mielke for thirty-two of the forty years the GDR existed, and its main task was spying on its own people. It developed a vast network of citizens who became informants, either by choice or under pressure. After the Berlin Wall fell and German reunification began in 1990, many Stasi officials were prosecuted for their crimes, and the Stasi files were opened so that any citizen could inspect their personal file on request. All of these events are featured in the 2006 German film *Das Leben der Anderen* (The lives of others), which touches on these political events but highlights the ability of art and of other human beings to affect our lives.

32. Overly conscientious and always caring for others, my father took on the unwanted task of trying to reform the prison system in Madison and St. Clair counties. He also was preparing to leave for a judges' conference and stayed late at the courthouse, working. He fell asleep at the wheel of the car on the way home and died at 3 A.M. in a one-car accident.

33. *The Testament of Mary*, Colm Tóibín's story of the crucifixion told from the point of view of Christ's mother, captures this brilliantly, as Mary seeks to escape not the terror of being watched and threatened by the political authorities, but rather the unbearable, horrifying

memory of her own mind. Tóibín describes so accurately the fear and pain I felt after my father died that I had difficulty getting through the first few pages of his brilliant book.

34. Perhaps it was the felicitous accident of rereading the Steinbeck book for another class, just as I was writing the conclusion to this book. Often described as Steinbeck's love letter to democracy, *The Moon Is Down* was crafted after Steinbeck's own bitter journey through the Great Depression and in the depths of World War II, when it was not at all clear that the Allies would win the war. Steinbeck's fictional characters articulate what the morally courageous in this book also tell us.

Bibliography

Adelman, Jeremy, ed. *The Essential Hirschman*. Princeton, NJ: Princeton University Press, 2013.
———. *Worldly Philosopher: The Odyssey of Albert O. Hirschman*. Princeton, NJ: Princeton University Press, 2013.
Andrews, Molly. *Narrative Imagination and Everyday Life*. Oxford and New York: Oxford University Press, 2014.
———. *Shaping History: Narratives of Political Change*. Cambridge and New York: Cambridge University Press, 2007.
Andrews, Molly, Corinne Squire, and Maria Tamboukou, eds. *Doing Narrative Research*. London and Thousand Oaks, CA: Sage Publications, 2008.
Anscombe, G. E. M. *Intention*. Oxford: Blackwell, 1957.
———. *Metaphysics and the Philosophy of Mind: Collected Philosophical Papers*. Vol. 2. Oxford: Basil Blackwell, 1981.
———. "On Brute Facts." *Analysis* 18, no. 3 (1958): 69–72.
Aquinas, Thomas. *The Cardinal Virtues: Prudence, Justice, Fortitude, and Temperance*. Translated by Richard J. Regan. Indianapolis, IN: Hackett, 2005.
Arendt, Hannah. *The Human Condition*. Chicago: University of Chicago Press, 1998.
Aristotle. *Nicomachean Ethics*. Translated by Terence Irwin. Indianapolis, IN: Hackett, 1999.
Avramenko, Richard. *Courage: The Politics of Life and Limb*. Notre Dame, IN: University of Notre Dame Press, 2011.
Baier, Annette. "Knowing Our Place in the Animal World." In *Ethics and Animals*, edited by Harlan B. Miller and William H. Williams, 61–77. Clifton, NJ: Humana Press, 1983.
———. "The Need for More than Justice." In *Feminist Theory: A Philosophical Anthology*, edited by Ann E. Cudd and Robin O. Andreasen, 243–250. Oxford, UK and Malden, MA: Blackwell, 2005.
Balot, Ryan Krieger. "Courage in the Democratic Polis." *Classical Quarterly* 54, no. 2 (2004): 406–423.
———. *Courage in the Democratic Polis: Ideology and Critique in Classical Athens*. Oxford and New York: Oxford University Press, 2014.
———. "The Dark Side of Democratic Courage." *Social Research: An International Quarterly* 71, no. 1 (2004): 73–106.

Barthes, Roland. *A Barthes Reader*. New York: Hill & Wang, 1982.
———. *Critical Essays*. Evanston, IL: Northwestern University Press, 1972.
———. *Criticism and Truth*. London: Athlone Press, 1987.
———. *How to Live Together: Notes for a Lecture Course and Seminar at the Collège de France (1976–1977)*. New York: Columbia University Press, 2013.
———. *New Critical Essays*. Berkeley and Los Angeles: University of California Press, 1990.
———. *The Responsibility of Forms: Critical Essays on Music, Art, and Representation*. Oxford: Basil Blackwell, 1985.
———. *The Semiotic Challenge*. Berkeley and Los Angeles: University of California Press, 1994.
Beauvoir, Simone de. *The Second Sex*. 1949. New York: Vintage Books, 2011.
Brockmeier, Jens. "Pathways of Narrative Meaning Construction." In *The Development of Social Cognition and Communication*, edited by Bruce D. Homer and Catherine Tamis-LeMonda, 291–313. Mahway, NJ: Lawrence Erlbaum, 2005.
———. "The Text of the Mind." In *The Mind as a Scientific Object: Between Brain and Culture*, edited by Christina E. Erneling and David Martel Johnson, 432–452. Oxford and New York: Oxford University Press, 2005.
Chapa, Olga, and Donna Stringer. "The Path of Measuring Moral Courage in the Workplace." *SAM Advanced Management Journal* 78, no. 2 (2013): 17–24.
Cicero, Marcus Tullius. *On Obligations*. Translated by P. G. Walsh. Oxford and New York: Oxford University Press, 2000.
Corlett, John. "Virtue Lost: Courage in Sport." *Journal of the Philosophy of Sport* 25, no. 1 (1996): 45–57.
Cox, David, Richard Hallam, Kieron O'Connor, and Stanley Rachman. "An Experimental Analysis of Fearlessness and Courage." *British Journal of Psychology* 74, no. 1 (1983): 107–117.
Dent, Nicholas J. H. "The Value of Courage." *Philosophy* 56, no. 218 (1981): 574–577.
Devereux, Daniel T. "The Unity of the Virtues in Plato's *Protagoras* and *Laches*." *Philosophical Review* 101, no. 4 (1992): 765–789.
Dickens, Charles. *A Tale of Two Cities: A Story of the French Revolution*. Edited and with an introduction and notes by Richard Maxwell. London: Penguin Classics, 2003.
Didion, Joan. *Slouching towards Bethlehem*. New York: Farrar, Straus & Giroux, 1968.
———. *We Tell Ourselves Stories in Order to Live*. New York: Everyman's Library, 2006.
Dobbs, Darrell. "For Lack of Wisdom: Courage and Inquiry in Plato's *Laches*." *Journal of Politics* 48, no. 4 (1986): 825–849.
Eisenberg, Nancy, Janusz Reykowski, and Ervin Staub, eds. *Social and Moral Values: Individual and Societal Perspectives*. Hillsdale, NJ: Erlbaum, 1989.
Eisenberg, Nancy, Tracy L. Spinrad, and Natalie D. Eggum. "Emotion-Related Self-Regulation and Its Relation to Children's Maladjustment." *Annual Review of Clinical Psychology* 6 (2010): 495–525.
Finfgeld, Deborah L. "Becoming and Being Courageous in the Chronically Ill Elderly." *Issues in Mental Health Nursing* 16, no. 1 (1995): 1–11.
Foot, Philippa. *Moral Dilemmas and Other Topics in Moral Philosophy*. Oxford: Clarendon Press, 2002.
———. *Natural Goodness*. Oxford: Clarendon Press, 2001.
———. *Virtues and Vices and Other Essays in Moral Philosophy*. Oxford: Blackwell, 1978.
———. *Virtues and Vices and Other Essays in Moral Philosophy*. Oxford: Clarendon Press, 2002.
Frankfurt, Harry G. *The Reasons of Love*. Princeton, NJ: Princeton University Press, 2004.

Friedan, Betty. *The Feminine Mystique*. New York: W. W. Norton, 1963.
Gable, Shelly L., and Jonathan Haidt. "What (and Why) Is Positive Psychology?" *Review of General Psychology* 9, no. 2 (June 2005): 103–110. https://doi.org/10.1037/1089-2680.9.2.103.
Gardner, Robert H., dir. *The Courage to Care* [documentary]. Produced by Robert H. Gardner and Carol Rittener. United Way Productions, Mutual of America, 1985.
Gay, Robert. "Courage and Thumos." *Philosophy* 63, no. 244 (1988): 255–265.
Gilligan, Carol. "Hearing the Difference: Theorizing Connection." *Hypatia* 10, no. 2 (1995): 120–127.
Greitemeyer, Tobias, Silvia Osswald, Peter Fischer, and Dieter Frey. "Civil Courage: Implicit Theories, Related Concepts, and Measurement." *Journal of Positive Psychology* 2, no. 2 (2007): 115–119.
Hacker-Wright, John, ed. *Philippa Foot on Goodness and Virtue*. Cham: Palgrave-Macmillan, 2018. Accessed October 2020, https://link.springer.com/book/10.1007/978-3-319-91256-1.
Hanisch, Carol. "The Personal Is Political." In Shulamith Firestone, *Notes from the Second Year: Women's Liberation: Major Writings of the Radical Feminists*, edited by Shulamith Firestone and Anne Koedt, 82–85. New York: Radical Feminism, 1970.
Hawkins, Sara F., and Janice Morse. "The Praxis of Courage as a Foundation for Care." *Journal of Nursing Scholarship* 46, no. 4 (2014): 263–270.
Hillman, Laura. *I Will Plant You a Lilac Tree: A Memoir of a Schindler's List Survivor*. New York: Atheneum, 2005.
Hobbes, Thomas. *Leviathan: With Selected Variants from the Latin Edition of 1668*, edited by Thomas Curley. 1651. Indianapolis: Hackett, 1994.
Hobbs, Angela. *Plato and the Hero: Courage, Manliness and the Impersonal Good*. Cambridge and New York: Cambridge University Press, 2000.
Houser, Rollen Edward. "The Virtue of Courage." In *The Ethics of Aquinas*, edited by Stephen J. Pope, 304–320. Washington, DC: Georgetown University Press, 2002.
James, William. *The Moral Equivalent of War*. United Kingdom: Read Books, 2013.
———. *What Pragmatism Means*. Edam, Netherlands: LM, 2017.
Kateb, George. "Courage as a Virtue." *Social Research: An International Quarterly* 71, no. 1 (2004): 39–72.
Keneally, Thomas. *Schindler's Ark*. London: Hodder and Stoughton, 1982. Published in the United States and later in Commonwealth countries as *Schindler's List*.
Kennedy, Caroline. *Profiles in Courage for Our Time*. New York: Hyperion, 2003.
Kennedy, John F. *Profiles in Courage*. Commemorative ed. New York: Harper Collins, 1962.
Kidder, Rushworth M. *How Good People Make Tough Choices: Resolving the Dilemmas of Ethical Living*. New York: HarperCollins, 2009.
———. *Moral Courage*. New York: William Morrow, 2006.
Knobe, Joshua. "What Is Experimental Philosophy?" *Philosophers' Magazine* 28 (2004): 37–39.
Knobe, Joshua, and Shaun Nichols. "An Experimental Philosophy Manifesto." In *Experimental Philosophy*, edited by Joshua Knobe and Shaun Nichols, 3–14. Oxford and New York: Oxford University Press, 2008.
Lakoff, George, and Mark Johnson. *Metaphors We Live By*. Chicago: University of Chicago Press, 1980.
———. *Philosophy in the Flesh: The Embodied Mind and Its Challenge to Western Thought*. New York: Basic Books, 1999.
Lapide, Pinchas. *Three Popes and the Jews*. New York: Hawthorn Books, 1967.

Lee, Harper. *Go Set a Watchman: A Novel*. New York: Harper Perennial, 2015.

———. *To Kill a Mockingbird*. New York: HarperCollins, 1960.

Lindh, Inga-Britt, António Barbosa da Silva, Agneta Berg, and Elisabeth Severinsson. "Courage and Nursing Practice: A Theoretical Analysis." *Nursing Ethics* 17, no. 5 (2010): 551–565.

Locke, John. *Second Treatise of Government*. Indianapolis: Hackett, 1980.

Lopez, Shane J., and Charles Richard Snyder. *Positive Psychology: The Scientific and Practical Explorations of Human Strengths*, 3rd ed. Thousand Oaks, CA: Sage, 2015.

Luther, Martin. *Amore et studio elucidande veritatis: hec subscripta disputabuntur Wittenberge. Presidente R. P. Martino Lutther . . . Quare petit: vt qui non possunt verbis eclarat nobiscum disceptare: agant id literis absentes*. Placard ed. Nuremberg: Hieronymus Höltzel, 1517. Published in pamphlet form as *Disputatio pro declaratione virtutis indulgentiarum* (Basel, 1517). Published in English in numerous editions, e.g., *The Ninety-five Theses: Disputation on the Power of Indulgences* (Musaicum Books, 2018).

MacIntyre, Alasdair. *After Virtue: A Study in Moral Theory*. 3rd ed. Notre Dame, IN: University of Notre Dame Press, 2007.

MacKinnon, Catherine A. *Feminism Unmodified: Discourses on Life and Law*. Cambridge, MA: Harvard University Press, 1987.

———. "Pornography as Defamation and Discrimination." *Boston University Law Review* 71, no. 5 (1991): 793–815.

———. *Sexual Harassment of Working Women: A Case of Sex Discrimination*. Foreword by T. I. Emerson. New Haven, CT: Yale University Press, 1979.

Madison, James. *Federalist* No. 51. In *The Federalist Papers*, edited by Clinton Rossiter, 320–325. New York: New American Library, 1961.

Mayeroff, Milton. *On Caring*. United Kingdom: Harper & Row, 1990.

McCain, John, and Mark Salter. *Worth the Fighting For: The Education of an American Maverick and the Heroes Who Inspired Him*. New York: Random House, 2003.

Mead, George. *Mind, Self and Society*. Chicago: University of Chicago Press, 1934.

Mill, John Stuart. *On Liberty and Other Writings*. Cambridge and New York: Cambridge University Press, 2009.

Miller, William Ian. *The Mystery of Courage*. Cambridge, MA: Harvard University Press, 2000.

Mills, C. Wright. *The Sociological Imagination*. New York: Oxford University Press, 1959.

Monroe, Kristen Renwick. *A Darkling Plain: Stories of Conflict and Humanity during War*. With Chloe Lampros-Monroe and Jonah Pellechia. Cambridge and New York: Cambridge University Press, 2016.

———. *Ethics in an Age of Terror and Genocide: Identity and Moral Choice*. Princeton, NJ: Princeton University Press, 2012.

———. *The Hand of Compassion: Moral Choice during the Holocaust*. Princeton, NJ: Princeton University Press, 2004.

———. *The Heart of Altruism: Perceptions of a Common Humanity*. Princeton, NJ: Princeton University Press, 1996.

———, ed. *Perestroika! The Raucous Revolution in Political Science*. New Haven, CT: Yale University Press, 2005.

Noddings, Nel. *Caring: A Relational Approach to Ethics and Moral Education*. Berkeley and Los Angeles: University of California Press, 1984.

———. "Stories and Affect in Teacher Education." *Cambridge Journal of Education* 26, no. 3 (1996): 435–447.

Nussbaum, Martha. *Cultivating Humanity: A Classical Defense of Reform in Liberal Education.* Cambridge, MA: Harvard University Press, 1998.

———. *The Fragility of Goodness: Luck and Ethics in Greek Tragedy and Philosophy.* 2nd ed. Cambridge and New York: Cambridge University Press, 2001.

———. *From Disgust to Humanity: Sexual Orientation and Constitutional Law.* New York: Oxford University Press, 2010.

———. "The Future of Feminist Liberalism." *Proceedings and Addresses of the American Philosophical Association* 74, no. 2 (November 2000): 47–79.

———. "Virtue Ethics: A Misleading Category?" *Journal of Ethics* 3 (1999): 163–201.

O'Byrne, Kristin Koetting, Shane J. Lopez, and Stephanie Petersen. "Building a Theory of Courage: A Precursor to Change." Paper presented at the 108th Annual Convention of the American Psychological Association, Washington, DC, August 4–8, 2000.

O'Connor, K., R. Hallam, and S. Rachman. "Fearlessness and Courage: A Replication Experiment." *British Journal of Psychology* 76, no. 2 (1985): 187–197.

Pangle, Lorraine Smith. "The Anatomy of Courage in Aristotle's *Nicomachean Ethics*." *Review of Politics* 80, no. 4 (2018): 569–590.

———. *The Moral Foundations of Aristotelian Political Philosophy.* Chicago: University of Chicago Press, 2020.

Penner, Terry. "What Laches and Nicias Miss—and Whether Socrates Thinks Courage Merely a Part of Virtue." *Ancient Philosophy* 12, no. 1 (1992): 1–27.

Pianalto, Matthew. "Moral Conviction." *Journal of Applied Philosophy* 28, no. 4 (2011): 381–395.

———. "Moral Courage and Facing Others." *International Journal of Philosophical Studies* 20, no. 2 (2012): 165–184. DOI: 10.1080/09672559.2012.668308.

Plato. *Plato: Laches; Protagoras; Meno; Enthydemus.* Translated by W. R. M. Lamb. Loeb Classical Library 165. Cambridge, MA: Harvard University Press, 1924.

———. *The Republic of Plato.* Translated by Allan Bloom. New York: Basic Books, 1991.

———. *The Trial and Death of Socrates: "Euthyphro," "Apology," "Crito," Death Scene from "Phaedo."* Translated by G. M. A. Grube. Indianapolis: Hackett, 1975.

Putman, Daniel. "Psychological Courage." *Philosophy, Psychiatry, & Psychology* 4, no. 1 (1997): 1–11.

Quinn, Warren. "Introduction." In *Morality and Action*, edited by Philippa Foot, ix–xii. Cambridge and New York: Cambridge University Press, 1993.

Rachman, Stanley. "Fear and Courage." *Behavior Therapy* 15, no. 1 (1984): 109–120.

Rate, Christopher R., Jennifer A. Clarke, Douglas R. Lindsay, and Robert J. Sternberg. "Implicit Theories of Courage." *Journal of Positive Psychology* 2, no. 2 (2007): 80–98.

Rawls, John. *Justice as Fairness: A Restatement.* Cambridge, MA: Harvard University Press, 2001.

———. *Political Liberalism.* New York: Columbia University Press, 1993.

Reykowski, Janusz. *Disenchantment with Democracy: A Psychological Perspective.* Oxford and New York: Oxford University Press, 2020.

———. "Intrinsic Motivation and Intrinsic Inhibition of Aggressive Behavior." In *Aggression and Behavior Change*, edited by Seymour Feshbach and Adam Frączek, 158–182. New York: Praeger, 1979.

———. "The Justice Motive and Altruistic Helping: Rescuers of Jews in Nazi-Occupied Europe." In *The Justice Motive in Everyday Life*, edited by Michael Ross and Dale T. Miller, 251–270. Cambridge and New York: Cambridge University Press, 2002.

———. *Motywacja, postawy prospołeczne a osobowość* [Prosocial motivation, prosocial attitudes and personality]. Warsaw: PWN 1979, 1986.

———. "Patriotism and the Collective System of Meanings." In *Patriotism in the Lives of Individuals and Nations*, edited by Daniel Bar-Tal and Ervin Staub, 108–128. Chicago: Nelson-Hall, 1997.

———. *Postawy i wartości Polaków a zmiany systemowe* [Values and attitudes of Poles and changes in the sociopolitical system]. Warsaw: Wyd. Instytutu Psychologii PAN, 1993.

———. *Potoczne wyobrażenia o demokracji: Psychologiczne uwarunkowania i konsekwencje* [The lay concepts of democracy: Their sources and consequences]. Warsaw: Wyd. IP, 1995.

———. "Social Motivation." *Annual Review of Psychology* 33 (1982): 123–154.

Reykowski, Janusz, Klaus Boehnke, Rainer K. Silbereisen, Nancy Eisenberg, and Augusto Palmonari. "Developmental Patterns of Prosocial Motivation: A Cross-National Study." *Journal of Cross-Cultural Psychology* 20, no. 3 (1989): 219–243.

Reykowski, Janusz, and Zuzanna Smoleńska. "Collectivism, Individualism and Interpretation of Social Change: Limitations of a Simple Model." *Polish Psychological Bulletin* 24, no. 2 (1993): 89–109.

Rorty, Amélie Oksenberg. *The Many Faces of Philosophy: Reflections from Plato to Arendt*. 1st ed. Oxford and New York: Oxford University Press, 2004.

———. *Mind in Action: Essays in the Philosophy of Mind*. Boston: Beacon Press, 1991.

———. "The Two Faces of Courage." *Philosophy* 61, no. 236 (1986): 151–171.

Rorty, Amélie Oksenberg, and Owen Flanagan, eds. *Identity, Character, and Morality: Essays in Moral Psychology*. New ed. Cambridge, MA: MIT Press, 1993.

Rousseau, Jean-Jacques. *Emile, or On Education*. Translated by Allan Bloom. New York: Basic Books, 1979.

———. *Rousseau: The Basic Political Writings*. Translated by Donald Cress. Indianapolis: Hackett, 2012.

Sanford, Jonathan J. "Are You Man Enough? Aristotle and Courage." *International Philosophical Quarterly* 50, no. 4 (2010): 431–445.

Scorza, Jason. "The Ambivalence of Political Courage." *Review of Politics* 63, no. 4 (2001): 637–661.

———. "Patriotism and Courage." In *The Handbook of Patriotism*, edited by Mitja Sardoc, 227–254. New York: Springer, 2020.

———. *Strong Liberalism: Habits of Mind for Democratic Citizenship*. Ann Arbor: University of Michigan Press, 2008.

Sekerka, Leslie E., and Richard P. Bagozzi. "Moral Courage in the Workplace: Moving To and From the Desire and Decision to Act." *Business Ethics* 16, no. 2 (2007): 132–149.

———, Richard P. Bagozzi, and Richard Charnigo. "Facing Ethical Challenges in the Workplace: Conceptualizing and Measuring Professional Moral Courage." *Business Ethics* 89, no. 4 (2009): 565–579.

Shelp, Earl E. "Courage: A Neglected Virtue in the Patient-Physician Relationship." *Social Science & Medicine* 18, no. 4 (1984): 351–360.

Shklar, Judith. *The Faces of Injustice*. New Haven, CT: Yale University Press, 1990.

———. "The Liberalism of Fear." In *Political Liberalism: Variations on a Theme*, edited by Shaun P. Young, 149–166. Albany: State University of New York Press, 2004.

———. *Ordinary Vices*. New York: Oxford University Press, 1984.

Simola, Sheldene. "Understanding Moral Courage through a Feminist and Developmental Ethic of Care." *Journal of Business Ethics* 130, no. 1 (2015): 29–44.

Staub, Ervin. "A Child in Distress: The Effects of Focusing Responsibility on Children on Their Attempts to Help." *Developmental Psychology* 2 (1970): 152–154. Reprinted in Judy F. Rosenblith, Wesley Allinsmith, and Joanna P. Williams (eds.), *The Causes of Behavior: Readings in Child Development and Educational Psychology*, 3rd ed., 214–267 (Boston: Allyn & Bacon, 1973).

———. *Positive Social Behavior and Morality: Social and Personal Influences*. New York: Academic Press, 2013.

———. "The Roots and Prevention of Genocide and Related Mass Violence." *Journal of Religion and Science* 47, no. 4 (2012): 821–842.

———. *The Roots of Goodness and Resistance to Evil: Inclusive Caring, Moral Courage, Altruism Born of Suffering, Active Bystandership, and Heroism*. Oxford and New York: Oxford University Press, 2016.

Staub, Ervin, Daniel Bar-Tal, Jerzy Karylowski, and Janusz Reykowski, eds. *Development and Maintenance of Prosocial Behavior*. New York: Plenum Press, 1984.

Steinbeck, John. *The Moon Is Down*. New York: Viking Press, 1942.

Taylor, Gabriele. *Pride, Shame, and Guilt: Emotions of Self-Assessment*. Oxford and New York: Oxford University Press, 1985.

Tessitore, Aristide. "Courage and Comedy in Plato's *Laches*." *Journal of Politics* 56, no. 1 (1994): 115–133.

Teichmann, Roger. *The Philosophy of Elizabeth Anscombe*. Oxford and New York: Oxford University Press, 2008.

Thoreau, Henry David. "Civil Disobedience" [1849]. In *Walden, or Life in the Woods and On the Duty of Civil Disobedience*, 85–104. New York: Bantam, 1962.

Tillich, Paul. *The Courage to Be*. New Haven, CT: Yale University Press, 2000.

Tilly, Charles. *Stories, Identities, and Political Change*. Lanham, MD: Rowan & Littlefield, 2002.

Tocqueville, Alexis de. *Democracy in America*. Edited and abridged by Richard D. Heffner. New York: New American Library, 1984.

Tóibín, Colm. *The Testament of Mary*. London and New York: Charles Scribner's Sons, 2012.

Vercors [pseud.; Jean Bruller]. *Le silence de la mer* [The silence of the sea]. Paris: Éditions de Minuit, 1942.

Ward, Lee. "Nobility and Necessity: The Problem of Courage in Aristotle's *Nicomachean Ethics*." *American Political Science Review* 95, no. 1 (2001): 71–83.

Wicklund, Robert A., and Peter Gollwitzer. *Symbolic Self-Completion*. New York: Routledge, 1982.

Waldron, Jeremy. "Superseding Historic Injustice." *Ethics* 103, no. 1 (1992): 4–28. Accessed October 2020, http://www.jstor.org/stable/2381493.

Williams, Bernard. *Ethics and the Limits of Philosophy*. Cambridge, MA: Harvard University Press, 1985.

———. *In the Beginning Was the Deed: Realism and Moralism in Political Argument*. Princeton, NJ: Princeton University Press, 2005.

———. *Morality: An Introduction to Ethics*. Cambridge and New York: Cambridge University Press, 2012.

———. "Practical Necessity." In *Moral Luck: Philosophical Papers, 1973–1980*, 124–131. Cambridge and New York: Cambridge University Press, 1981.

———. *Shame and Necessity*. Berkeley and Los Angeles: University of California Press, 1993.

———. *Truth and Truthfulness: An Essay in Genealogy.* Princeton, NJ: Princeton University Press, 2002.

Yearly, Lee H. *Mencius and Aquinas: Theories of Virtue and Conceptions of Courage.* Albany: State University of New York Press, 1990.

Zuccotti, Susan. *Under His Very Windows: The Vatican and the Holocaust in Italy.* New Haven, CT: Yale University Press, 2002.

Index

AARP. *See* American Association of Retired Persons (AARP)
abortion, 63–64, 208n5
Abu Dhabi (United Arab Emirates), 96
ACLU. *See* American Civil Liberties Union (ACLU)
Action Committee for Decent Childcare (ACDC), 28
Adelman, Jeremy, 207n1
Aeschylus, vii
Affordable Care Act, 4, 56, 185
AFL-CIO, 56
African Americans, 54–55, 58, 66, 73, 138, 185, 216n1, 223n19
Agamemnon (Aeschylus), vii
agency, 2, 24–25, 146–49, 183–86, 219n18
agonistic choice, 65, 145, 167, 171–72, 174–76, 187, 208n11, 221n5
Alabama, 69, 139
Alinsky, Saul, 28
altruism, 25–26, 30, 182–83, 189, 219n8
Alzheimer's disease, 82, 86–88
Amal (pseudonym), 216n1, 220n25; and anti-Muslim bullying, fighting against, 5, 29, 96–107, 138, 147, 151–52, 155–58, 163, 173, 182–93
American Association of Retired Persons (AARP), 76
American Civil Liberties Union (ACLU), 53
American Civil War (1861–1865), 15, 216n1
American Electoral College, 202
andreia, masculine bravery of soldiers during wartime as courage, 14–15, 19
Andrews, Molly, 214n3
animus, and ideology, 23
Anscombe, Elizabeth, 212n79

anti-Semitism, 46, 154, 185
Apel, Dennis, 51–52, 216n3
Apology (Plato), 20
Arendt, Hannah, 25
Aristotle, 14–16, 19, 23–24; Aristotelian analysis, 2; Aristotelian ethics, 221n4; on traditional courage, 210n31
Athens, Greece: democracy, 12, 18–21; polis, 18–19; politics, 20
Austria-Hungary, 43
authenticity, 17–18, 21; and integrity, 11, 18; and liberalism, 11–12, 211n49
Avramenko, Richard, 15, 25

Bagozzi, Richard, 25
Bahá'í religion, 109; Bahá'í of America, 109
Barbosa da Silva, António, 25
Barthes, Roland, 214n6, 228
Beauvoir, Simone de, 214n9
Beirut, Lebanon, 95
Berg, Agneta, 25
Berlin Wall, 198, 224n31
Biden, Joe, 9, 23, 70–72
Black Lives Matter, 9, 18, 56, 70
Black Maverick (Beito and Beito), 63
Bloom, Anne, 52
Boleyn, Anne, 224n28
Boleyn, Elizabeth, 224n28
Bond, Julian, 55
Booth, Heather: as activist, feminist, and political strategist, 28–29, 32, 34–36, 54–74, 135–40, 142–43, 146–48, 162, 173, 184–87, 195, 202, 208n8, 215n13, 216n1, 216n4, 219n5, 224n25; documentary, 29, 56; on moral courage, 4–5, 190–91; on social activism, 54–74; on values, 135
Booth, John Wilkes, 178

bravery, xiii, 3–4, 14–15, 19–20, 24, 36, 151, 155, 180–82, 196, 209n3, 209n9. *See also* heroism and heroes
Bridgeport, Connecticut, 42
Bright, Rick, 9
Brown, Jerry, 45, 125, 146, 194
Brown, Pat, 125, 194
Brown, Sherrod (senator), 72
Brown v. Board of Education, 59
Bruller, Jean. *See* Vercors (pseudonym)
Buena Park, CA, 180
Burma, Asia, 153
Bush, George, 55, 93, 114–15, 202
Bush v. Gore, 202

California, 31, 60, 81, 97, 104–5, 108–24, 160
California Public Utilities Commission (PUC), 29, 108, 116–21, 166, 170; commissioner, 5, 112, 123, 159–60; Public Utilities Code, 113
California State Superintendent of Public Instruction, 111, 217n4
California Supreme Court, 113
Cambodia, Asia: activist, 30, 152, 158, 167; government, 30, 32
Cameroon, Central Africa, 96, 217n2
Camus, Albert, 203
Canada, 96
cancel culture, 22
Capitol Hill Police (CHP), 180
care ethics, 24–25, 212n87, 215n10
caregiving and caregivers, 16, 75–76, 83, 95, 212n87
Caring (Noddings), 215n10
Carter, Jimmy, 108–9
Carton, Sydney (fictional character), 144, 181–82
caste, discrimination in India, 4, 21, 29, 34, 128–32, 151, 154–62, 185, 194
Catholics, 51, 108, 169–70, 222n11; Catholic Worker community (CA), 216n3; church, 10, 169
Ceballos, Richard: lawsuit over workplace corruption and free speech, xii–xiii, 30, 149, 159, 171, 174, 184, 191, 207n4, 209n9, 219n4
Center for Human Rights, 53
CFPB. *See* Consumer Financial Protection Bureau (CFPB)
Chagall, Marc, 207n2
Chaney, James, 58, 216n1
character, 108, 125, 174–76, 193, 199; and identity, 143, 174, 176; and presidency, 1, 127, 170, 188, 202; and self-respect, 162; and virtue, 23
Chemerinsky, Erwin, 145–47, 159–60, 172–73, 191–96, 220n20, 222n8; lawsuit against Trump, 28, 31–32, 34, 49–53, 150, 179–80, 193–94, 220n19; on moral courage, 49
Cheney, Liz, 9, 209n9
Chicago, IL, 30, 49, 54–55, 63, 69, 200
China, 30, 73, 152, 169, 208n8

Choo Tee Lim (pseudonym): and fighting sale of children in China, 30–31, 147, 150, 153, 164–65, 169, 185, 191, 196, 208n8, 219n4, 224n27
CHP. *See* Capitol Hill Police (CHP)
Christians, 188; Christianity, 97, 221n4; non-Christians, 99; schools, 5, 97–98
Christmas, 97, 102, 113
Cicero, Marcus Tullius, 14
Citibank, 116
Citigroup, 116, 217–18nn8–9
Citizen Labor Energy Coalition, 55
Citizens for Responsibility and Ethics in Washington organization, lawsuit against Trump, 53
Civil Rights Labor Organizing Drive, 54
civil rights movement, 54, 61, 64, 138–39, 173, 216n4
Civil War (1861–1865), 15, 216n1
Clarke, Jennifer, 13
Clinton, Bill, 126–27, 170, 217n8; administration, 5, 29, 114–15, 175; campaign, 110, 127; health-care plan, 55
Clinton, Hilary, 110, 127
Clostridium difficile (*C. diff.*), 89
cognitive psychology, 209n1
Collinsville, Illinois, 78
Combahee River Collective (Boston, MA), 35
Community Resources Against Street Hoodlums (CRASH), Los Angeles Police Dept., Rampart division, 215n1
Confucius, 17, 213n87
confusion, 62, 139; and despair, 2, 37, 188, 202, 204; and uncertainty, xiv, 191
connectedness, 70, 152–55, 172, 176
conscience, 3, 5, 34, 166, 172, 176, 194
Consumer Financial Protection Bureau (CFPB), 56
Corlett, John, 25
courage, 142–44; and agency, 24–25, 146–49, 183–86; defined, 11–14; and democracy, 25; vs. fear, 7; and human behavior, 24–25, 144; in illiberal democratic politics, 12; and liberal democracy, 25; and liberalism, 11, 209n3; and liberal values, 25; physical, 15–16, 146; traditional, 210n31; and values, 209n3; vital, 11–12, 15–17; vital/health, 16–17; and wisdom, 20. *See also* moral courage
Courage to Care, The (documentary), 191, 220n28
Court of Appeals. *See* US Court of Appeals
COVID-19 pandemic, xiv, 9, 16
Covington, Mary White, 223n19
CRASH. *See* Community Resources Against Street Hoodlums (CRASH)
Current TV, 217n5

Daley, Richard J. (mayor), 55
Darkling Plain, A (Monroe), 197, 224nn29–30, 230

INDEX

Davis, Gray (governor), 5, 29, 111–27, 166, 170, 175, 194, 217n4, 218n12, 221n31
Deep South, 138
democracy, 19–23, 225n35; American, 9, 13, 22; Athenian, 12, 18–21; and courage, 25; and justice, 54, 73, 136; liberal, xiii, 10–12, 18–23, 25, 211n49; and liberalism, 12, 206; and tyranny, 70; and values, 73, 136
democratic liberal values, 19–23
Democratic National Committee, 55
Democratic National Convention, 200
Democratic Party, 55, 57, 66–67, 72, 110–11, 124–27, 217n3, 217nn4–6
Demosthenes, 12, 19–20
DePaul University (Chicago, IL), 49
Depression. *See* Great Depression
Deputy, The (Hochhuth), 222n11
Deregulation Bill of 1966 (CA), 112
De Roche, Monica, 209n1, 221
despair, vii, 1–3, 41, 170–71, 181, 192, 200, 202–4; and confusion, 2, 37, 188, 202, 204
Dickens, Charles, 144, 181–82
Didion, Joan, 195, 215n11, 220n27
Dimmesdale, Arthur (fictional character), 95, 164
Dirie, Waris, 214n9
Disenchantment with Democracy (Reykowski), 224n26
Dobbs, Darrell, 20
Dobbs v. Jackson Women's Health Organization, 68, 208n5
Dodd-Frank Bill, 55
Doing Narrative Research (Andrews, Squire, and Tamboukou), 214n3
"doing the right thing," 109, 136, 159, 168–72, 176–77, 218n3
Douala, Cameroon, 96, 217n2
Douglas, Lindsay, 13
DREAMers, 31, 43, 156–57, 219n4, 220n24
Dreyman, Georg, 198–200
Du Bois, W. E. B., 223n19
Duke University (Durham, NC), 49
Durden, Nino, 50

Ear, Sophal, as Cambodian activist against Cambodian government, 30–32, 152, 158, 167, 193, 220n22
Easter, 97
Eastin, Delaine, 111, 217n4
Egypt, 109
Eid al-Fitr (Festival of Breaking the Fast), 97, 217n3
Einstein, Albert, 222n11
Ellsberg, Daniel, 208n2, 209n9
El Salvadoran refugees, 190
Emergency Rescue Committee (ERC), 207n2
emotional intelligence, 190–92, 200

empathy, 4, 148–49, 152–55, 172, 176, 190, 203, 215n16, 219n18
England, Tudor, 177–78, 209n9, 224n28
Enron Corporation, 180; crisis/scandal, 5, 29, 108–27, 166, 175, 217n7, 218n9; lawyers, 122
Environmental Protection Agency (EPA), 57
ERC. *See* Emergency Rescue Committee (ERC)
Essential Hirschman, The (Adelman), 207n1
ethics, 177–78, 187, 192–95, 209n9, 219n8, 221; African, 213n87; and agonistic choice, 221n5; Aristotelian, 221n4; Confucian, 213n87; consequentialist, 213n87; deontological, 213n87, 215n10; feminist, 24, 213n87; Kantian, 24, 213n87, 215n10, 221–22n5; and law, 159; and morality, 3, 215n10; and politics, xii, 34, 194; in real world, 174; teaching of, 223–24nn23–24; utilitarian, 24, 213n87, 215n10, 221n5; and values, xvii, 66. *See also* care ethics; virtue ethics
existentialism, 221n2
Exit, Voice, and Loyalty (Hirschman), 207n1

family values, 164, 168–70
fanaticism, xiii–xiv, 1, 3, 6, 141, 176–78, 183, 209n3, 223n15
Fashion Forward (non-profit company), 96
fatwa, 123
Fauci, Anthony, 9
Federal Bureau of Investigation (FBI), 61–62, 139
Federal Energy Regulatory Commission (FERC), 109, 114–15, 121–22, 217n2
Feinstein, Dianne (senator), 109, 111, 217n3
female genital mutilation, 214n9
Feminine Mystique, The (Friedan), 34–35
feminist activists, 35, 214n9
feminist ethics, 24, 213n87
feminist theory, 34–35, 212–13n87
FERC. *See* Federal Energy Regulatory Commission (FERC)
Feuchtwanger, Lion, 207n2
Finch, Atticus (fictional character), xii
Foot, Philippa, 183, 212n79
Fragility of Goodness, The (Nussbaum), 188–89, 212n79, 223n23
Frankfurt, Harry, 18
Freedom Summer (Mississippi, 1964), 4, 28, 63, 69, 139, 168, 180, 185, 216n1
Freeman, David, 121
Freudian framework, 197
Friedan, Betty, 34–35, 214n9
Friendship Clinic (Chicago, IL), 63
Fry, Varian, xi, 207nn1–2

Garcetti, Eric, 45, 146
genocide, 2, 26
German Democratic Republic (GDR), 198, 224n31
Gestapo (Nazi secret police), 163, 191

Gilligan, Carol, 212n87
Girl Scouts, 80
Glass Menagerie, The (Williams), 91
Golden Globe Awards, vii
Goldman Sachs, 126, 217–18n8
Gonzalez, Jessica, 209n1, 221
Goodman, Andrew, 58, 216n1
Goodman, Eugene, 13, 18, 210n7
Gore, Al, 112, 114–15, 202
Go Set a Watchman (Lee), xii, 207n3
Gramsci, Antonio, 36, 60, 195
gratitude, and giving back to society, 149, 155–58, 172, 176
Great Depression, 77, 119, 160, 169, 225n34
Greece, classical, and courage, 14–15, 208–9n9. *See also* Sparta, Greece
Gregory, Dick, 72, 216n3
Guadalupe, California: Catholic Worker community, 216n3
Guantanamo Bay Detention Camp (Cuba), 50–51

Hahn, James K. (mayor), 215n1
Hamer, Fannie Lou, 66–67
Hand of Compassion, The (Monroe), 214n4, 214n7, 219n11, 222n12, 223n22, 230
Hanisch, Carol, 35, 214nn8–9
Hardy, Thomas, 95, 164
Harkin, Tom, 110
Harvard University (Cambridge, MA), 49, 206
Hawkins, Andrew, 59, 70, 219n5
Hawkins, Cheryl Nichol, 206
Hawkins, Mary Lou, 59, 70, 219n5
Hawkins v. Town of Shaw, 59, 219n5
Hawthorne, Nathaniel, 94–95, 221n29
Hayakawa, Samuel Ichiye (senator), 109
Heart of Altruism, The (Monroe), 214n2, 219n11, 222n12, 223n22, 230
Heather Booth: Changing the World (documentary), 29, 56
Hecker, Jim, 115
Hegelianism, 221n2
Held, Virginia, 212n87
Henry VIII, execution of wives, 224n28
heroism and heroes, 15, 18, 24, 25–26, 44–45, 117, 131, 146, 151, 155, 168–69, 177, 213n95. *See also* bravery
Hiroshima, Japan, bombing of, 216n3
Hirschman, Albert Otto, xi, 203, 207nn1–2
Hitler, Adolf, 177–78, 207n1, 222n11, 223n15. *See also* Holocaust; Nazis; Third Reich
Hobbes, Thomas, 14
Hochhuth, Rolf, 222n11
Hollywood, 64
Holocaust, 26, 30, 138, 145, 163, 179, 189, 191, 220n21, 222n11. *See also* Hitler, Adolf; Nazis
Homer, 19

Hong Kong, China, 73
hope, 5, 45, 71, 92, 95, 147, 189, 197–204, 216n1
Howard, T. R. M., 63–64
Hoyt, Benjamin (Ben), 206, 209n1, 212n68, 221
humanity, 3, 106, 136, 138–39, 148–49, 153–55, 172, 176, 184, 197–98
humility, 150–51, 179
Humphrey, Hubert, 72, 216n3
Hyatt, Joel, 112, 217n5
Hyatt Legal Services, 112, 217n5

IBEW. *See* International Brotherhood of Electrical Workers (IBEW)
ICE (United States Immigration and Customs Enforcement), 43, 148
identity: and altruism, 182; and character, 143, 174, 176; and virtue ethics, 143–44
Immigration Justice Campaign, 56
Independence, Missouri, 108
Independent System Operator (CA), 112
India, 139; caste discrimination in, 4, 21, 29, 34, 128–32, 151, 154–62, 185, 194; constitution, 155; Council on Foreign Relations, 128; government, 34, 128, 131, 164, 194; history, 128; politics, 132
Indonesia, tsunami (2004), 138, 157, 220n25
insurrection (January 6, 2021). *See* US Capitol
integrity, v, 11–12, 15, 17–18, 20–21, 101, 161–62, 198, 201, 204, 206
International Brotherhood of Electrical Workers (IBEW) 119, 170
Iran-contra war crimes, 110
Islam, 97–98, 221n4

James, William, 209nn2–3, 212n84
Jane Collective, 28, 63–64, 208n5
Jane movement, 4, 74, 173
Janes, The (film), 69
Jesus Christ, 98
Jews, 26, 30, 138, 144–45, 151, 155, 161, 163, 168, 179, 187, 189, 191, 197, 220n21, 222n11
Johnson, Lyndon Baines, 72
Johnson, Mark, 186
Judaism, 97, 221n4
Justice Department (US), Civil Rights Division, 57

Kant, Immanuel, 24, 66, 213n87, 215n10, 221n1, 221–22n5
Kateb, 209nn2–3
Keker, John, 110
Keker and Brooke law firm, 110, 113
Kennedy, John Fitzgerald, 115
Khmer Rouge, 193
King, Martin Luther, Jr., xvi, 45, 50, 55, 156
King, Rev. Ed, 67
Kittay, Eva Feder, 212–13n87

INDEX

Koran, 221n4
Kuehl, Sheila, 117, 218n10
Ku Klux Klan (KKK), 58, 63

Laches (Plato), 19–21, 24
Laches, General, 20
Lakoff, George, 186
Landowska, Wanda, 207n2
Lapide, Pinchas, 222n11
Latinos, 109–10
LAUSD. *See* Los Angeles Unified School District (LAUSD)
Lay, Kenneth, 115, 217n7
LBD. *See* Lewy body dementia (LBD)
Lebanon, 96–97, 104
Lee, Harper, xii, 68
Lee, Spike, 20–21
Left Behind (film), 98
Lewis, John, 45, 156
Lewy body dementia (LBD), 29, 82, 88, 90, 167
liberal democracy, xiii, 10–12, 18–23, 25, 211n49
liberalism, 19–23, 25; and authenticity, 11–12, 211n49; and courage, 11, 209n3; and democracy, 12, 206
Lim. *See* Choo Tee Lim (pseudonym)
Lincoln, Abraham, 178
Lincoln Project (DC), 209n9
Lindh, Inga-Britt, 25
Lindsay, Douglas, 13
Lives of Others, The (film), 198–200, 224n31
Lockyer, Bill, 120
Loeb & Loeb LLP (Los Angeles law firm), 123, 218n12
Lopez, Shane, 13
Los Angeles Chamber of Commerce, 51–52
Los Angeles County Board of Supervisors, 109, 218n10
Los Angeles County District Attorney's Office, 30
Los Angeles Legal Aid, 109
Los Angeles Police Department, 49–50, 172–73, 179, 215n1, 222n8
Los Angeles Police Protective League, 50
Los Angeles Times, 108
Los Angeles Unified School District (LAUSD), 5, 28, 31, 35, 41–42, 135, 195
Luther, Martin, 177–78, 207n5, 209n9, 223n15
Lynch, Loretta: and Enron/energy crisis, 5, 29, 108–27, 133, 147–49, 159–67, 170, 173, 175, 184, 187, 193–94, 215n13, 217n7, 218n9, 218n12, 224n25

MacIntyre, Alasdair, 14
MacKinnon, Catherine, 214n9
Madison, James, 25
Mahler, Alma. *See* Werfel, Alma Mahler
Mann, Thomas, 207n2
Mayeroff, Milton, 212n87

McCain, John, 65, 209n9
Medical Committee for Human Rights (MCHR), 61–63, 74, 139, 173
Medicare, 58, 76
Mencius, 17
Metzenbaum, Howard, 112, 217n6
Mexican Legal Defense Fund, 53
Middle East, 96, 157
Midwest Academy (Chicago, IL), 28, 54–55, 185, 223n18
midwestern America, 4
Mielke, Erich, 224n31
Mills, C. Wright, 34–35
Mississippi, 54–55, 58–67, 139–40; Freedom Democratic Delegation, 67; Freedom Democratic Party, 66; Freedom Summer, 4, 28, 63, 69, 139, 168, 180, 185, 216n1; Mississippi Burning murders, 216n1; Shaw (town), 59, 219n5
Missouri, 78, 108, 110
Molina, Gloria, 110
Monroe, James Oliver, Jr., v, 201–2, 206, 224n32, 225n33
Monroe, Kay, 208n4; and caring for elderly mother, 3–4, 29–35, 75–95, 137, 144–47, 157–58, 164, 167, 172–73, 185, 187, 193–96, 206, 219n16; and hope, 95
Monroe, Kristen Renwick, 1, 230
Moon Is Down, The (Steinbeck), 198, 225n34
moral courage, 9–10, 142–43; central components of, 26–27; complex nature of, 3; as concept, 7, 11–15, 175; and concern for others, 24–25, 154; data, 28–30; defined, 1–6, 10, 11, 13–14, 17–19, 135–43; delayed impact of, 189–90; and duty toward others, 154, 168–70; empirical examination of, 11, 23, 27, 135, 174, 186, 209n3; and facing others, 219n14; and future work, 174–87; and human behavior, 24–25; insights into, 174–87; kinds/types of, 11–12, 14–19; model of, 11, 12–14; and polis, 21–23; relationships and support for, 163–65; and restraint, 151–52; rethinking, 186–87; as richly faceted, 133; spontaneous vs. impulsive, 182; as taught, 213n95; types/kinds of, 11–12, 14–19; understanding, 3, 39. *See also* courage
moral imagination, 33, 36, 192, 195–96, 199–200
morality, 46, 189, 192; and ethics, 3, 215n10
moral muscle, xv, 5, 65, 171–73, 177, 188–89, 199–200, 203
"Moral of the Story, The" (political science class, UCI), xii, 188, 205
moral psychology, 11, 211n49
moral relativism, 3, 177–78, 207n5, 223n15
More, Thomas, 10, 177, 207n5, 209n9, 223n15
Moseley Braun, Carol, 55
MoveOn Resistance Summer (2017), 4
Muslims, 101, 182–85; anti-Muslim sentiment, 29, 96–107, 138, 152; assimilated, 97; bigotry against,

Muslims (cont.)
163, 185; bullying of, 5, 29, 96–107, 138, 151–52; discrimination against, 188–89; fasting, 217n3; holidays, 217n3; prejudice against, 5
Myth of Sisyphus (Camus), 203

NAACP. *See* National Association for the Advancement of Colored People (NAACP)
narrative analysis, 29, 32–33, 187, 214n3
narrative imagination, 36, 196
Narrative Imagination in Everyday Life (Andrews), 214n3
narratives, 5, 29–37, 152–54, 172–73, 187, 192–204; alternative, 196; counter-narratives, 33, 193; drawback of, 215n16; micro- and macro-narratives, 34, 194; political, 34, 194. *See also* oral histories; stories
National Abortion Rights Action League (NARAL), 55
National Association for the Advancement of Colored People (NAACP), 185, 223n19; National Voter Fund, 55
National Collegiate Athletics Association (NCAA), 108
Nazis, 138, 151, 163, 167, 177–78, 185, 187, 191, 198, 207n2, 207n5, 209n9, 222n11; Nazi Germany, 10; Nazi occupation, 145, 154, 198; Nazi Party, 178. *See also* Hitler, Adolf; Holocaust; Third Reich
Nelson, Dorothy Wright (judge), 109, 217n1
Netherlands, 139, 155, 191
Newark, Arkansas, 110
Newsom, Gavin (governor), 218n13
New York Times, 9, 210n7, 212n77
Nicias, 20
9/11, 50, 97–99, 141, 178, 209n3
Nini (Dutch woman): as teenager rescued Jews during Holocaust, 30, 138–39, 144–46, 151–55, 167–68, 179, 185, 187, 190–91, 218n4, 219n12, 220n21
Nixon, Richard, 72, 126, 194, 216n3
Noddings, Nel, 212n87, 215n10
North, Oliver, 110
Northwestern University (Evanston and Chicago, IL), 49
Nussbaum, Martha, 188–89, 212n79, 221–22n5, 223n23

Oath Keepers, 71
Obama, Barack, xvi, 43, 56, 119, 126, 160
Obama, Michelle, 101
Office of Planning and Research (OPR), 111
Olson, Culbert, 125, 194
On Caring (Mayeroff), 212n87
oral histories, xvi, 30, 190, 196
Orange County Register, 52

Pacific Coast Highway (PCH), 51, 216n3
Pacific Gas and Electric (PGE), 116, 118, 167
Palmer, Alice, 55
Parkinson's disease, 82
Parks, Bernard (police chief), 215n1
patriotism, militarized, politics of, 10
patriots, 208n2, 209n9
PCH. *See* Pacific Coast Highway (PCH)
Pearl River, 59
Pelosi, Nancy, 126
Pennsylvania, 71
Perestroika! (Monroe), 214n5
perestroika movement, in political science and methodological pluralism, 214n5
Perez, Rafael, 50
Pericles, 12, 19–20, 24
PGE. *See* Pacific Gas and Electric (PGE)
phenomenology, 221n2
Philadelphia (film), 112
philosophy, 11–12, 14, 209n1; continental, 221n2; and moral courage, 11, 174–76; and political theory, 10–11; and virtue ethics, 221nn1–2, 221n4; Western, 187
Phi Phi Islands, Thailand, 217n4
Phuket, Thailand, 105, 217n4
Pianalto, Matthew, 147, 184, 219n14, 219n17
PIES, in healing circles, 70
Pine Lake, (Collinsville, IL), 201
Pius XII (pope), 222n11
Planned Parenthood, 53, 55, 185
Plato, 12, 17, 19–21, 24
pluralism, in political science, 32, 214n5
Poland, 139, 144, 167, 180, 196, 222n11; Round Table Talks for democracy, 30, 36, 148, 161, 195; trade union Solidarność (Solidarity) 30, 148, 161. *See also* Warsaw, Poland
police corruption, 215n1
Polish Academy of Sciences, 163
Politburo, 195
political science, xiv, 10, 32
political theory, 10–11, 213n87
Polleta, Francesca, 215n16
pornography, as civil rights violation, 214n9
Positive Social Behavior and Morality (Staub), 213n95
Prichard, Marion, 163, 191
Progressive Era, 119, 160
Prynne, Hester (fictional character), 94–95, 164, 221n29
psychology, 11–12, 14. *See also* cognitive psychology; moral psychology; social psychology
public service, 9, 59, 111, 125, 171, 194
Purple Heart, 110

Q-Anon movement, 212n78
Quick Response Team, in Arkansas, 110
Quran, 97

INDEX   241

Ramadan, Muslim holy month of fasting, 97, 217n3
Rampart scandal, 49–50, 172–73, 179, 215n1, 222n8
Rate, Christopher, 13–14, 209
Reagan, Roland, 55
Redstockings (feminist nonprofit organization), 35
Reformation Europe, 177–78
Reid, Bruce, 110
Renwick, Robert Hart, v, 206
Republic, The (Plato), 20
Republican Party, 9, 55, 71, 109, 111, 126, 194, 208n2, 209n9, 218n12
Reykowski, Janusz: fighting for Polish democracy, 30, 32, 36–37, 139, 142–48, 161, 163, 167, 169–70, 180, 195–96, 206, 215n14, 218n4, 219nn8–9, 224n26
risk(s), 26, 135, 144–46, 172, 175, 178–81, 214n99
Rivlin, Lilly, 56
Roe v. Wade, 63, 68–69, 208n5
Romney, Mitt (senator), 9, 209n9
Roosevelt, Franklin Delano, 7
Rorty, Amélie, 212n79
Rubin, Robert "Bob" (Secretary of the Treasury), 116–17, 217–18nn8–9
Ruddick, Sara, 212n87
Russia, 73

Sanders, Bernie (senator), 47, 140
Scarlet Letter, The (Hawthorne), 94–95, 221n29
Schindler, Oskar, 144, 181–82
Schindler's List (film), 144, 181–82
Schumer, Charles, 126
Schwarzenegger, Arnold (governor), 218n12
Schwerner, Michael, 58, 216n1
Scorza, Jason, 209nn2–3
Sekerka, Leslie E., 25
self-respect, 18, 162–63
self-sacrifice, 25, 165–68
self-worth, 162–63, 175
Selma, Alabama, 45, 156
Senator Joe (California state senator): and breaking with political party over matters of principle, 30, 121–22, 135, 148, 156, 158–59, 162, 166, 169, 171, 180, 184, 218n1, 219n4, 220n23
Severinsson, Elisabeth, 25
sexual harassment, 108, 159; as sex discrimination, 214n9
Shaping History (Andrews), 214n3
Shklar, Judith, 12, 23
Sierra Club, 55
Silence of the Sea, The (Vercors), 198
Slouching towards Bethlehem (Didion), 220n27
SNCC. *See* Student Nonviolent Coordinating Committee (SNCC)
Snowden, Edward, 209n9

Snyder, Charles, 13
social activism, 4, 54–74, 138, 148
Socialist Unity Party of Germany, 224n31
social psychology, 10–11, 13, 15, 25–26, 32, 142, 174, 209n1, 213n95
social science, 10, 32, 201
Social Security, 76
Sociological Imagination, The (Mills), 34–35
Socrates, Platonic, 12, 20
Southern Poverty Law Center (SPLC), 71
Sparta, Greece: and courage, 10, 19, 209n3; and militaristic courage, 19
Speer, Albert, 177, 207n5, 209n9, 223n15
SPLC. *See* Southern Poverty Law Center (SPLC)
spying and spies, 198–99, 209n9, 224n31
Squire, Corinne, 214n3
Stalinist undertones, 21
Stangl, Franz, 177, 207n5, 209n9, 223n15
Stasi (Ministry for State Security), for GDR, 224n31
State and Local Leadership Project, electoral training organization, 55
Staub, Ervin, 25–27, 206, 213n95, 219n18
Steinbeck, John, 198, 225n34
Sternberg, Robert, 13
St. Louis, Missouri, 78, 80, 82–83, 201
St. Louis University (SLU), SLUCare Geriatric Psychiatry, 88–89
stories, xiii, xvi, 3, 5–6, 30–37, 41, 172–73, 192–204, 215n16; analysis of, 33; data and research methodology, 28–37; and ethical life, 192–95; and moral imagination, 195–96. *See also* narratives; oral histories
Story, Moorefield, 223n19
Streep, Meryl, vii
Stuckart, Wilhelm, 177, 207n5, 209n9, 223n15
Student Nonviolent Coordinating Committee (SNCC), 54–55, 58
Summers, Lawrence, 115
Supreme Court of California, 113
Supreme Court of the United States, 51, 55–59, 159, 202, 208n5, 220n19
Switzerland, 151
Syrian refugees, 190

Tale of Two Cities, A (Dickens), 144, 181–82
Taliban, 190
Tallahassee River, 59
Talmud, 220n21, 221n4
Tamboukou, Maria, 214n3
Tej, Vikram (pseudonym): fighting caste discrimination in India, 4, 29, 31, 34–36, 128–32, 137–41, 146, 151, 154–62, 165, 171, 185, 187, 191, 194, 196, 218nn1–2; on parenting, 4, 128, 129, 158, 165
Ten Commandments, 23, 221n4

Tess of the d'Urbervilles (Hardy), 95, 164
Testament of Mary, The (Colm), 224–25n33
Thailand, 102–5; government, 105–6, 157; islands, 217n4; Straits of Malacca coast of, 217n4; tsunami (2004), 138, 157, 220n25
Third Reich, 177–78, 207n1, 209n9, 223n15. *See also* Hitler, Adolf; Nazis
Thoreau, Henry David, 17
Three Popes and the Jews (Lapide), 222n11
Tobis, Jerome (Jerry), 216n4
Tocqueville, Alexis de, 25
Tóibín, Colm, 224–25n33
To Kill a Mockingbird (Lee), xii, 68–69
tolerance, 2, 22, 97
Torres (refugee from Central America), 157–58, 220n26
Tripp, Linda, 209n9
Tronto, Joan, 212–13n87
Trump, Donald, xi–xii, xiv, 1–3, 9, 22, 28, 31, 34, 45–47, 56–57, 70–72, 113, 140–42, 171–73, 179–80, 202–3; administration, 125–26, 193–94, 220n19; constitutional violations, 53, 150, 173, 193, 220n19; dehumanized issues, 41, 45, 137; and elite, 47, 141; impeachment, 208n2; lack of equality and fairness, 140; lawsuit against, 28, 31–32, 34, 49–53, 150, 179–80, 193–94, 220n19; legal and ethical behavior, 220n19; as manifestation of incredible divisiveness and hate, 202; moral courage in age of, 37, 209n9; and Muslims, treatment of, 101; politics, 2, 211; politics and ethics in age of, xii; public morality of, 171; and rogue Republicans, 209n9; selfishness, 170–71; and ugliness of political life, 1, 203
Trump International Hotel (DC), 52–53
Tudor England, 177–78, 209n9, 224n28

UC Berkeley. *See* University of California, Berkeley
UCI. *See* University of California, Irvine (UCI)
Under His Very Windows (Zuccotti), 222n11
undocumented students, 5, 28, 30, 35–36, 135–36, 148, 173, 190, 195, 219n4; protection of, 41–48
University of California, Berkeley, 102, 157; Civil Justice Research Initiative, 51; Institute of Governmental Studies, 123; Public Policy School (Goldman), 123; School of Law, 28, 173, 220nn19–20
University of California, Irvine (UCI): Ethics Center, xiv, 66, 205–6, 207n6, 209n1, 212n68, 215n16, 221; School of Law, 28, 49, 51, 150; School of Medicine, 216n4
University of Chicago (Chicago, IL), 63, 185
University of Illinois, 67, 80
University of Southern California (Los Angeles), 49, 108

US Capitol: January 6, 2021, insurrection and uprising, 12–13, 18, 180, 210n7
US Court of Appeals: 2nd, 220n19; 4th Circuit, 220n19; 5th Circuit, 219n5; 9th Circuit, 50–51, 108, 120, 217n1; women appointees, 108–9
US Immigration and Customs Enforcement (ICE), 43, 148
US Justice Department, Civil Rights Division, 57
US Supreme Court. *See* Supreme Court of the United States

values, 149–72, 208n10, 209n9, 211n49, 222–23n15; and character, 158; core, xiii, 1, 5, 10, 12, 17–18, 22, 26, 68, 135, 136–43, 158–63, 166, 171–72, 175–82, 189–90, 207n5; and courage, 209n3; and ethics, xvii, 66; family, 164, 168–70; and identity, 175; liberal, 25; and virtues, 212n80
Vancouver, 81
Van de Kamp, John, 109–11, 119, 170, 217n3
Vandenberg Air Force Base (Lompoc, CA), 51, 215–16nn2–3
Vatican City, 222n11
Vercors (pseudonym), 198
Vietnam War, 17, 72, 110, 200–202
Villaraigosa, Antonio, 215n1
virtue ethics, 23–24, 66, 175, 212nn79–80; and agnostic choice, 187; and identity, 143–44; limitations of, 221n1; and moral principles or rules, 221n4; and philosophy, 221nn1–2, 221–22nn4–5; and values, 212n80
virtues, 11–13, 15–17, 21–23, 25, 143, 175, 183–84, 187, 212n80
vital courage, 11–12, 15–17
vital/health courage, 16–17
voting rights, 56–59, 69–70, 109–10, 142–43, 216n1
Voting Rights Act, 58–59, 70, 109

Wallace, George, 216n3
Wall Street, 114, 218n8
Warren, Elizabeth, 72
Warsaw, Poland, 36, 148, 163, 196; Jewish Ghetto, 161; Uprising, 161, 169
Washington, D.C., 49, 52–53, 56–57, 109–11, 114–15, 142
Washington University (St. Louis, MO), Memory Diagnostic Center, 82
well-being, 13, 17, 22, 25–26, 142, 159–62, 171–72, 176, 180, 185, 187, 212n87, 213n95
Werfel, Alma Mahler, 207n2
Werfel, Franz, 207n2
Western philosophy, 2, 187
whistleblowers, 17–18, 30, 209n9
Whitewater controversy, 110–11
Wiggin, Geoffrey, 209n9
Williams, Bernard, 12, 23, 212n79
Williams, Fran, 91

Williams, Robin, 82
Williams, Tennessee, 91
Wilson, Pete (governor), 112, 122, 217n4
Wilson, Rick, 209n9
Women's March, 56, 70
Woolworths (F. W. Woolworth Co.), 54
Worldly Philosopher (Adelman), 207n1
World Trade Center (9/11), 50, 97–99, 141, 178, 209n3
World War I, 43
World War II, 15, 60, 151, 154–55, 167, 169, 181, 197–98, 209n9, 220n21, 222n11, 225n34

Yad Vashem medal, 151, 220n21
Yale Law School (Haven, CT), 108, 110
Yiddish speaking/speakers, 42–43, 168

Zimmer, Stephen (Steve): helping immigrants and protecting undocumented students, 5, 28, 31, 35–36, 39, 41–48, 135–37, 140–41, 146–50, 153–56, 168–69, 173, 187, 195, 209n9, 220n21, 222n11, 225n34
Zosia (Reykowski grandniece), 36–37, 196
Zuccotti, Susan, 222n11

www.ingramcontent.com/pod-product-compliance
Lightning Source LLC
Chambersburg PA
CBHW022047290426
44109CB00014B/1013